UNNATURAL SELECTIONS

UNNATURAL SELECTIONS

EUGENICS IN AMERICAN MODERNISM
AND THE HARLEM RENAISSANCE

DAYLANNE K. ENGLISH

The University of North Carolina Press \ Chapel Hill and London

Designed by April Leidig-Higgins
Set in Mrs. Eaves by Copperline Book Services, Inc.
Manufactured in the United States of America

Publication of this work was aided by a generous grant from the Z. Smith Reynolds Foundation.

The paper in this book meets the guidelines for permanence and durability of the Committee on Production Guidelines for Book Longevity of the Council on Library Resources.

Library of Congress Cataloging-in-Publication Data
English, Daylanne K.
  Unnatural selections: eugenics in American modernism and the Harlem Renaissance / by Daylanne K. English.
    p. cm.
Includes bibliographical references (p.) and index.
ISBN 0-8078-2868-8 (cloth: alk. paper)
ISBN 0-8078-5531-6 (pbk.: alk. paper)
    1. American literature—20th century—History and criticism.   2. Eugenics in literature.   3. American literature—African American authors—History and criticism.   4. American literature—White authors—History and criticism.   5. Modernism (Literature)—United States.   6. African Americans in literature.   7. Harlem Renaissance.   8. Race in literature.
I. Title.
PS228.E84E54   2004
810.9'3556—dc22   2003021778

cloth   08 07 06 05 04   5 4 3 2 1
paper   08 07 06 05 04   5 4 3 2 1

Chapter 1 has been adapted from "W. E. B. Du Bois's Family Crisis," *American Literature* 72, no. 2 (June 2000): 291–319; copyright © 2000 Duke University Press. Chapter 3 originally appeared, in somewhat different form, under the title "Gertrude Stein and the Politics of Literary-Medical Experimentation," in *Literature and Medicine* 16, no. 2 (1997): 188–209; copyright © 1997 The Johns Hopkins University Press. Used with permission of the copyright holders.

I DEDICATE THIS BOOK TO THE STAFF AND PATIENTS
OF LYNN COMMUNITY HEALTH CENTER IN LYNN,
MASSACHUSETTS. THEIR EXPERIENCES AND MINE
WITH THEM ARE THE ORIGIN OF THIS PROJECT.

CONTENTS

ILLUSTRATIONS

ACKNOWLEDGMENTS

Many colleagues have made it possible for me to write this book. My first and deepest thanks go to Deborah E. McDowell, whose incisive intellect and unflagging spirit have shaped this project throughout. I extend thanks as well to Sian Hunter, who has been central to its realization. I also owe a great deal to the readers for the University of North Carolina Press, whose thoughtful close readings and rigorous questioning improved the manuscript tremendously. I acknowledge Mason Stokes for his steadfast and stimulating friendship and colleagueship of many years. My thanks are due as well to the following scholars who have, by their intellectual guidance, professional example, and personal support, helped bring this project to completion: Michael Levenson, Sara B. Blair, Houston Baker, Jacqueline Goldsby, Susan Stanford Friedman, Suzanne Poirier, Joan Bryant, Dorothy Denniston, Eric Lott, Michelle Wright, Rita Felski, Stephen Arata, Derek Nystrom, Thomas Glave, Brenda DoHarris, and Lawrence Buell. I also thank the editorial staff at the University of North Carolina Press, including Paul Betz, Paula Wald, and David Hines, for their invaluable contributions. Finally, this book would be greatly diminished if not for the suggestions and insights of readers for and editors at *American Literature* and *Literature and Medicine*.

Many others made the research process possible. I thank the American Philosophical Society Library, particularly curator Robert Cox. I also thank curator Judith May-Sapko and librarian Emily Doak of the Pickler Library at Truman State University. My thanks go as well to curator JoEllen ElBashir and librarian Donna Wells at Howard University's Moorland-Spingarn Research Center. I owe much to the librarians and staff at Bowie State University's Thurgood Marshall Library, for handling my many interlibrary loans. For their financial support, I thank the National Endowment for the Humanities and the University System of Maryland Women's Forum. I also thank my students at Brown, Brandeis, and Bowie State Universities, whose agile minds often prodded my own into action.

Perhaps most important, I wish to acknowledge friends and family who have sustained me and this project, especially Michael Furlough, Robin Dougherty, LaVonne Jackson, Anna Shenk, Leslie Loveless, David Forman, Andrea Hibbard, Paul Shenk, and Dorilyn English. Finally, thank you to Patricia Dougherty English and Eugene Shenk, whose care and presence made it all worthwhile.

UNNATURAL SELECTIONS

The person taking the eugenic family history should be thoroughly, scientifically trained. The history is perhaps the most important item of the examination, and it is also the most difficult task of all to secure a complete and consistent record from the imperfect recollections and limited information of most families. In Kansas this unit is directed by the Professor of Eugenics from the State University. Social workers, trained in case record work, may take very good histories.—"Fitter Families for Future Firesides, a Report of the Eugenics Department of the Kansas Free Fair" (1924)

The [Negro] race is faced with a startling fact. Our birth rate is declining; our infant mortality is increasing; our normal rate of increase must necessarily be slowing up; our educated and intelligent classes are refusing to have children; our women are going into the kind of work that taxes both physical and mental capacities, which of itself, limits fecundity.—Alice Dunbar-Nelson, "Woman's Most Serious Problem" (1927)

I have no doubt that the paper [the *Criterion*] will appear too conservative to some and too radical to others, but I have gone on the principle of trying to secure the best people of each generation and type.—T. S. Eliot, letter to John Quinn (1922)

INTRODUCTION

Eugenics, the science of breeding better human beings, saturated U.S. culture during the 1920s. It seeped into politics. It permeated social science and medicine. It shaped public policy and aesthetic theory. It influenced the nation's literature. It affected popular culture. Eugenic thinking was so pervasive in the modern era that it attained the status of common sense in its most unnerving Gramscian sense. From eugenics' inception in late-nineteenth-century England to its peak in the United States during the postwar years of the late 1910s and 1920s, few challenged the notion that modern nations, especially those beset by immigration, must improve their human stock in order to remain competitive, indeed viable, in the modern world. G. K. Chesterton, H. L. Mencken, Nella Larsen, Angelina Weld Grimké, and a few representatives of the Catholic Church were among the handful of oddly disparate protestors against the utopian idea that a nation's human stock, like its livestock, could *and should* be improved on—with some professional, state, and institutional intervention, that is. Margaret Sanger,

Alice Dunbar-Nelson, W. E. B. Du Bois, and T. S. Eliot, on the other hand, were among the scores of equally disparate American activists and writers who endorsed some form of eugenics in the 1920s.[1]

Only recently have scholars begun to acknowledge the profound influence of eugenic thought on modern white American and British writers, including not only Eliot but also Ernest Hemingway, F. Scott Fitzgerald, Charlotte Perkins Gilman, Virginia Woolf, and W. B. Yeats.[2] We must acknowledge, as well, that some version of eugenics appeared in the writings of modern African American intellectuals, including not only Du Bois and Dunbar-Nelson but also Jean Toomer, George Schuyler, and E. Franklin Frazier. In the end, there were not nearly as many outright refutations of eugenics in modern America as there were competing versions of it. As Zygmunt Bauman has argued, the ideal of weeding out defectives from the well-ordered garden of modernity "permeated modern society and remained arguably the most salient feature of its collective spirit."[3]

Eugenic ideology was "salient" for so many modern thinkers across political and racial lines because, unlike more general discourses of race, it eased the conflict between individual and collective forms of identity—a conflict fundamental to the modern liberal-democratic state. Both black and white intellectuals were able to negotiate intraracial class tensions via eugenic thinking: to improve the collective (race or nation), they simply had to determine which individuals should breed (based on class or race or both). As a result of that circumvention of the characteristically modern—and politically inflected—individual-collective dialectic, eugenics in some form can (and often does) show up on almost anyone's ideological map between 1890 and 1940.[4] In turn, because it was both so widespread and so variable, eugenics serves as an ideal lens through which to examine often overlooked commonalities —as well as significant disjunctions—among Progressive Era public policy and social science, Harlem Renaissance aesthetic visions and class politics, and American modernist literary experimentation and racial politics.

Indeed, in the United States of the 1910s and 1920s, eugenics became so widely accepted that it might be considered the paradigmatic modern American discourse. Along with its ability to assess and express the individual's relationship to the collective, there were a number of other reasons for the particular success of eugenics in the United States. First, it represented scientism and progress—a combination that appealed to a wide variety of modern American intellectuals. Second, the United States's particular historical circumstances in the early twentieth century—including widespread immigration and migration, a shift to an urban industrial economy, and the country's emergence as a dominant global power—help further explain the rise of an ideology that promised to increase national competitiveness and efficiency. Finally, the long and distinguished intellectual history of eugenics lent it credibility. Over a century of dominant European social philosophy, evolutionary theory, and scientific racism culminated in the late-nineteenth-century English and American invention of eugenics.

REACHING BACK TO THE late eighteenth century, well before English social scientist Sir Francis Galton coined the term "eugenics" in 1883, we can find the utopian roots of eugenic thinking, along with a precedent for its characteristic social urgency and national protectiveness (both characteristics resonate still in contemporary public policy debates, particularly around welfare and immigration). In his 1798 *Essay on the Principle of Population*, English economist and social philosopher Thomas Malthus set forth the idea, later to inspire both Spencer and Darwin, that the earth's ability to provide food for people would soon be outstripped by human fertility. There is a "constant tendency," explained Malthus, "in all animated life to increase beyond the nourishment prepared for it."[5] The result, he believed, would be the inevitable elimination of many as a result of starvation, disease, and "vice and misery"—all natural "checks which repress the power of population" (12–13). Malthus argued that the nature of those checks varied according to a particular population's developmental "stage." Among "savages" such as the Tierra del Fuegans, the Africans, and the American Indians, "positive checks"—ones that increase the mortality rate— were most prevalent and effective; they included famine, war, disease, cannibalism, and infanticide. But for societies at a "higher stage," "preventive checks"—ones that decrease the birthrate—functioned as the primary means of keeping the population in balance with national resources. Chief among the preventive checks was "moral restraint," a quality Malthus associated exclusively with the advanced states of "modern Europe" (12–13). Malthus did acknowledge that vice and misery could function as positive checks even in England—but solely among the lower classes (294).

Eugenics Building at the Kansas Free Fair, 1929. Courtesy of the American Philosophical Society.

Malthus's hierarchical population theory finds an obvious descendant in Spencer's theory of "social evolution" organized by the principle of survival of the fittest. Indeed, although many consider Francis Galton to be the father of eugenics, and his 1869 *Hereditary Genius* to be its urtext, English social philosopher Herbert Spencer had laid the ideological groundwork for Galtonian eugenics two decades earlier. Spencer, who coined the phrase "survival of the fittest" (often mistakenly ascribed to Charles Darwin),[6] took the crucial step of equating the "social state" with a biological organism. As he put it: "We commonly enough compare a nation to a living organism. We speak of the 'body politic,' of the functions of its parts, of its growth, and of its diseases, as though it were a creature. But we usually employ these expressions as metaphors, little suspecting how close is the analogy, and how far it will bear carrying out. So completely, however, is a society organized on the same system as an individual being, that we may perceive something more than analogy between them."[7] From Spencer's "something more than analogy," it was a small step to the equation of social undesirables with bodily impurities: "We should think it a very foolish sort of benevolence which led a surgeon to let his patient's disease progress to a fatal issue, rather than inflict pain by an operation. Similarly, we must call those spurious philanthropists who, to prevent present misery, would entail greater misery on future generations. . . . [U]nder the natural order of things society is constantly excreting its unhealthy, imbecile, slow, vacillating, faithless members. . . . [Charity and the poor laws] absolutely encourag[e] the multiplication of the reckless and incompetent . . . [and] bequeathe [sic] to posterity a continually increasing curse."[8] Spencer thus neatly anticipated and summarized the eugenic policies to come in the late nineteenth and early twentieth centuries in the United States, policies that concentrated on the study, institutionalization, and sterilization of the poor and unfit, rather than on financial or social relief measures.

Charles Darwin often enjoys some degree of critical exemption from the scientific racism and elitism readily assigned to Spencer, and it is certainly true that social Darwinism is a misnomer for a doctrine perhaps more appropriately termed social Spencerianism. Nevertheless, Darwin too followed in Malthus's footsteps. Darwin himself described *The Origin of Species* as "the doctrine of Malthus, applied to the whole animal and vegetable kingdom."[9] Furthermore, at the same time that *Origin* appeared in 1859, the business of scientific racism, bolstered by the 1853 publication of French naturalist Comte de Gobineau's influential work on "l'inégalité des races humaines," was booming, and Darwin was not immune to its influence. In fact, both Spencer and Darwin extended and elaborated, rather than supplanted, an inherited eighteenth- and early-nineteenth-century hierarchy of human races. And both unquestionably supplied some of the essential theoretical tools used by American and English eugenicists between 1880 and 1930.

In Darwin's 1871 *The Descent of Man*, a hierarchy of racial difference emerges clearly and repeatedly, while it explicitly extends *Origin*'s theory of natural selection to human beings.[10] Darwin speaks in *Descent* of "the different races or species of mankind, whichever may be preferred."[11] He goes on to construct a new, evolution-based human hierarchy that still fits neatly with prior racial orders offered by French naturalists Buffon in the eighteenth century and Gobineau in the nineteenth.[12] Darwin declares that the "variability or diversity of the mental faculties in men of the same race, not to mention the greater differences between men of distinct races, is so notorious that not a word need here be said" (109–10). Darwin regularly relies on the self-evidentiary nature of racial differences to establish his theory of global natural selection among humans. He concludes that at "some future period the civilised races of man will almost certainly exterminate and replace throughout the world the savage races" (201). As expected, for Darwin the "Western nations stand at the summit of civilisation" (178); thus, like Malthus and Spencer before him, Darwin selects his own form of nationhood as fittest. Perhaps even more significant for the eugenics movement that followed, he selects his *own family* as particularly fit. Darwin observes in his 1871 *Descent* that his cousin Francis Galton had already established in *Hereditary Genius* the fact that "genius tends to be inherited" (110).

In the very first sentence of his 1869 *Hereditary Genius*, the first explicitly eugenic text, Sir Francis Galton explained that the "idea of investigating the subject of hereditary genius occurred to me during the course of a purely ethnological inquiry, into the mental peculiarities of different races."[13] The independently wealthy Galton developed new statistical methods (some still in use today) as a means of pursuing his chosen life's work—the quantification of human, particularly racial, differences.[14] The bulk of *Hereditary Genius* consists of studies, including genealogies, of genetically worthy and accomplished families among the English aristocracy. But in his penultimate chapter, "The Comparative Worth of Different Races," Galton announces his discovery of "a difference of not less than two grades between the black and white races, and it may be more"(338–39). It perhaps comes as no surprise that Galton's innovative statistical methods confirm a racial hierarchy inherited from earlier white European social scientists.[15] Also not surprising is the positioning of Galton's own family at the very top of his hierarchy. He included—as the clearest possible proof that genius runs in families—an extensive fold-out self-genealogy.[16] Galton's study of hereditary genius culminated in his *Inquiries into Human Faculty and Its Development* (1883), wherein he coined the term "eugenics," observing that "we greatly want a brief word to express the science of improving stock," a word that will connote the project of giving "the more suitable races or strains of blood a better chance of prevailing speedily over the less suitable."[17]

His cousin was already well aware of the possible dangers in permitting "less suitable" human beings to prevail. In *Descent*, Darwin argued that, while Galton had established the hereditary nature of genius, "on the other hand, it is too certain that insanity and deteriorated mental powers likewise run in the same families" (111). In one short passage,

Darwin, in a kind of intrafamilial conversation with Galton, deftly sets the stage for full-blown eugenics. He proceeds to select the cast and sketch the plot. "We civilised men," he claims, "do our utmost to check the process of elimination; we build asylums for the imbecile, the maimed, and the sick; we institute poor-laws; and our medical men exert their utmost skill to save the life of every one to the last moment. There is reason to believe that vaccination has preserved thousands, who from a weak constitution would formerly have succumbed to small-pox. Thus the weak members of civilised societies propagate their kind. No one who has attended to the breeding of domestic animals will doubt that this must be highly injurious to the race of man." But Darwin fails to bring this eugenic script to a climax. However reluctantly, he rejects the enactment of eugenic policies, insisting that "if we were intentionally to neglect the weak and helpless, it could only be for a contingent benefit, with a certain and great present evil" (169). Darwin concludes that "we must bear without complaining the undoubtedly bad effects of the weak surviving and propagating their kind," thereby accepting that a type of unnatural selection will inevitably accompany modern social and scientific innovations such as the asylum and vaccination (169).[18] Spencer, however, disagreed with Darwin's stoic policy.

Spencer advocated both active and passive race- and class-based eugenics (although he did not use the term) precisely to counter modern technologies of health and the emergence of the welfare state. Like Darwin, he regretted that natural selection among humans had been "greatly interfered with by governments," but his response to that unnatural state of affairs was far less humanitarian and resigned. Spencer declared that "the continuance of [governmental] interferences may retard, if not stop, that further [human] evolution which would else go on. I refer to those hindrances to the survival of the fittest which in earlier times resulted from the indiscriminatory charities of monasteries and in later times from the operation of the Poor Laws."[19] Although Spencer approves of voluntary charity as morally uplifting for the upper classes, he wants such charity to be quite limited (he wants far fewer than a thousand points of light), while he contrasts the poor laws unfavorably with the killing off of weaker animals by predators. He seeks a social state more in keeping with a natural order wherein "all vitiation of the race through multiplication of its inferior samples is prevented."[20] For example, he describes the "harsh fatalities" among the widows and orphans of dead English laborers as "full of beneficence—the same beneficence which brings to early graves the children of diseased parents, and singles out the intemperate and the debilitated as the victims of an epidemic."[21]

Spencer extends his class-based evolutionary model to race by focusing on the Irish as a distinct and inferior, yet troublesomely fecund race. Because the Irish represent the less fit for Spencer, they help him develop the notion of differential birthrate (meaning that the lower classes and races are multiplying faster than the higher classes and races), so crucial for later eugenicists. Spencer observes that "the Irish, . . . though not well fed, multiply fast."[22] He must therefore make adjustments to his theory of "survival of the fittest," given his observation that the "civilized races" are "less prolific" than the "uncivilized races." To put this another way, if Spencer were to rely strictly on a theory of natural selection, then the greater reproductive success he assigns to "uncivilized races" such as the Irish and Africans would also necessarily signal their greater fitness because, at least according to Darwin, the organisms that multiply most successfully *are* the fittest.[23] Like the American eugenicists who would follow him, Spencer explains away differential birthrate by blaming modernity itself for the uncanny success of the Irish and other (to him) obviously less fit humans.

Spencer offers "changes of conditions" to account for the different "rates of multiplication" of differentially evolved races and classes.[24] In his view, the modern apparatus of the welfare state, along with shifting gender roles in the nineteenth century, have made for a most unnatural selection process wherein the least fit have become the most reproductively successful—the central paradox of eugenic ideology. According to Spencer: "That absolute or relative infertility is commonly produced in women by mental labour carried to excess, is . . . clearly shown. Though the regimen of upper-class girls is not what it should be, yet, considering that their feeding is better than that of girls belonging to the poorer classes, while, in most other respects, their physical treatment is not worse, the deficiency of reproductive power among them may be reasonably attributed to the overtaxing of their brains."[25] In other words, if upper-class girls weren't thinking so much, they could certainly match the fertility of their working-class counterparts. As historian Gail Bederman observes, Spencer believed that "as civilized races gradually evolved toward perfection, they naturally perfected and deepened the sexual specialization of the Victorian doctrine of spheres."[26]

Thus, for Spencer, rigidly maintained traditional gender and class identities, along with laissez-faire social policy, offer the most natural, indeed the ideal prescription for continued evolution and progress of the national body.

Spencer welcomed the social scientific proof of his philosophy of national well-being and survival of the fittest that came in 1877 with the publication of the first sociological, eugenic family study in the United States. During an 1874 investigation of recidivism at a New York state prison, amateur U.S. sociologist Robert Dugdale noted that a number of the inmates were blood relatives. That observation led him to pursue a hereditarian study he published as *The Jukes: A Study in Crime, Pauperism, Disease and Heredity*. Adapting Francis Galton's (eugenic) family-study methodology of the 1870s, Dugdale presented the first genealogical-behavioral analysis of a single, obviously genetically flawed (dysgenic) family, whose identity he veiled with the pseudonym the "Jukes." Spencer commented approvingly on Dugdale's study, pointing out that it "rarely happens that the amount of evil caused by fostering the vicious and good-for-nothing can be estimated. . . . Was it kindness or cruelty which, generation after generation, enabled these [Jukes] to multiply and become an increasing curse to the society around them?"[27]

Dugdale, like Spencer, was a Lamarckian; that is, he believed in the hereditary transmission of acquired traits.[28] But unlike Spencer's, Dugdale's eugenic program was relatively liberal as a result. In contrast to later, Mendelian eugenicists, Dugdale advocated, at least initially, broad reforms to improve the lot of the American poor.[29] Because "environment tends to produce habits which may become hereditary, especially so in pauperism and licentiousness," Dugdale recommended training and more sanitary living conditions; an improved environment should lead, he believed, to improved heredity.[30] But Dugdale failed to sustain this relatively humane approach to eugenics. He ultimately decided that the "tendency of heredity is to produce an environment which perpetuates that heredity" (66). Thus, in the case of some dysgenic individuals—habitual criminals, for example—the only option that remains is to "sternly cut [them] off from perpetuating a noisome progeny" (114). So, despite his pre-1900, Lamarckian understanding of heredity, Dugdale developed a eugenic stance that paved the way not only for later, more repressive policies for the purification of the national gene pool (particularly the compulsory sterilization of male inmates), but also for many more class-biased studies of the native-born

American dysgenic. *The Jukes* was only the first of over a dozen studies, published between 1877 and 1926, of apparently dysgenic U.S. families,[31] studies termed "melancholy genealogies" by Lothrop Stoddard.[32] All promoted the sterilization or institutionalization of the American unfit. One family-study author concluded that "man must complete the work which nature begins in limiting the procreation of the obviously unfit."[33] Another study author echoed Spencer even more clearly: "The people of the community, in giving constant financial relief and shelter in county institutions, although they are being humane, are also defeating nature's attempt to eliminate the unfit."[34] Herbert Henry Goddard, author of the most famous and widely read family study, *The Kallikak Family* (1912), argued that because "humanity is steadily tending away from the possibility" of "the lethal chamber" for the "low-grade idiot," segregation and sterilization stand as the likely, if not "final solution of this problem."[35] These studies, rather chillingly, gave American eugenics what Nicole Rafter aptly terms "its central, confirmational image."[36]

But the popularity of the family studies, as well as the overall success of eugenics in the United States between 1880 and 1940, can only be partly explained by a European intellectual genealogy so distinguished that it included not only Spencer and Lamarck but also Malthus, Darwin, Galton, Buffon, Gobineau, and Mendel. In his study of eugenics' influence on English writers, Donald Childs rightly argues that "the science of eugenics . . . interested everyone in the early years of the twentieth century."[37] But in the United States, unlike in England, that interest translated into a great deal of explicitly eugenic legislation and jurisprudence. Indeed, eugenics achieved a pervasive influence in the United States (not only on public policy but also on social science, literature, and popular culture) that far outstripped its degree of influence in Europe (with Germany the obvious exception in the 1930s and 1940s). Between 1907 and 1930, twenty-four states enacted statutes permitting compulsory sterilization of feebleminded or otherwise dysgenic state residents, with the result of at least 60,000 compulsory sterilizations being performed between 1907 and 1964 for explicitly eugenic reasons.[38] Those state sterilization statutes actually served as a model for the Nazi Sterilization Law of 1934. It is important to understand what led to such widespread enactment of eugenic policies in the United States, well before their far more horrifying application in Nazi Germany.

A NUMBER OF historical and social contingencies in the late nineteenth to early twentieth centuries created a cultural climate in the United States that was congenial for eugenics.[39] Whereas English eugenics arose in a context of fears regarding degeneration (as Donald Childs has rightly argued),[40] American eugenics arose in a context of nascent superpower in tension with anxieties regarding widespread foreign immigration and domestic migration. In other words, when Great Britain's imperial might was waning, the United States was becoming the dominant economic, industrial, and political world power, while in the midst of substantial domestic demographic change. As of the first decade of the twentieth century, Americans were already becoming "accustomed to taking up the white man's burden," as Gail Bederman puts it, in an ever-expanding list of nations, including the Philippines, Cuba, Panama, and the Dominican Republic.[41] Particularly after a hard-won victory in World War I, the United States sought ever greater efficiency in order to consolidate its new status as the greatest imperial power, the fittest among competitor nations.[42] At the turn of the century Theodore Roosevelt had deployed an alarmist rhetoric of "race suicide" to encourage all (white) Americans to breed,[43] but interwar notions of ideal breeding became more precise; not all white native-born Americans, it turned out, were fit to reproduce. With a domestic protectionist mood taking hold in the postwar era, an urgent question emerged: how to sustain this new American power, along with a more vigorous and distinctive Americanness, in an era of increasingly competitive, globalized geopolitics and economics (as evidenced by the Great War itself)?[44]

As Calvin Coolidge stated in his inaugural address of 1925, "We are not without our problems, but our most important problem is not to secure new advantages but to maintain those which we already possess."[45] Coolidge offered the following prescription: "The very stability of our society rests upon production and conservation. For individuals or for governments to waste and squander their resources is to deny these rights and disregard these obligations. The result of economic dissipation to a nation is always moral decay." By 1925, U.S. industry, at least, had already achieved greater "production and conservation." Henry Ford had opened his Highland Park auto factory in 1910; it operated according to a system which "depended on standardization, mechanization, speed, efficiency, and careful control of production and workers."[46] Frederick Taylor had published his *Principles of*

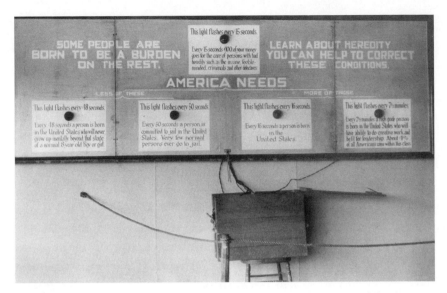

Exhibit used at fitter families contests in the 1920s. Courtesy of the American Philosophical Society.

Scientific Management in 1911. According to the principles of scientific management, or Taylorism, laborers were first to be selected to do work for which they were fit; they were then to be trained to perform ever more specialized tasks in an increasingly efficient system of manufacture.[47] Just as Fordism and Taylorism promised greater economic efficiency — and thus international competitiveness for the United States — so eugenics promised greater reproductive efficiency by producing laborers fit for the modern American workplace and managers fit to oversee them in that workplace. As the authors of one family study put it, eugenics, along with intelligence testing, effectively addresses "the amount of intelligence necessary to enable one to get along tolerably with his fellows and to keep somewhere in sight of them in the thousand and one kinds of competition in which success depends upon mental ability. . . . It is possible that the development of civilization, with its inevitable increase in the complexity of social and industrial life, will raise the standard of mental normality higher."[48] Eugenics functioned as the social-biological arm of a broad American program for becoming more fit — thereby, in Coolidge's words, also becoming "more and more American." Any potential internal threat to U.S. power and enhanced Americanness — including inferior immigrant intelligence, as well as criminal activity or insufficient "production and conservation" among native-born Americans—would be confronted and, if necessary, eliminated.

Coolidge went on in his 1925 address to outline the potential consequences for those Americans who threatened the nation's stability and prosperity: "Those who want their rights respected under the Constitution and the law ought to set the example themselves of observing the Constitution and the law. While there may be those of high intelligence who violate the law at times, the barbarian and the defective always violate it. Those who disregard the rules of society are not exhibiting a superior intelligence, are not promoting freedom and independence, are not following the path of civilization, but are displaying the traits of ignorance, of servitude, of savagery, and treading the way that leads back to the jungle." The link among biological inferiority, immorality, and regressiveness evident in Coolidge's address both undergirded and justified the national eugenic policies that reached maturity in the inter-war years. Indeed, the President was certainly right that "the barbarian and the defective" would fail to have their Constitutional rights "respected." Defectives would be held, in the 1927 *Buck v. Bell* Supreme Court decision upholding compulsory sterilization of the feebleminded, as obviously not meriting the same Constitutional rights as "those of high intelligence." In the often-quoted words of Justice Oliver Wendell Holmes in his majority opinion in *Buck v. Bell*: "Three generations of imbeciles are enough." Using the precedent of vaccination as a compulsory medical procedure justified by state interests, Holmes effectively brought full circle Darwin's earlier anxieties regarding the dysgenic effects of modern public health measures.[49] Eugenic national policies would help correct for the unnatural selection resulting from vaccination; the morally and biologically inferior, though they might survive childhood at a greater (indeed an unnatural) rate, would not be permitted, as adults, to breed lesser Americans. Those who "squander resources," along with the criminal, the barbarian, and the defective, did not belong in Coolidge's picture of a nation that would be ever more "openly and candidly, intensely and scrupulously, American."[50] Or as Harry Laughlin, assistant director of the United States Eugenics Record Office, put it, "Approximately 10 percent of our population, primarily through inherent defect and weakness, are an economic and moral burden on the 90 percent and a constant danger to the national and racial life."[51] But native-born Americans who were feebleminded or insufficiently productive (while being overly reproductive) represented only one such "danger to the national and racial life."

Immigration represented an equally potent perceived threat to Americans' "national and racial life." Roughly twenty-eight million immigrants came to the United States between 1880 and 1920.[52] As Philip Reilly has noted, starting at around 1905, worries about these immigrants began to appear regularly in the popular press.[53] Coolidge again weighed in, citing "restrictive immigration" (clearly referring to the Johnson Immigration Restriction Act, passed in 1924)[54] as a "helpful influence" on American prosperity. By this time, a number of books, many written for a lay audience, were warning of the dire consequences of foreign immigration for the national gene pool; they included Madison Grant's 1916 *The Passing of the Great Race*, Lothrop Stoddard's 1920 *The Rising Tide of Color against White World-Supremacy*, Albert E. Wiggam's 1923 *The New Decalogue of Science* and his 1924 *The Fruit of the Family Tree*—all of which were popular, white supremacist tracts urging the purification and improvement of the national family. Literary scholar Walter Benn Michaels has offered a compelling analysis of this 1920s American preoccupation with race and family, hypothesizing that during that decade the "family becomes the site of national identity."[55] Although Michaels's hypothesis is correct, his conclusion—that, as a result, "nationality becomes an effect of racial identity" (8)—is not. Because the family is never solely a racial site, neither, then, is the modern nation. Race, despite Michaels's often compelling argument, is itself only one (though arguably the most powerful and pernicious one) among multiple categories of collective modern subjectivity, and as such cannot resolve what he rightly identifies as the fundamental "crisis of liberalism" in the modern United States: the irreconcilability of individuality and collectivity (103).[56] Eugenics, however, can.

EUGENICS EMERGED as a central national ideology—one that influenced public policy, juridical discourse, medical care, popular culture, literature, and aesthetic theory—most of all because it so effectively addressed that crisis of modern American subjectivity. Eugenics, while it is fundamentally about the family, can accommodate the *full range* of perceived human differences contained, represented, and reproduced within the (individual, racial, or national) family, even as it sustains and promotes various still-intact modern social hierarchies.

In the 1910s and 1920s, eugenic ideology promised to allow Americans to pick their fellow citizens, their national relatives—not simply on the basis of race but also on the basis of ethnicity, class, region, intelligence, efficiency, and even beauty. Thus, although Michaels argues persuasively that the 1920s witnessed an "intensification of the commitment to race" (137), his suggestion that this "new racism" (67) in turn brought about both a "new indifference to class" among black writers (53) and an abandonment of "universalist white supremacy" among white writers (140) is far less persuasive.

I would argue that, on the contrary, the 1920s witnessed "intensification" not only of race but also of other social categories; the decade can actually be characterized by a greater awareness of class, region, ethnicity, gender, and intellect—as the enactment of a great deal of regionalist and elitist (and not always explicitly racial) eugenic policies in the United States clearly demonstrates.[57] Eugenics reached the peak of its influence in the United States in the 1920s, with thousands of compulsory sterilizations performed during that decade on generally rural —and generally white—lower-class Americans, all of whom had been deemed hopelessly feebleminded or irrevocably immoral or chronically poor.[58] As one journalist has recently reported, compulsory sterilizations for eugenic reasons became "so frequent . . . especially among poor Southerners, that researchers would later label them 'Mississippi appendectomies.' "[59] But class and region were not the only hierarchical social categories that remained intact and enforced, via state eugenic statues in the 1910s and 1920s; racial distinctions and hierarchies were enforced above all else. David Levering Lewis points out that it was in 1923 that *Birth of a Nation* was rereleased and that the Dyer antilynching bill failed in the Senate.[60] And it was in 1924 that the Race Registration Act was passed in Virginia and the Immigration Restriction Act became federal law. Matthew Guterl describes the paramount importance of race in the United States of the 1920s: "When push came to shove, the color line between 'the Negro' and everyone else mattered far more to patrician Americans than the markers within whiteness" (49).

In the end, both white supremacy and class hierarchy were often simply taken for granted by many (though certainly not all) white eugenicists of the 1920s. In his 1923 best seller, *The New Decalogue of Science*, American journalist and eugenics popularizer A. E. Wiggam succinctly expressed the racial, ethnic, and class "givens" of mainstream nativist white American eugenics: "In addition to this ominous phenomenon [differential birthrate among social classes in the United States], you have deliberately introduced within the past two decades at least two million oppressed peoples of other lands, of lower intellectual ability than your ten million or more Negroes already on hand."[61] Lothrop Stoddard declared in his 1924 *Revolt against Civilization* that "the intelligence of the colored population averages distinctly lower than the intelligence of native American whites, and somewhat lower than the intelligence of our least promising east and south European elements" (65). Ironically, it was its continued commitment to class that permitted eugenics to cross racial lines. Despite having an obvious immediate ancestor in the late-nineteenth-century white supremacist eugenics of Francis Galton (as the above passages from Wiggam and Stoddard demonstrate), early-twentieth-century U.S. eugenics sidestepped the period's intensively enforced racial divisions precisely because it engaged forms of modern identity other than race.

Regardless of their race, many modern American intellectuals addressed intraracial class anxieties by means of eugenics. Indeed, eugenics adapted quite readily to the racial segregation that served as the nation's primary post-Reconstruction legal and social modality. Like movie theaters and schools, eugenics became intraracial, though by means of voluntary articulated theory rather than law. Many African American writers and activists in the 1920s, including W. E. B. Du Bois and Alice Dunbar-Nelson, were attracted to and wrote about racial uplift achieved through selective breeding, particularly in the context of the New Negro and the Great Migration. Between 1890 and 1920, over 1.2 million African Americans migrated from the southern to the northern and western United States, with at least 300,000 migrating in a single decade, between 1910 and 1920.[62] A kind of intraracial cultural contact resulted, especially in the North, with many already settled, urban African Americans reacting with ambivalence to the influx of black migrants into a setting of residential racial segregation (and so forced class mixture). Du Bois produced the first large-scale social scientific documentation of (even as he registered concern about) the Great Migration in his landmark 1899 urban study, *The Philadelphia Negro*. Du Bois worried that the urban and urbane New Negro, who "forms the realized ideal of the group" and provides the standard by which the group as a whole should be "understood and finally judged," would have to contend with "untrained and poorly ed-

ucated [Negro] countrymen, rushing from the hovels of the country
. . . into the strange life of a great city."[63] By the 1920s, Du Bois offered
a kind of intraracial reproductive solution to the problem of New
Negro subjectivity in the modern United States, arguing in a *Crisis* editorial that the race must begin to "train and breed for brains, for efficiency, for beauty."[64] Likewise, Dunbar-Nelson worried that "educated
and intelligent" New Negro women would choose childlessness.[65] But
Dunbar-Nelson's and Du Bois's intraracial version of eugenics, while
it may have been elitist, was not racist or regressive—it rejected white
supremacy while it called for an egalitarian revision of the political
and social status quo. Some leftist white intellectuals of the period
embraced a similar version of eugenics. As eugenics historian Daniel
Kevles puts it, "The left mixed its eugenics with the socialist reconstruction of society."[66] Along with Havelock Ellis and Margaret Sanger,
Du Bois and Dunbar-Nelson advocated the equalization of social and
economic opportunity, yet at the same time encouraged, in Du Bois's
words, "families of the better class" to have more children.[67] Clearly,
eugenics was not necessarily accompanied by a platform of white supremacy or, for that matter, even racial purity.

Little noted even in recent treatments of modern eugenic thinking
are those (admittedly few) eugenicists (many, although not all, of them
African American) who believed in "hybrid vigor" and therefore advocated racial mixture as a means to improve the individual American
and the nation as a whole. Shawn Michelle Smith has asserted that "eugenicists, committed to a notion of Anglo-Saxon superiority, adamantly
opposed racial mixing as a threat to the progress (and dominance) of
the Anglo-Saxon race."[68] Smith argues further that Pauline Hopkins's
turn-of-the-century novels, with their mixed-race characters, "provide complicated examinations of racial character and of racial mixing
that challenge the fundamental tenets of eugenics" (188). But, as we
have seen, not all eugenics sympathizers were white supremacists; nor
were all white; nor did all advocate racial purity.[69] Hopkins can in fact
be seen as constructing an early "hybrid vigor" version of eugenics.[70]
When a Hopkins character declares that "amalgamation has taken place;
it will continue, and no finite power can stop it," the narrative is clearly
associating the progress and destiny of the nation with racial mixture.[71]
This association of more vigorous Americanness with racial mixture
would be more fully and explicitly articulated during the 1920s and
1930s, particularly by several writers of the Harlem Renaissance. The

new mixed-race American, rather than the New Negro, stood at the center of this particular vision of national improvement. For example, African American satirist and journalist George Schuyler and his wife, white Texan heiress Josephine Cogdell, conducted a kind of conscious, intrafamilial breeding experiment in the form of their daughter Philippa, born in 1931. As Philippa Schuyler biographer Kathryn Talalay explains, Philippa's parents designed her to be the ideal product of "hybrid genetics, proper education, and intensive education."[72] Jean Toomer, too, believed in hybrid vigor. As Diana Williams has recently argued, Toomer "saw the keys to cultural superiority not in racial *purity* but in racial *mixture*,"[73] and she notes that he "expressed great admiration for the writings of Herbert Spencer" (190). But Diana Williams, like Shawn Michelle Smith, is mistaken in then concluding that Toomer was less "progressive" because of his Spencerian sympathies or that his advocacy of racial mixture meant that he "differed from eugenicists" (189). As I have argued throughout this introduction, eugenics, regardless of the racial or class politics underlying it, must be seen *in its historical context* as a progressive ideology, one with the widely shared, utopian aim of improving the national or racial stock by conscious intervention. In fact, eugenicists like Toomer and Schuyler who advocated racial mixture as a source of genetic superiority could, perhaps even more legitimately than could the racial purists, consider their version of eugenics truly progressive and truly Darwinian, for Darwin had noted in *The Origin of Species* "that a cross between very distinct individuals of the same species . . . gives vigour to the offspring" (281). And it was not only African American thinkers who were drawn to the notion of hybrid vigor. As Robert von Hallberg has argued, William Carlos Williams, Marianne Moore, and even Ezra Pound "were all fascinated by exogamy, hybridity, [and] crossings," while a character like Williams's heroic Jatacqua of *In the American Grain* (1925) derives her power from "being both European and Indian."[74] Regardless of the scientific plausibility of assigning Darwinian "hybrid vigour" to mixed-race human beings (given that biological racial distinctions themselves have since been discredited), the important point here is that Toomer, Schuyler, and Williams were, in fact, contributing to eugenic discourse; it is just that their *version* of that discourse was non–white supremacist and pro–racial mixture—a quite real, but also a relatively rare and powerless version in the United States of the 1920s.

We must acknowledge that A. E. Wiggam's version of eugenics, with

Examiners for a fitter families contest at the Michigan State Fair. Courtesy of the American Philosophical Society.

its assumption of white and native-born American supremacy—not Du Bois and Dunbar-Nelson's interracially egalitarian, intraracially elitist version and certainly not Schuyler and Toomer and Williams's interracial, hybrid vigor version—represents the dominant form of eugenics in the United States in the 1920s, what Daniel Kevles usefully terms "mainline" eugenics.[75] Nativist *and* white supremacist *and* elitist, mainline American eugenics was constructed and perpetuated not just by popular journalists like Wiggam, but also by academics and professionals—including a "Professor of Eugenics from the State University" in Kansas and the women social workers who conducted white fitter family examinations at state fairs and collected data for the eugenic family studies.[76] Thus, as shared and various as it was, eugenics also serves especially well to reveal the social and racial fissures of the modern era. The differences between W. E. B. Du Bois's eugenics (elitist, yet accompanied by a platform of equal social and economic opportunity) and T. S. Eliot's eugenics (elitist, and accompanied by a platform of sustained class difference and a return to tradition) express a fundamental, indeed a nationally constitutive racial-cultural divide. As

Matthew Guterl cogently argues, regardless of the actual demographic makeup of the modern United States, the period witnessed "a new American sense of race as color, as a simple matter of blackness and whiteness," with intellectuals across the color line accepting and contributing to that "bi-racialism" (9, 6).

IN ITS ANALYSIS OF the racially divided eugenic constitution of the modern United States, *Unnatural Selections* travels from the literary aesthetics and politics of Du Bois, Grimké, Eliot, and Stein to the professional social science of the eugenics field workers—and to the popular culture of the American heartland. I thereby trace the route of eugenic discourse from Harlem to Baltimore, from urban flats to Minnesota timberland, from the suburban Long Island offices of the Eugenics Record Office to Kansas state fairs, and from the *Crisis* to the *Criterion*. I devote a great deal of space to the writers of American modernism and the Harlem Renaissance, agreeing with Walter Benn Michaels that "any account" of a modernist "conception of culture," especially one that focuses on race and class, "would end up making American literary history central" (141). But equally central to this book is the notion that literary developments serve as signifiers of historical change and that historical change, in turn, cannot be easily separated from scientific, political, and social contexts. We cannot fully understand either modernism or the Harlem Renaissance, or the period as whole, without taking into account what Michaels calls the "wider range" of scientific, social, and cultural "phenomena" that are so clearly intertwined with the form and the content of the period's literature (142). But this is not to argue that literature functions merely as a mirror of history; I examine literature extensively precisely for its ability to achieve at least some degree of what Robert von Hallberg terms "deviance from social, political, and institutional history."[77] Modern American literature, especially during the 1910s and 1920s, offered significant complications of, and at times the sole challenges to, the period's dominant social and scientific project of bio-national improvement.

I do not, however, endorse thoroughgoing literary exceptionalism in this book. I read literary texts alongside medical and sociological texts in order to explore the ways that science—in this case, eugenics—refracts and reconfigures cultural, including literary, values. In general, the period—along with its science, its social science, its industrial and managerial techniques, much of its literary culture, and even its visual culture—appeared to take enthusiastically and unquestioningly as its motto T. S. Eliot's 1922 "principle" in editing the *Criterion*: namely, "trying to secure the best people of each generation and type."[78] But, as I will argue in chapter 2, Eliot himself, though undeniably a literary and cultural elitist, was not always and everywhere the eugenicist that critics have made him out to be. Yes, Eliot was undeniably influenced by eugenics, as Juan León and Donald Childs have amply demonstrated, but so was everyone in the modern era.[79]

Indeed, given the pervasiveness of eugenics, I could have easily examined other writers and other literary, photographic, historical, political, and scientific texts and found its influence. This book is not intended to be a literary "influence" study, but rather an interdisciplinary cultural study designed to bring to the surface the deep structure of a period variously called the "Progressive Era" by historians, "modernism" by Americanist literary scholars, and the "Harlem Renaissance" by African Americanist literary scholars and historians. Of course, each of these terms has been subject to extensive scholarly contestation. Nearly every modernist critic has noted the amorphousness of the definition as well as the periodization of "modernism."[80] Modernist literary scholars generally end up separating *modernity*, what Rita Felski succinctly terms a "constantly shifting set of temporal coordinates," from *modernism*, "a specific form of artistic production, serving as an umbrella term for a mélange of artistic schools and styles which first arose in late-nineteenth-century Europe and America."[81] In this book, I aim to bring modernity, its temporality and its material conditions, closer to American aesthetic and intellectual modernism by revealing the ways that a great deal of the modern literature (especially its innovative and avant-garde) and the public policy from 1890 to 1930 in the United States can be decisively, and often alarmingly, located not only according to the temporal but also the political and scientific "coordinates" supplied by eugenics.

An ulterior motive of this book, then, is to bridge gaps, where possible and logical, among competing disciplinary nomenclatures for the modern period in the United States, particularly the decades from 1910 to 1930. To that end, I use the lens of a widely shared, exceptionally flexible ideology in order to scrutinize and challenge, although not always to refute, habitual bifurcations of the period by discipline and by writers' and reformers' race, gender, and political affiliation. As my title suggests, I aim to provide an inclusive cultural context for studies of the modern United States. For example, in placing the work of Du Bois and Dunbar-Nelson and Grimké in the context of eugenics, I challenge the still-common segregation of modern African American intellectuals from the dominant literary, philosophical, and scientific debates of the modern period. In such exploration of cross-racial cultural and political discourses, I am indebted to and sympathetic with the recent work of Ann Douglas in *Terrible Honesty: Mongrel Manhattan in the 1920s* (1995), George Hutchinson in *The Harlem Renaissance in Black and White* (1995), and Walter Benn Michaels in *Our America: Nativism, Modernism, and Pluralism* (1995). Yet I do not wish to argue that all "gaps" between modernism and the Harlem Renaissance can or should be bridged by contemporary scholars. Some gaps remain distinct in this project if only because there were quite separate spheres dictated by both law and social practice in the modern period. My aim, then, is not to flatten the substantial material and political differences among the thinkers, writers, and activists I consider, but instead to analyze the differences among their various, often competing, versions of improved human breeding. I have distinguished carefully among the various adaptations of—and occasional challenges to—eugenics as they appear in the work of W. E. B. Du Bois, E. Franklin Frazier, T. S. Eliot, Gertrude Stein, Angelina Weld Grimké, Mary A. Burrill, Nella Larsen, and the many white women eugenics field workers. As a result, this book has less in common with the works of Douglas, Hutchinson, and Benn Michaels, all of which emphasize cross-racial cooperation or participation in modern political discourse and cultural production, than it does with Kevin Gaines's *Uplifting the Race: Black Leadership, Politics, and Culture in the Twentieth Century* (1996), Gail Bederman's *Manliness and Civilization: A Cultural History of Race and Gender in the United States, 1880–1917* (1995), and Sandra Adell's *Double Consciousness/Double Bind: Theoretical Issues in Twentieth-Century Black Literature* (1994). Gaines, Bederman, and Adell examine the shared intellectual contexts of white and black modern writers, while acknowledging that differing material realities (including those produced by race, class, gender, sexuality, and the contingencies of individual lives) necessarily shaped their thinking and their texts.

What I have termed the "nation's primary post-Reconstruction legal and social modality," segregation, generally caused eugenics to take distinct forms for black and white writers; I found few instances of interracial eugenic thought or texts.[82] Middle-class white American moderns were, to adapt Coolidge's words, faced with a "problem": "not to secure new advantages but to maintain those which [they] already possess[ed]." Thus a figure like Eliot combines a utopian religious vision with a desire to return to social and literary tradition. African American middle-class moderns, on the other hand, needed both to secure new advantages and to maintain the few they already possessed. For a figure like Du Bois, that dual agenda translated into sustaining and expanding the Negro middle class while combating Jim Crow social and legal practices and white racial terrorism. This American racial-cultural divide means that the Harlem—or, as its participants identified it, the New Negro—Renaissance, both as a movement and as a term, must still be acknowledged as being, in some significant ways, distinct from white American modernism.

Of course, the Harlem Renaissance, too, is one of those "vague terms" that "still signify," to adapt Michael Levenson's words regarding modernism.[83] And, like scholars of modernism, scholars of the Harlem Renaissance disagree about the name as well as about the dates and significance of the movement.[84] Most agree that a cultural outpouring by African Americans took place in the first several decades of the twentieth century, with the peak of this period of literary and artistic production taking place during the 1920s, and perhaps centered in Manhattan. In my argument, the Harlem Renaissance was a movement, both cultural and political, that aimed to create—via art, literature, photography, and biological reproduction—a "New Negro," an improved black American who would slip what Du Bois termed "the bonds of medievalism" to become an authentically modern and representative Negro subject.[85] Beginning in the late nineteenth century and peaking in the 1920s, this increasingly biological, as well as explicitly intraracial and familial, uplift project aimed to produce and represent through cultural production an ever more intelligent, beautiful, and efficient black American subject. Of course, as with literary modernism, that aesthetic-political project cannot be separated from its particular historical contexts during the 1910s and 1920s, a context that includes the Great Migration, immigration from the West Indies, the return of black veterans from World War I, the expansion of a college-educated black middle class, segregation throughout the United States, race riots in a number of American cities, and ongoing white racial terrorism.

But there was an especially powerful historical context that American modernist and New Negro movement writers shared: theirs was the Era of Reform and Progress.[86] Michael North has observed that Ezra Pound and T. S. Eliot wanted "to overcome a stultified society and make with the tools of art a new future."[87] W. E. B. Du Bois and Angelina Weld Grimké shared that desire. But, at the same time, others were using the tools of legislation, public policy, and jurisprudence to accomplish similar ends. The "new future" of the United States would be peopled by New Americans, black and white and of mixed race, whose ideal appearance was imagined not only in the period's novels, photographs, essays, plays, and poems, but also in its statutes, Supreme Court decisions, sociological studies, management techniques, factory designs, and public health and penal policies. By examining American modernism, the Harlem Renaissance, and the Progressive Era together through the lens of Coolidge's newly intense and scrupulous Americanness, we will end up with a clearer picture of the period as a whole. In this picture, eugenics stands as the middle figure between politics and aesthetics; many modern intellectuals and reformers, regardless of race, gender, or political affiliation, saw the progress of the "body politic," the evolution of collective subjectivities, as inextricably linked with improved cultural production *and* with selective biological reproduction. My chosen authors, reformers, and texts are bound together both by their acute awareness of social categories and hierarchies (including racial, class, national, regional, and intellectual hierarchies) and by their desire to improve modern America. Although not all the figures I consider agreed that those categories and hierarchies could or should change, nearly all agreed that the selection process among modern humans could be improved, preferably by producing more people like themselves. To be more precise, what such apparently dissimilar figures like Du Bois, Dunbar-Nelson, Toomer, Eliot, Grimké, and Stein share with Malthus, Spencer, Darwin, and Galton is the habit of *self-selection*. Obviously, the image of a eugenically ideal national subject could not remain stable as it moved across lines of race, class, gender, sexual orientation, and politics; but the overall project of imagining and propagating that ideal citizen-self was widely shared across those social lines.

IN CHAPTERS 1, 2, and 3, I reexamine canonical literary figures—Du Bois, Eliot, and Stein—who have generally been perceived as essentially unlike one another (in terms of literary, political, sexual, ethnic, and racial affiliations and identities). I do so in part to document African American intellectuals' often overlooked or underestimated participation in mainstream cultural and academic trends and discourses, and in part to challenge blunt assessments of the period's politics and literature by authorial identity. I choose these three figures not so much because they are representative but because they are now *considered* representative, as they were during their own time. As such, they had disproportionate influence in their own cultural moments and continue to have that degree of influence in critical and historical treatments of modernism and the Harlem Renaissance. I have selected W. E. B. Du Bois, then, for his power as an arbiter of the New Negro movement; he sustained his role as editor, literally of the *Crisis* and symbolically of the race itself, by continuously documenting and promoting his vision of an ideal New Negro family, particularly during the 1910s and 1920s. In fact, David Levering Lewis, in the second volume of his definitive biography of Du Bois, frequently refers to his subject, shorthand, as "the editor."[88] I have selected T. S. Eliot for his analogous role as a kind of intraracial editor, not only of the *Criterion* but of Anglo-American modernism as a whole; he frequently wrote broad cultural and social prescriptions according to "the principle of trying to secure the best people of each generation and type."[89] I have chosen Stein, like Du Bois and Eliot, for her status as metonymic representative—but of an avant-garde modernism often represented in contemporary scholarship as an alternative to Eliot and Pound's brand of modernism and of politics. Although often hailed for her highly experimental, deeply literary-aesthetic sensibility, Stein turns out to be particularly useful in demonstrating the inseparability of the scientific, social, and historical from the literary, especially in the modern period. Indeed, compared with the work of all of the other literary figures I consider, Stein's is perhaps most thoroughly grounded in and structured by the material conditions of American modernity, especially as those conditions affected women. Her *Three Lives* (1909), in particular, explores the physical and medical consequences of modern social and professional formations, particularly the rise of obstetrics, for African American and immigrant women. While Stein's first published book was racialist, and at times racist, it also expressed a degree of sympathy for its protagonists, especially female immigrant domestic laborers, whose fertility represented—and arguably still represents—a modern political and social preoccupation.

In chapter 4, I consider how New Negro women writers themselves, particularly Angelina Weld Grimké, Mary Burrill, Georgia Douglas Johnson, and Alice Dunbar-Nelson, represented the politics of black women's fertility in the modern United States. Like such white women moderns as Stein and Sanger, New Negro women writers of the 1920s understood that women necessarily had to contend, in distinctly personal and bodily ways, with any national or racial breeding project. Dunbar-Nelson, for example, considered dysgenic trends within the Negro race to be "*Woman's* Most Serious Problem" (emphasis added), the title of her 1927 *Messenger* article about the declining birthrate, increasing infant mortality rate, and differential birthrate among modern African Americans. She explicitly linked New Negro womanhood with decreased fertility, observing that "our women are going into the kind of work that taxes both physical and mental capacities, which of itself, limits fecundity" and that "our educated and intelligent classes are refusing to have children."[90] Although Dunbar-Nelson's suggestion that modernity has had dysgenic effects on the Negro race may sound to our ears patently elitist and eugenic, she nonetheless rightly identified an extraordinarily complex, vexed, and recurrent topic for the college-educated, middle-class, African American women writers I consider, writers who offered some of the period's strongest challenges to mainline eugenics. For that reason alone, their work merits far more scholarly attention than it has garnered to date.

New Negro women writers' challenges to eugenics emerged most clearly in a genre invented in the 1910s by Grimké, Burrill, and Dunbar-Nelson—the antilynching drama. As I explore in detail in chapter 4, although these dramas have struck many contemporary scholars as repetitive, retrograde, and sentimental (particularly in their loving representations of domesticity), these plays were in fact very much of their time in that they show that no performance of an idealized black family—that is, no eugenic breeding project—could possibly be enacted in a modern national setting that included pervasive racism and white racial violence. Indeed, the plays' authors were quite alert to the implicit racial subtext in Coolidge's aim to exclude Americans who are "treading the way that leads back to the jungle." For example, Grimké's 1916 antilynching play, *Rachel*, challenges a eugenics based on white supremacy, even as it worries about despair and sterility among the well-educated Negro middle class (of which Grimké was, of course, a member). In her notes about *Rachel*, Grimké wrote: "I drew my characters, then, deliberately from the best type of colored people."[91] But in the play that "best type" is clearly selected against in the setting of the modern United States, where the best black men are lynched, and the best black women choose childlessness as a result of repeated violent racial trauma within their families. *Rachel* demonstrates that America's racism and its tolerance of lynching (not public health measures, as white supremacist and elitist eugenicists from Spencer to Wiggam had argued) have resulted in unnatural selection for both blacks and whites. Lynchers, the worst of the whites, remain unpunished and free to propagate their kind—as one of the characters in *Rachel* says, "The scum of the earth shall succeed."[92] By contrast, the lineages of the "best type of colored people" are abruptly and violently terminated. At play's end, the heroine Rachel—her father killed by lynchers and her adopted son suffering from racist taunts—wonders hysterically whether it would be "kindness to kill" black children before they experience the full extent of American racism.[93] The play—with its linked preoccupations with racial violence, reproduction, and the quality of the individual subject—exposes the fundamental illogic of mainline eugenic thinking in the United States—that is, the version that was being advanced by A. E. Wiggam in the 1910s and 1920s and that had been originated by nineteenth-century English thinkers.

Spencer and Darwin had feared that increasingly democratic social and economic structures (as represented by poor laws and universal vaccination) would result in excessive health and fecundity among lower classes and races. For them, modernity led to unnatural selection among human beings. Lothrop Stoddard offered the plainest American version of the belief in unnatural selection in his 1924 *Revolt against Civilization: The Menace of the Under Man*: "Civilization [has] meant a change from a 'natural' to a more or less artificial, man-made environment, in which natural selection was increasingly modified by 'social' selection. And social selection altered survival values all along the line. In the first place, it enabled many weak, stupid, and degenerate persons to live and beget children who would have certainly perished in the state of nature. . . . The strong *individual* survived even better than *before—but he tended to have fewer children*" (emphasis in the original).[94] Grimké may have agreed that the best individuals were having fewer children, but she disagreed about the reasons. *Rachel* argues that the true source of "unnatural selection" in the modern United States was not "civilization" but a kind of lack of civilization in the form of ongoing social injustice and racism.[95] I have focused on *Rachel*, as well as other antilynching dramas, for that rare challenge to, and effective redefinition of, the period's prevailing eugenic notion of "unnatural selection." Ironically, it was another set of "New Women," also largely overlooked in contemporary scholarship, who offered one of the strongest endorsements of mainline eugenics and who directly enabled its enactment.

In chapter 5, I consider the white women eugenics field workers of the U.S. family studies, who carried out the often appalling project of improving the breeding of Americans in the interwar years. The field workers located and evaluated native-born dysgenics in order to "sternly cut [them] off from perpetuating a noisome progeny," to use the words of the very first family study.[96] Although only a handful of historians have examined their work, the field workers were central in the enactment of a particularly vigorous and orthodox version of nativist, elitist, and sexist (Kevles's "mainline") eugenics. In fact, they were eager to heed Coolidge's inaugural call to abrogate the constitutional rights of "the barbarian and the defective," who "are not promoting freedom and independence, are not following the path of civilization, but are displaying the traits of ignorance, of servitude, of savagery." During the 1910s and 1920s, hundreds of college-educated women were traveling throughout the United States under the supervision of the Eugenics Record Office in Long Island, narrating and quantifying the genetic toll on the national germ plasm being exacted by feebleminded, poor, and backward rural white Americans.

Like the more obviously literary writers I consider, the field workers envisioned a "new future" for America, while the "tools" they used were both literary and scientific. In the field workers' unpublished notes and in their published studies, race, nation, gender, region, and class meet biological reform and social progress to create a new interdisciplinary genre: a mixture of short story, personal narrative, travel narrative, sociology, and statistics. Indeed, the field workers' writings can be seen as a kind of inverse (and equally intraracial) counterpart to the new genre created by Grimké, Burrill, and Douglas Johnson.[97] But whereas the antilynching plays assume an inequality of opportunity (brought about by racism) that has resulted in unnatural selection (the best black people die out); the field workers' writings, by contrast, assume an equality of opportunity (provided by public schools and charity) that has resulted in another kind of unnatural selection (the white dysgenic are fecund and prolific). Yet, quite unlike any of the literary figures I consider, the field workers were directly responsible for the institutionalization (often for the purposes of sterilization) of thousands of ostensibly dysgenic people—all in the name of progress and more "scrupulous" Americanness. Their professional activities and writings thus partake of, but also clearly exceed, the relatively metaphorical eugenics of modern poets, novelists, and playwrights. Given the field workers' clear and original engagement with, and inscription and enactment of, mainline American eugenics, it is remarkable that they have been nearly ignored in contemporary scholarship on the reform era. Indeed, despite their production of directly competing forms of what I have termed the paradigmatic modern American discourse (eugenics), neither the field workers nor the antilynching dramatists have ever been considered "representative" by literary scholars or historians. Their presence in this project is meant to reposition them at the center of studies of the period and to supplement, and at times to challenge, the representativeness traditionally and readily assigned to Du Bois, Stein, and especially Eliot. Eliot has repeatedly—and mistakenly —been labeled an enthusiastic eugenicist in part because of his reactionary politics, his whiteness, his literary racism, and his status as the preeminent Anglo-American modernist. But eugenics, as we have seen, was neither inherently reactionary nor inherently white; in fact, Eliot's conservative social and religious agenda actually served to distance him from eugenics, which, in any incarnation, calls for active, distinctly nonmetaphorical interventions in individual reproductive lives in the name of collective (racial or national) progress.

THIS PROJECT, by its textual selection and methodology, implicitly argues that democratic, historically grounded, highly nuanced literary and cultural study offers a useful—though not the only—means to assess a social, scientific, political, and aesthetic phenomenon as flexible and pervasive as eugenics. In turn, it shows that the study of eugenics itself permits us to develop a fuller and more precise picture of the modern period in the United States, particularly the 1910s and 1920s. Because so many writers and reformers shared eugenic ideals in those decades, eugenics allows us to examine the period, including its cultural production and political activism, in a broad and inclusive context. At the same time, because individuals tailored eugenic discourse to their own subject positions and to their own political and social agenda, we can also develop sharp local views of the period and its writers. *Unnatural Selections* bears witness to the ways that literature, medicine, and social science contributed to disturbing eugenic national goals, even while it acknowledges that writers like Stein and Grimké could never have had the direct influence on American lives that the field workers so clearly had.

Because the field workers brought about (often devastating) "real-life" effects even as they produced a kind of new creative writing, their work in particular calls for a carefully interdisciplinary approach. Therefore, in the chapter on the field workers, I have combined the literary-critical with the historical and sociological; some would argue that, in so doing, I have, as Eric Lott readily admits he has, "unquestionably poached."[98] But Lott's admission, as disarming and forthright as it is, also perpetuates notions of academic territorialism and transgression that this project contests. I, without hesitation or apology, blend theories—including black feminist, deconstructive, new historical, historical-materialist, and psychoanalytic—in a mixture that assumes and values impurity in literary, historical, and cultural study. But while I protect the mixture, I do not protect the ingredients. I often challenge the usefulness of some theoretical approaches for some texts. For example, the chapter on antilynching drama argues that psychoanalytic theory of both the period and the present fails to account for either these playwrights' or their characters' (raced and gendered and classed) experiences of, and performances within, an ailing and racist modern United States. Similarly, the chapter on the field workers explores the limitations of both feminist theory and new historical theory in assessing the role of these politically reactionary and socially conservative "New Women." In the case of the field workers, searching for their texts' political unconscious was not as crucial as analyzing their quite conscious, and clearly dangerous, sociopolitical intent and effect.

Overall, the project insists on what one scholar terms "rigorous historicization."[99] Aware of and sympathetic with recent calls for literary scholars to return to the archives, I have done just that. I recognize that, in the process, I myself have unquestionably been selective—and certainly in at least some ways of which I am not aware. This is an in-

Winners of fitter families contests at the Kansas Free Fair, 1923–24.
Courtesy of the American Philosophical Society.

evitable part of any scholar's enterprise. As the Kansas fitter family examiners realized, "The history is perhaps the most important item of the examination, and it is also the most difficult task of all."[100] Of course, although they did not recognize it themselves, their own highly politicized, ideological goal—to improve the breeding of Americans—was a greater obstacle to getting "a complete and consistent record" than were the "imperfect recollections and limited information of most families," which the examiners explicitly recognized as obstacles to a complete and accurate examination of the past.[101] And although my goal in this book will, I hope, be clearly seen as fundamentally opposed to that of the fitter family examiners, I realize that the record I have compiled is necessarily incomplete.

Stein scholar John Whittier-Ferguson has recently challenged academics' imperfect retrieval of the past, charging that faulty or highly selective historicization utterly fails an author like Stein, who made it her business to expose the innate shortcomings of memory and time and their intellectualized offspring, history. He suggests that our current trips to the archives, even when we acknowledge their partial results, will not necessarily bring us "closer than ever before to unprecedentedly accurate, psychologically nuanced positioning of texts, authors, and events in time."[102] Accurate representation of a complete past, including its authors and texts, is, of course, impossible. And I agree, too, that Stein's work, like that of any writer, deserves careful critical and historical consideration wherein we are "honoring the shapes of the texts" (117). But Stein does not merit special historiographic or literary-critical treatment simply because she herself resisted temporal positioning or because her politics were inscrutable or inconsistent. Authors, for better or worse, cannot dictate the critical terms by which their work is assessed. More important, the notion that our current archival turn is all about accurate remembrance of the past may miss the mark.

Current literary and historical methodologies say as much, and perhaps more, about the present as they say about the past. In other words, the more interesting question here is not whether we are getting the past right but rather what our chosen methodology (regarding the past) says about the present. What politics of aesthetics and of aesthetic inquiry are we now enacting? When we believe that we can truly "know" an author or a text by means of volumes of historical minutiae, we are participating in a wider, cross-disciplinary (and perhaps overconfident) discourse of knowledge and identity. For example, the human genome project promises to know us all—at once individually and collectively—in an apparently democratic mapping of the identity of all humankind, in a kind of contemporary and scientized *Everybody's Autobiography*. As the head of the National Human Genome Research Institute puts it, "We are learning at a very rapid clip how we are all the same and all different."[103] Such a melding of the individual and the collective within a national context in order to determine, finally, the nature of our identity represents a social, scientific, and literary (and inevitably political) notion of human subjectivity that looks remarkably similar to the modern era's eugenic hubris.

I am skeptical about elevating either science or literature, then or now, above the ideologies and politics of its time. As Toni Morrison has suggested, Gertrude Stein, though often held separate from Eliot and Pound in negative assessments of modernist politics, cannot be seen as wholly outside the racialist thinking of her period.[104] Though she undeniably registered feminist protest against conventional literary and medical techniques, Stein also perpetuated quite conventional racist portraiture of black Americans. In other words, radicalism of literary form does not comfortably or consistently correspond to the representation of radicalized social formations. In my chapter on Stein, I combine new historicism with more recent historical-materialist methodology to assess her texts' investment in some of the major and unquestionably ideological and political struggles of American modernity. I place her *Three Lives* within the context not only of eugenics but also of the related battle between obstetrics and midwifery that was taking place at the time of its publication.

Of course, it is not news to us that writers cannot transcend their times. In the 1910s and 1920s, eugenics was so pervasive that it became nearly invisible as an ideology, appearing in a remarkably wide range of texts by an equally wide range of authors. Though some Americans objected to eugenics, no one thought to be ashamed of it until much later. Only in the aftermath of the Holocaust, when survivors and liberators told their stories, did "selection" take on a new bodily and horrifying meaning within the context of the Nazis' almost fully realized eugenic program. Although the National Socialists of Hitler's Germany clearly took the selection process to inhuman extremes, we must not forget what Stefan Kühl has termed the "connection" between Anglo-American eugenic discourse and policy and the "final solution" enacted in the Holocaust.[105] The cultural-racial improvement project of modern American writers and activists, white and black, must be remembered and told because such processes of self-selection cannot always be neatly contained within temporal, discursive, literary, racial, national, or familial boundaries. Even within the United States, modern writers' relatively benign, largely metaphorical eugenics—in which they represented national and racial improvement as inseparable from cultural improvement—had its malignant, nonmetaphorical counterpart in much of the nation's public policy, including federal immigration restrictions and the Supreme Court—sanctioned compulsory sterilization statutes enforced by the field workers. As discredited as it is now, in the 1910s and 1920s eugenics was, for the vast majority of the U.S. population, simply "true"—just common sense. In my conclusion, I explore the very real possibility that there is some way of thinking, some scientific innovation, or some social or political phenomenon

that we, in the present, have accepted as thoroughly and as unquestioningly. And what is perhaps an even more pressing question: what
saturating, permeating ideology within our national culture will look
to later generations as dangerous, as *unnatural*, as eugenics now appears
to us?

James was aghast. "But Helga! Good heavens! Don't you see that if we—I mean people like us—don't have children, the others will still have. That's one of the things that's the matter with us. The race is sterile at the top. Few, very few Negroes of the better class have children, and each generation has to struggle again with the obstacles of the preceding ones, lack of money, education, and background. I feel very strongly about this. We're the ones who must have the children if the race is to get anywhere."

"Well, I for one don't intend to contribute any to the cause."
—Nella Larsen, *Quicksand* (1928)

W. E. B. Du Bois's Family Crisis

The mission of racial uplift has a long, rich, but problematic history. Although the idea of racial improvement has been in place since the beginning of the African American literary tradition, writers have constructed the means and ends of the improvement process differently, depending on their personal, historical, social, and political circumstances. In the 1770s Phillis Wheatley did not use the term "uplift," but she promoted correction of what she termed "errors" engendered by the paganism of Africa.[1] For Wheatley, at least in her public discourse, conversion to Christianity was essential if "*Negros*, black as *Cain*" were to become "refin'd."[2] With Frederick Douglass's *Narrative* in 1845, Christianity as prerequisite for freedom and racial advancement was supplemented, and perhaps supplanted by, literacy and physical and political resistance. By the late nineteenth century, the term "uplift" was not only common in intellectual and literary parlance; it had also found a more clearly intraracial expression, at least partly in response to segregation's emergence as the nation's dominant social, political, and legal modality.

A number of scholars have begun to limn the sometimes troubling history of uplift in the late 1800s. Kevin Gaines, in his wide-ranging and impressive *Uplifting the Race*, argues, as I do, that uplift and "self-help" ideology at the turn of the century "functioned," to a degree, "as an accommodation to blacks' noncitizenship status."[3] The intraracial, or class, distinctions at the heart of this version of uplift allowed many African American intellectuals to view themselves as racial exemplars, constituting, in Gaines's words, "evidence of what they called racial progress."[4] Hazel Carby has pointed out that as of 1893 W. E. B. Du Bois, for one, explicitly linked the "advancement of the race" with "his own personal achievements as an intellectual."[5] She also delivers a compelling critique of Du Boisian uplift, as envisioned in his 1903 *Souls of Black Folk*, finding it both patriarchal and highly moralistic.[6] In the Reconstruction and post-Reconstruction eras, many African American activist-writers, both male and female, constructed uplift as a middle-class leadership's bestowal of enlightenment—represented by literacy, bourgeois sensibility, and standard English diction—on a dialect-speaking, "Negro" folk.[7]

Then, from about 1900 to 1930, uplift took on a more disturbing quality as the period's notions of racial improvement (for both white and black people) became ever more tightly intertwined with the emerging science of genetics. As Laura Doyle puts it, the "era of the Harlem Renaissance and of modernism was also the era of eugenics."[8] However, Doyle specifically exempts W. E. B. Du Bois from eugenic thinking, arguing that he, along with Franz Boas, "spoke openly against racialism of all kinds throughout this period."[9] Similarly, Shawn Michelle Smith likens Du Bois's archive of photographs of African Americans for the Paris Exposition of 1899 to Francis Galton's explicitly eugenic composite photographs of ideal English types in his *Inquiries into Human Faculty and Its Development* (1883), yet she avoids the obvious conclusion that Du Bois, too, was engaging in a kind of eugenic visual documentation. Smith argues instead that Du Bois's use of the photos undercut the sort of "essential, physical racial identity sought by eugenicists and white supremacists."[10] But Du Bois's choice and use of photographs under the rubric "Types of American Negroes" cannot be interpreted solely as a reaction to white supremacism; he was, at the same time, advancing his own intraracial agenda, one that cannot be so easily divorced from eugenic thinking and portraiture.[11] Neither eugenic photographic representation nor eugenics itself was solely white supremacist or wholly interracial. Indeed eugenics, including eugenic expressions of visual culture, found a ready partner in the period's class-based, intraracial improvement project for African Americans — that is, uplift.[12] One could speak out against racialism and white supremacy and yet embrace some form of eugenic (and, indeed, even racialist) thought and representation. As Gaines observes, in the modern era, "the majority of writers and intellectuals [both black and white] inescapably drew on deeply problematic varieties of knowledge about race."[13] Often overlooked by literary critics and cultural historians alike is the fact that modern African American writers and intellectuals were not necessarily entirely alienated, as a result of their racial identity, from now-discredited but then-normative ideologies.[14]

The writing and editorializing of W. E. B. Du Bois, a passionate and brilliant student of and contributor to Western philosophical and political discourse, provide an especially good site for exploring how discourses on race, genetics, and social improvement could converge. In general, of course, Du Bois was acutely aware of (and often built his public identity on) his distance from mainstream national, political, and social ideologies; moreover, he often measured that distance in specifically racial terms. He famously and prophetically proclaimed the "color-line" to be "the problem of the twentieth century."[15] It was certainly his own central "problem"—he even subtitled his second autobiography "An Essay toward an Autobiography of a Race Concept."[16] Raised in the working- and middle-class Massachusetts town of Great Barrington and Harvard-educated, Du Bois says in his third autobiography, published posthumously, that "had it not been for the race problem early thrust upon me and enveloping me, I should have probably been an unquestioning worshiper at the shrine of the established social order." Given his background, that is, he "should" have embraced the status quo, but, as he puts it, "apparently [race] . . . alone saved me from complete conformity with the thoughts and confusions of then current social trends. . . . Otherwise I might easily have been simply the current product of my day."[17] Leaving open the possibility that he may be in partial conformity with the "thoughts and confusions" of his day, Du Bois nevertheless invites here and elsewhere just the sort of critical misreading that has, until recently, held him too far apart from the social, scientific, and philosophical "trends" of his day —including the eugenic thinking that was pervasive, even ubiquitous, in the United States during the 1920s. In a 1922 issue of the *Crisis*, Du Bois's interest in eugenics is clear: "The Negro has not been breeding for an object" and therefore must begin to "train and breed for brains, for efficiency, for beauty."[18]

Many historians and literary and cultural critics of the period have underestimated eugenic ideology's power and significance (indeed, its singular appeal) for modern, male African American intellectuals. Eugenics, in at least some form, underpinned not only James Vayle's uplift discourse in Nella Larsen's *Quicksand*, but also the political and social discourse of many other "race men" during the 1920s and 1930s. During that period, E. Franklin Frazier, A. Philip Randolph, Chandler Owen, James Weldon Johnson, Du Bois's great rival Marcus Garvey, and especially Du Bois himself—all endorsed some version of eugenics. Among modern African American writers and leaders, fewer women than men, however, espoused eugenic ideology. Helga Crane in *Quicksand* was certainly not alone, then, in resisting any assigned role as reproducer for a racial cause.[19] As Ann Douglas confirms, many of the artistic and intellectual "new women" of the 1920s, both black and white, were "reluctant breeders."[20] Indeed, as I will explore in a later chapter, New Negro women writers—Angelina Weld Grimké and Georgia Douglas Johnson, in particular—produced some of the period's few challenges to eugenic thinking. But eugenics did appeal to many male, as well as a significant number of female, especially white female, American writers and activists, regardless of their political orientation or, in the case of men, their race. Eugenics provided them with a seemingly effective—and seemingly scientific—response to the conditions of modernity, especially foreign immigration and domestic migration. In fact, the scientific dimension of eugenics helped establish its appeal for the "race men" of the 1920s. In a 1922 *Crisis* editorial, Du Bois argued that "birth control is science and sense applied to the bringing of children into the world, and of all who need it we Negroes are the first. We in America are becoming sharply divided into the mass who have endless children and the class who through long postponement of marriage have few or none."[21] Uplift in this period often participates in, and partakes of, not only evolutionary theory (as Gaines rightly argues)[22] but genetic theory as well. And in the 1920s and 1930s at least, genetics and eugenics were inseparable.

Although Gregor Mendel had published the results of his experiments with peas in 1866, his work languished in obscurity until its rediscovery (simultaneously in three countries) in 1900.[23] Mendelian genetics permitted the association of an astonishingly wide array of undesirable human behaviors with heritable unit traits. Geneticists in the 1920s identified pauperism, wanderlust, alcoholism, and especially feeblemindedness, as unit characters inherited according to a simple dominant-recessive chi-square pattern. Mendelian genetics was particularly useful for twentieth-century eugenicists who wished to assign "dysgenic" status to ever-expanding categories of people (the poor, the unemployed, immigrants, migrants, the non-English-speaking, and so on). As a result, the post-1900 acceptance of Mendelian inheritance laws corresponds, chronologically and theoretically, both with increasing anxiety in the United States regarding sociodemographic change and with an increasing illiberalism in the agenda of many American eugenicists.[24]

Between 1880 and 1920, unprecedented levels of foreign immigration to and domestic migration within the United States provided perhaps the clearest stimulus for many Americans' turn to Mendelian eugenic thinking. Roughly 28 million immigrants came to the United States during that time.[25] In addition, between 1890 and 1920, over 1.2 million African Americans migrated from the southern to the northern United States, with at least 300,000 migrating in a single decade, between 1910 and 1920.[26] Around 1905 worries about these tides of migration and immigration began to appear in the popular press.[27] By the 1920s, many white supremacist tracts (written for a lay audience, and several of them best sellers) were raising the alarm about racial threats to the national gene pool.[28] There were even white "fitter family contests" held at state and county fairs in the 1910s and 1920s.[29] But eugenic anxiety was not confined to white American popular culture, nor did it originate there. Social scientific, scientific, and political formulations (and legislative enactments) of eugenic policy had become commonplace in the United States well before the 1920s. The period from 1882 to 1924 witnessed the passage of ever more restrictive immigration policies in the name of protecting the nation from "foreign defective germ plasm."[30] At the same time, registration, suspension of financial relief measures, segregation by institutionalization, and compulsory sterilization were emerging as the preferred eugenic prescriptions for containing America's native dysgenic population. At least 60,000 people in the United States were compulsorily sterilized for eugenic reasons between 1907 and 1964.[31]

But despite the obviously protectionist, elitist, and white supremacist nature of much of the period's eugenic activism, U.S. eugenics in the 1920s cannot be characterized as an exclusively white or reactionary phenomenon. As eugenics historian Daniel Kevles has shown, there were two distinct "strains" of eugenic thinking in the modern United States: one was espoused by progressive social reformers, and the other (which he terms "mainline" eugenics) by social conservatives.[32] Both Havelock Ellis and Margaret Sanger, for example, had eugenic sympathies. In *The Problem of Race-Regeneration*, Ellis insists that "we need to extend and deepen social reform"; but he cautions that while we are thereby "smoothing the path for the fit," we are also "making the path smoother for the unfit." He concludes that we must therefore apply our "efforts to raise the level of civilisation," but "at the right spot."[33] Sanger drew similarly eugenic conclusions, writing in 1926: "I am glad to say that the United States Government has already taken certain steps to control the quality of our population through the drastic immigration laws. . . . But while we close our gates to the so-called 'undesirables' from other countries, we make no attempt to discourage or cut down the rapid multiplication of the unfit and undesirable at home."[34] It is important to understand the broad appeal and ideological flexibility of eugenics: how else could such a range of modern writers and thinkers embrace the goal of improving human breeding?

Because eugenics focuses simultaneously on the quality of the individual "breeder" and the quality of the collective body (variously constructed as the race, an elite within the race, the nation, a class within the nation), it effectively bridges the theoretical distance between the individual and the collective modern subject. That such a tension between the collective and individual subject exists (as a byproduct of the modern liberal democratic state) stands as a critical-historical commonplace. In her biography of Sanger, Ellen Chesler describes "postwar disenchantment with collectivist solutions to social problems."[35] Chesler argues that Sanger's advocacy of birth control in the modern United States was aimed at alleviating social problems by changing individual behavior. In other words, the widespread use of birth control, implemented as part of a national eugenic program, represented a means of "propagating individuals capable of meeting the rigorous demands of modern life."[36] By contrast, eugenics historian Carl Degler concludes that because eugenics worries primarily about the quality of a collective gene pool, it thoroughly subordinates the individual to the collective. "In the name of its philosophy," Degler argues, eugenics "put society's good above that of the individual; it countered selfish individualism with social responsibility."[37] Unlike both Chesler and Degler, I am arguing that the ideology of eugenics effectively bridges the individual and the collective, thereby undermining binary constructions of modernism or of the Harlem Renaissance. This bridging quality also effectively distinguishes eugenics from evolutionary theory and from more general discourses of race.[38]

For Du Bois, eugenic thinking helped resolve the obvious tension between himself, as an elite yet paradoxically representative individual leader, and the Negro masses apparently so sorely in need of uplift. Michael North has observed a similar dynamic among some white, even conservative and reactionary, modernists. Pound, like Yeats and Eliot, North argues, "conceives of the elite as a universal class, a minority that represents best because of its difference from the majority."[39] This paradoxical relationship between the enlightened modern intellectual leader and the unenlightened masses exposes, in North's words, the "logical contradictions of [an] elitism in which the elite bases its claims both on its resemblance to and its difference from the mass."[40] Of course, Pound's and Eliot's social and political goals were not compatible with those of Du Bois or Sanger or Ellis. But for eugenic advocates of any political orientation or racial identity, the "reconstruction of society" (whether as antiracist, socialist, aristocratic, oligarchic, or racially "pure") ideally would be engendered by the preserving and multiplying—that is, selecting—of individuals like themselves. In this limited, intraracial sense, then, Du Bois's famous "Talented Tenth" is not wholly unlike Eliot's "international fraternity of men of letters . . . whose business" it was "to maintain intellectual activity on the highest level."[41] Both groups represent a collection of superior, modern, intraracial, yet international, intellectual leaders.

From the beginning of the 1903 essay in which he first uses the term, Du Bois describes the "Talented Tenth" in gendered sociobiological terms as "exceptional men" and as the "Best of the race," who must "guide the Mass away from the contamination and death of the Worst."[42] Here Du Bois has clearly "absorbed and transformed" one dominant cultural and eugenic text,[43] adapting it quite early in his career to launch what was to become, in the 1920s, an increasingly biosocial version of uplift. In fact, throughout his career, the "Talented Tenth" served to metonymize an intraracial form of elitism; but, in Du Bois's writing from the twenties, the "Talented Tenth" is identified with an explicitly biological superiority. Thus, although a great deal of

Du Bois criticism of the past twenty years has focused on his possibly biological definition of "race" (that is, his potential for racial essentialism), it is in fact his far more clearly and consistently biological definition of both an intraracial hierarchy within the United States and an international elite of color (particularly as envisioned in his 1928 novel, *Dark Princess*) that merits closer attention. Kwame Anthony Appiah rigorously and productively probed Du Bois's changing constructions of race in a well-known 1985 article, "The Uncompleted Argument: Du Bois and the Illusion of Race." Arguing that Du Bois never completely abandoned an essentialist, biologically based definition of race, Appiah suggested that even Du Bois's assertion of a common black history (made in his 1940 autobiography, *Dusk of Dawn*) "simply bur[ies] the biological conception below the surface" and thus fails to "transcend it."[44] Appiah's argument, while compelling and at times completely convincing, perhaps too relentlessly dissects Du Bois, who stated quite plainly in 1933 that "race is psychology, not biology."[45] On the other hand, Paul Gilroy has rightly noted Du Bois's "complex and shifting positions" on race throughout a long and prolific career; positions so complex and shifting, in fact, that I would argue that we simply cannot be sure about Du Bois's views concerning the reality of race; he defined "race" variously in order to accommodate varying circumstances and strategies.[46] But we can be sure that throughout his career Du Bois sustained a vision of a naturally able leadership of color. In the 1920s, that natural ability generally coincided, for Du Bois, with good breeding.

The intersection of elite leadership, racial redemption, and biological reproduction was articulated so vividly and sensuously in Du Bois's 1928 *Dark Princess* that the novel might be termed a kind of eugenic fantasy. Set in the years 1923 to 1927, *Dark Princess* follows the many, often torturous, political and amorous adventures of its handsome and talented African American male protagonist, Matthew Towns, to their climax in his marriage to an Indian princess, Kautilya, who is "of royal blood by many scores of generations of direct descent."[47] Claudia Tate has recently argued that we must begin to take into account what she terms the "textual desire" of black writing, particularly in novels.[48] For Du Bois, she argues, the "public satisfaction of racial equality is connected and somewhat analogous to the private pleasure of eroticism, for eros and polity are mutually signifying" (49). Tate finds this interrelationship especially apparent in *Dark Princess*, a work that, as she points out, Du Bois considered his "favorite" among all his writings (55). Certainly, Tate is right in setting up the equations that structure the novel: "propaganda = art = erotic desire" and "propaganda = freedom = erotic consummation" (50). But consummation does not bear a simply structural or metaphoric relationship to freedom in *Dark Princess*; by the end of the novel, the union of an African American Talented Tenth man and a royal Indian woman has led to a literal product in their eugenic progeny. In other words, Du Bois's heterosexual equation is both political and genetic. Near the end of the book, Towns declares that the birth of their son "changes the world" (308), while the final words of *Dark Princess* are spoken in chorus by "The Great Central Committee of Yellow, Black, and Brown" (296)—a group of racial and national representatives who declare the baby to be the "Messenger and Messiah to all the Darker Worlds!" (311). Du Bois tries to denaturalize this clearly reproductive vision of an international Talented Tenth of color by articulating his own racial-political desires through Princess Kautilya: "And, oh, my Matthew, your oligarchy as you conceive it is not the antithesis of democracy—it is democracy, if only the selection of the oligarchs is just and true. Birth is the method of blind fools. Wealth is the gambler's method. Only Talent served from the great Reservoir of All Men of All Races, of All Classes, of All Ages, of Both Sexes—this is real Aristocracy, real Democracy—the only path to that great and final Freedom which you so well call Divine Anarchy" (285). Du Bois's attempt here to erase "birth" as the source of his elite international leadership is far outweighed by the novel's ongoing, explicit, and implicit investment in Towns's "sudden love for a woman" as being "more than romance—it was a longing for action, breadth, helpfulness, great constructive deeds" (42). Their erotic and political partnership would, in the end, initiate the construction of a great leadership consisting of a new and "different kind of man" (272). The Princess came to Towns "quite naturally" (209), bringing her generations-long royalty together with his "inherent polish [and] evidence of breeding" (203) to produce a "Maharajah," a Messiah, of "royal blood" (308).

Granted, Du Bois largely abandoned explicitly eugenic rhetoric after the 1920s, as I will discuss in my conclusion. But even as late as 1948, and despite his increasingly leftist politics, Du Bois still used biological metaphors to describe his superior set of race leaders. In his 1948 Wilberforce speech, "The Talented Tenth: A Memorial Address," he ostensibly aims to reject the problematically aristocratic, if not oligarchic, model of "Talented Tenth" racial leadership when he adds the "basic requirement of character" to his list of criteria for "successful leadership."[49] Ironically, however, he ends up not with a talented tenth but with a "guiding hundredth"![50] This new, even more select group would consist of the old guard joined by a "screened young membership" of "predominantly active, virile men."[51] Du Bois asserts that the resulting "body" would be "large enough to represent all," yet "small enough to insure exceptional quality." What links Du Bois's "body" of leading race men in 1903 with his international elite of color in 1928 and his "body" of leaders in 1948 is not only his (gendered) biological rhetoric but also his own role as arbiter: he will choose the individual men who constitute that "body." Careful, "just and true"—that is, *natural*—selection emerges as Du Bois's tool of choice for constructing the national "Talented Tenth" in 1903, the international "Great Central Committee of Yellow, Black, and Brown" in 1928, and the "guiding hundredth" in 1948 as elite, yet representative groups.

Du Bois exercised his power of selection perhaps most dramatically and effectively from his post as editor of the *Crisis*, the official organ of the NAACP. As David Levering Lewis argues, the journal "was the expression, in monthly installments, of its editor's intellectual and moral personality."[52] Indeed, from its inception in 1910 to the editor's resignation in 1934, the *Crisis* mirrors a Du Boisian ideal of social, economic, and political—but also genetic—racial uplift, wherein the Talented Tenth are naturally representative of, but also superior to, the Negro masses. For example, Du Bois declared in 1912 that the production of the Talented Tenth must begin with the commitment of "honest colored men and women" not "to bring aimless rafts of children into the world, but as many as, with reasonable sacrifice, we can train to largest manhood."[53] Having procreated responsibly, the "immediate program" of the "American Negro" must then be to "seek out colored children of ability and genius to open up to them broader, industrial opportunity and above all, to find that Talented Tenth and encourage it by the best and most exhaustive training in order to supply the Negro race and the world with leaders, thinkers and artists."[54] Thus, Du Bois's "Talented Tenth" comprises not just an already uplifted representative body but a carefully bred, selected, and trained elite. Although such an ideology of racial uplift by a few talented leaders is inherently elitist, it need not necessarily be *eugenic*; however, Du

Bois's rhetoric in the *Crisis* in the 1920s demonstrates that uplift ideology adapted quite readily to the period's characteristic eugenic thinking. In a 1926 editorial, Du Bois describes the problem: "There are to be sure not enough children in the families of the better class."[55] Clearly he is concerned about a population "crisis" as well as a racial-political one. In fact, from 1910 to 1934, the *Crisis* advocated a kind of intraracial family planning. During his editorship, Du Bois helped construct a fully illustrated narrative of a successfully eugenicizing racial family. By cataloging and photographing the accomplishments of African Americans, the *Crisis* documented the nonexceptionality, as well as the expansion, of modern black middle-class urbanity.

This positive representational project works, in a way, to counter the more negative, class-based intraracial analyses in Du Bois's earlier work. For example, while Du Bois's use of the term "Talented Tenth" is quite well known, few scholars cite his coinage of the term "submerged tenth" in *The Philadelphia Negro*, his groundbreaking 1899 urban sociological study. In *The Philadelphia Negro*, Du Bois divided the families of Philadelphia into "four grades," with "Grade 4" being the "lowest class of criminals, prostitutes and loafers; the 'submerged tenth.'"[56] *The Philadelphia Negro*, along with a number of later black and urban sociological studies, documented the apparently unregulated behaviors of migrant and working-class "Negroes" in American cities, as well as their potentially deleterious effects on the African American uplift project. *The Philadelphia Negro*'s sometimes elitist intraracial politics emerge out of Du Bois's anxious awareness of the influx of "untrained and poorly educated [Negro] countrymen, rushing from the hovels of the country . . . into the strange life of a great city" (45) in tension with his reification of an already established urban Negro upper class. For Du Bois, that upper class "forms the realized ideal of the group" and provides the standard by which the group as a whole should be "understood and finally judged" (7).

This combination of anxiety about inferior migrants and elevation of an elite yet representative intraracial minority recurs in the work of other modern African American male intellectuals. E. Franklin Frazier, in his landmark black family studies of the early 1930s, echoes Du Bois, noting the "breakdown in family life and the disorganization of the community" in a section of Chicago "occupied chiefly by migrant families."[57] Frazier likewise speaks of a "small group of Negroes, mostly mulattoes, who represented the vanguard of the race," and who "attempted to escape from the less energetic and lower elements in the Negro population" (104). Frazier's "vanguard" consists of an elite intraracial class in Chicago (those descended from free blacks) who can boast of "the complete assimilation of the highest ideals of family life" and whose "leavening power in the masses of Negroes has not been unfelt" (45). Thus Frazier establishes his own version of a biosocially superior Talented Tenth, one that derives its "class distinctions . . . partly . . . [from] a tradition of free ancestry in the best families" (55).[58] Frazier even offered an explicit, class-based, regional, and intraracial version of eugenics in a 1925 essay titled "Eugenics and the Race Problem": "There is no apparent danger that the best mentally endowed Negroes will debase their intellectual inheritance by mating with feebleminded persons. But there is a danger that the proper institutional controls, which should control the procreation of the colored feebleminded, will be lacking among colored people. In the South where little notice is taken of the colored feebleminded, they are permitted to breed at a rapid rate."[59] Whereas Frazier associates the dysgenic tendencies of southern Negroes with unregulated reproduction, with biology, he associates the high achievement of the northern urban middle class—and even the Harlem Renaissance itself—with "the socializing process": "Most of the present outburst of creative effort on the part of Negroes in New York is surely attributable to a stimulating cultural environment rather than to any formal breeding process" (92). In this view, the modern urban setting itself produces the kind of natural selection the race needs to counter the unnatural selection taking place in the South. "In the large cities of the North," claims Frazier, "where competition is severe and family life in some sections of the population tends to disappear, a part of the population will die out" (252). He concludes that this "selection and segregation process" will lead to more "efficiency" in a city like Chicago (256, 252), where "ills" such as "illegitimacy" result from "social" rather then genetic "heritage" (202, 251). So even Frazier, from the relatively liberal Park school of sociology,[60] could not hold out completely against the period's eugenic anxiety, particularly that stemming from regionalist and elitist fears surrounding migration.

James Weldon Johnson's 1930 *Black Manhattan* offers the period's clearest articulation of the urban north, New York in particular, as *the* site where a modern intraracial elite is to be produced and maintained. Generically unstable and remarkably innovative, *Black Manhattan* establishes through photographs, sketches, anecdotes, statistics, and historical details Johnson's construction of the ideal modern African American subject—that is, one who is urban, urbane, and northeastern. Johnson observes that "in such a wholesale migration" of blacks as that which took place during and after World War I, it "could not be otherwise . . . that many who came were ignorant, inefficient, and worthless, and that there was also a proportion of downright criminals."[61] He argues that it "was not until the return of more normal [postwar, postmigration] conditions that the process of elimination of the incapable and unfit set in" (152). In other words, Negro modernity is normally and *naturally* urban. For Johnson, the most likely candidates for "elimination" are those who ended up in "the manufacturing cities of the Middle West" and who were largely "migrants from the cotton-raising regions of the lower Mississippi Valley, from the rural, even the backwoods, districts, Negroes who were unused to city life or anything bearing a resemblance to modern industry" (152). New York, by contrast, "drew most of her migrants from cities and towns of the Atlantic seaboard states, Negroes who were far better prepared to adapt themselves to life and industry in a great city" (152–53). Ultimately, despite the many and varied new Negroes arriving in the urban North, the "New Negro" would, ideally and inevitably (through a process of natural selection), look very much like Frazier, Johnson, and most especially Du Bois. As Johnson put it, "Dr. Du Bois, more than any other one man, has paved the way for the 'New Negro' " (141).

Du Bois's *Crisis* of the 1910s and 1920s repeatedly represents such men as paradigmatic New Negroes within an ever-improving racial family. For example, the *Crisis* reported in October 1916 on the "sturdy family of a teacher" who was doing his part to prevent "race suicide."[62] "One thinks," reads the copy above a photograph of the (male) teacher's three well-dressed children, "of the families of colored people as growing smaller, and they are. Particularly the educated and careful folk have few or no children; but some are willing to bear the burden of the next generation and to train little men and women to go forth and fight." The next sentence, set off as a paragraph unto itself, reads: "Here are the protagonists from one family."[63] Although this statement does not advocate a strictly hereditarian, or biological, view of racial improvement (acknowledging that families must "train" the next generation), nevertheless, "the educated and careful" are undeniably being urged to "bear" more children.

"The sturdy family of a teacher" illustrating the "Men of the Month" feature, *Crisis*, October 1916.

Overall, despite any evidence to the contrary, Du Bois's *Crisis* wants to believe its own family story: that talented "protagonists" within the Negro race are overcoming the evils of differential birth rate (the period's code term for overpropagation by the lower classes) and other potentially dysgenic familial trends. As Du Bois puts it, "[The Negro] finds himself surrounded in the modern world by men who have been bred for brains, for efficiency, for beauty. He is beginning carefully to train and breed for the same purposes in varying proportions. He is beginning to appear in the colleges of the North in appreciable numbers . . . In time efficiency and brains and beauty are going to be well-bred in the American Negro race."[64] The *Crisis* of the 1920s both envisions and documents the emerging eugenic breed, produced through a combination of nature (breeding) and nurture (training), that Du Bois hypothesizes. And it is only this well-trained and well-bred "New" Negro who will succeed in the modern world.

Under Du Bois's editorship, the *Crisis* is thus a kind of eugenic "family album," a visual and literary blueprint for the ideal, modern black individual.[65] The journal's many photographs of degreed and pedigreed African Americans disclose a middle class actively picturing into being its own collective ego ideal. This racialized version of a mirror stage impossibly free of alienation is documented particularly well by two features: "Men of the Month" (added in May 1911—quite early in the journal's history—and continued for over a decade) and "The Horizon" (added in August 1916). The "Men of the Month" column celebrates, largely through photographs, the increasing fitness of the race. "The Horizon" generally lists newsworthy accomplishments by African Americans, such as a sixteen-year-old boy's triumph at an oratorical competition.[66] The latter column of course functions to counter racist representations of African Americans by the white press; but, given the predominantly black readership of the *Crisis*, such compulsive cataloging also serves to keep the "family" updated on its members' activities. "The Horizon" works, then, not so much as a social register than as a family newsletter. The quaint, even banal nature of many of its listings simply heightens the illusion that the "Negro family" coheres enough and adheres enough (to a middle-class norm) to permit exhaustive (and wholly positive) representation.[67]

But the most starkly eugenic feature in the *Crisis* must be the NAACP "prize baby contests" published in its annual "Children's Number" every October (except one) during Du Bois's editorship.[68] Each Children's Number includes dozens of photographs, sent in by readers, of glowingly healthy, impeccably groomed children, with captions such as "One of Manhattan's 'Finest'" and "A Great Grandfather's Great Grandson."[69] The latter, a photo of Frederick Douglass III, underscores the Children's Numbers' primary function: to document a high-quality genealogical and relational narrative—that is, a eugenic family story. Du Bois observes, in the 1914 Children's Number, "True, these are selected children; but careful consideration of the total pictures received by the *Crisis* . . . makes it seem certain that there is growing up in the United States a large and larger class of well-nourished, healthy beautiful children among the colored people."[70] These prize baby contests acquire an international and historical-political context one year later, in an editorial written by Archibald Grimké for the 1915 Children's Number: "If we strive earnestly to make [our children] Puritan in morals and German in efficiency and English in love of liberty, there will be no baffling Negro problem a generation hence. For these children of ours . . . will be fit. . . . The weak and unfit who are fighting against them will fail, will ultimately be overcome."[71] Grimké's use

NAACP "prize babies," *Crisis*, December 1925.

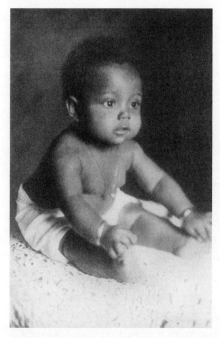
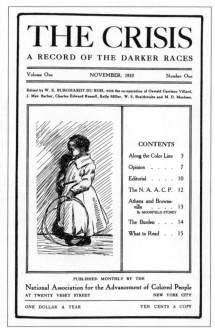

Left: A prize baby—"One of Manhattan's 'Finest' "—in the 1914 Children's Number of the *Crisis*.

Right: The cover of the initial issue of the *Crisis*, November 1910.

of the first person plural implicitly affirms the collective breeding and training project that Du Bois later explicitly outlines in the 1916 Children's Number: "After all, these are not individual children . . . they belong to a great people and in their hands is that people's future."[72] By way of proof that there exist great children to guide the future of the race, the 1927 Children's Number includes a photograph of "Five Exceptional Negro Children," along with their IQ scores—but not their names.[73] Du Bois's *Crisis* inscribes and prescribes the parameters of *collective* modern "Negro" subjectivity; "our children" constitute an obvious locus for such intraracial prescription (the cover of the very first issue, dated November 1910, depicts a child in a tidy, Victorian outfit, playing with a hoop and stick).

The annual Children's Numbers proved to be one of the journal's most popular features, so readers of the *Crisis* were regularly shown the "fit" progeny of "a great people." The only exception to the Number's annual publication from 1910 until 1934 (suggestively, the Children's Numbers disappeared just as Du Bois was leaving his post as editor) occurred in October 1920, when Du Bois replaced it with a "Homes Number," in order "to publish pictures of the most beautiful Negro homes in America—interiors and exteriors."[74] Du Bois tried to appease disappointed readers, rationalizing that "we are to have not one [Children's] number but twelve numbers," along with the addition of a new children's feature, the "Brownies' Book."[75] Of course, both the "Children's" and the "Homes" numbers served to enact the journal's agenda of presenting eugenic racial portraiture. Du Bois's assignment of "race" ("Negro") to "homes" suggests that the beauty of the architectural structure containing the family unit corresponds to the beauty of the genetic structure of a successfully breeding bourgeois Negro family. From a eugenic perspective it makes perfect sense to replace "children" with "homes": both constitute material expressions of high-quality "Negro" family life. Du Bois's politics in this context are, on one (interracial) level, quite progressive; he wants financial capital— material well-being—for all black Americans. But some houses and some families within the (intraracial) domestic picture have been pre-selected for representation by the *Crisis* as a result of their having a visible—and photogenic—abundance of genetic as well as material capital.[76]

The *Crisis* of the 1920s and 1930s is filled with beautiful photographs that arrive "raced" by both subject and production. In the 1923 Children's Number, Du Bois laments: "Why do not more young colored men and women take up photography as a career? The average white photographer does not know how to deal with colored skins and having neither sense of the delicate beauty of tone nor will to learn, he makes a horrible botch of portraying them."[77] Du Bois is suggesting here that "colored men and women" can subvert the white gaze through a black lens, or mirror. The (aesthetic) politics of representation become literally "colored," then, with the advent of photography. Authentic photographic portrayal presumes an authentic (racial) representative as subject and as objective representor. And when Du Bois explains in 1924 to *Crisis* readers that "we want all the good clear pictures of healthy human babies that we can get," representation collapses into corporeality.[78] Obviously, "good clear pictures of healthy human babies" are standing in for the vitality and presence of the babies themselves—that is, "we want" not just photos but "all the . . . healthy human babies we can get." Du Bois, however, does not rely solely, or perhaps even primarily, on the children of the race for the visual representation of its eugenicizing tendency. He returns to his paradigmatic New Negro, the middle-class man, for visual confirmation of the genetic uplift of the race.

Photographs in "Men of the Month," like advertisements in the *Crisis* for "Pictures of Distinguished Negroes . . . Excellent Photographs 11×14,"[79] simultaneously construct and commodify, promote and advertise, the racial family itself—or at least one branch of it. Identified by and with their professions ("A Dentist," "A Physician," "Attorney at Law"), the "men of the month" have achieved uplift both individually and categorically. They function as singularly successful subjects, professionally and photographically, and as metonymic racial representatives. However, with the October 1916 *Crisis*, the "Men of the Month" feature changes format. The original layout placed photos separately on the pages, accompanied by their own copy. The revised layout collects the photos on a single page, with captions below each that list profession and name (and sometimes just a profession). The new, contiguous layout assumes and creates a visual logic of relationship where in fact none exists. Mimicking a page from a family album, the photographs imply a blood relation among subjects whose interconnections are actually social. The men of the month share only race, class, and gender (and modernity).

As the title "Men of the Month" attests, such racial collectivization frequently occurs at the expense of black women. Women do occasionally appear in the column (Jessie Fauset was a "man of the month" in the November 1919 issue), but the *Crisis* apparently cannot "see"—and certainly does not acknowledge—the gendered contradiction between title and content that results. Then, in January 1920, the column undergoes another change in its layout, a change I call the "floating patriarch phenomenon." The "men of the month" photos remain clustered on a single page, but one photograph of an older man is accorded visual supremacy. Larger than the others and centered, his picture overlaps the edges of several other photos. Although "Men of the Month" stopped appearing in the late 1920s, "The Horizon" continued such visual representations of distinguished men anchored by the floating patriarch throughout the 1920s; women and young men rarely appeared in this position of photographic privilege. The *Crisis* thus constructed its visual rendering of the ideal racial family literally around and through a father figure.

Du Bois himself functions as the *über*father of the *Crisis*, the implicit

Presidents of the seven largest branches of the NAACP, *Crisis*, January 1927.

floating patriarch presiding over the whole of its family story. His presence shifts the journal's representational mode from metonymy to synecdoche. It is not simply the Talented Tenth who will represent the Negro race, but Du Bois himself. With the June 1916 *Crisis*, Du Bois's editorial column moves to the beginning of each issue. Three years later, just a few months before the floating patriarch arrives in "Men of the Month," Du Bois's editorial column is renamed "Opinion of W. E. B. Du Bois." Du Bois's nominal and editorial primacy works against the potentially radical, collectivizing political (interracial) mission of the journal but *with* its more conservative social (intraracial) aim of establishing the "college-bred," middle-class, urban, intellectual man as the authentic representative of an ideal racial family.[80] That ideal racial family turns out, for a brief time at least, to be Du Bois's own.

The June 1928 *Crisis* is perhaps most famous for Du Bois's pairing of Nella Larsen and Claude McKay in his joint review of *Quicksand* and *Home to Harlem*.[81] But the issue includes yet another provocative coupling that discloses even more dramatically Du Bois's problematic ideal for a modern racial-family portrait. The issue is, in large part, given over to photos and an article (titled "So the Girl Marries") covering the April wedding of his daughter, Yolande Du Bois, and poet Countée Cullen.[82] With an elegant, full-page photo of the bride, the *Crisis* becomes, quite literally, her wedding album, and thus her father's family album (186). Du Bois takes the editorial-paternal opportunity to ponder "the problem of marriage among our present American Negroes" and asks, "Should we black folk breed children or commit biological suicide?" (192). With sixteen bridesmaids and thirteen hundred invited guests, the wedding represents, for Du Bois, the foundational moment of a eugenic dynasty for "black folk." He describes, rapturously, the guests leaving the ceremony, exulting that it "was a new race" (208–9). The elaborate, bourgeois trappings of the wedding suggest just how Du Bois pictures that "race." He distances himself from the material excess of the ceremony, however, claiming that "the girl" (meaning his daughter) wanted it that way. But he does take credit for an "admittedly small" but "not altogether negligible" part in "mate-selection": "We talked the young men over—their fathers and grandfathers; their education; their ability to earn particular sorts of living; their dispositions" (208).[83] But father and daughter—although they may or may not have considered the quality of the (adopted) Cullen's

Wedding portrait of Mrs. Yolande Du Bois Cullen, *Crisis*, June 1928.

patrilineage—apparently neglected to discuss the selected "young man's" sexual orientation.[84]

In his editorial for the October 1922 "Children's Number," Du Bois speaks presciently of the trouble with weddings between a member of the Talented Tenth and a "modern young colored woman":

Here is a man and a woman. The natural and righteous cry of their bodies calls for marriage to propagate, preserve and improve mankind. But there are difficulties. First, as to ideals: the man—an educated Negro American of 1922—is himself a spoiled child. He has been catered to and petted by a mother. . . .

To increase the complication the modern young colored woman has her own ideas and ideals. . . .

Thus, practically, marriage must be a compromise and if the compromise is based on common sense and reasonable effort, it becomes the center of real resurrection and remaking of the world.[85]

Du Bois's odd figuration here of the male New Negro as "spoiled" by an over-indulgent mother clearly locates the origins of racial pathology in the black mother. At the same time, the heterosexist imperative of Du Bois's (and for that matter, any) eugenic racial ideal clearly emerges in the terms "natural" and "righteous."[86] And although Du Bois seems to believe that his daughter's "picture perfect" wedding marks just such an occasion of "real resurrection and remaking of the world," the picture develops as a false one. Two months after what David Levering Lewis describes as a "short, awkward honeymoon" with Yolande in Atlantic City and Philadelphia, Cullen traveled to Paris with his father and with his longtime companion and best man, Harold Jackman, "leaving the bride to find her own way to Paris [one month] later."[87] Mason Stokes aptly describes this series of events: "If the wedding itself symbolized the Harlem Renaissance's aristocratic self-image, Jackman symbolized the contradictions under the surface."[88] The couple certainly would not "procreate" in order to "improve" the race. By year's end, Countée Cullen and Yolande Du Bois Cullen had settled, not on "compromise," but on divorce.

Both "marriages" in the *Crisis* "wedding album" of June 1928—Larsen and McKay, Cullen and Yolande Du Bois—seem to exist almost solely as Du Bois–authored textual artifacts. In both, the "bride" is constructed as a dutiful daughter of the Harlem Renaissance and of Du Bois himself. In Du Bois's ideal racial picture, the woman (or, "the girl") takes up a compliant, relational position (Mrs. Cullen; Mrs. Imes, Larsen's married name that he uses in the review of *Quicksand*). Moreover, just as Claude McKay was the prodigal son who disrupted Du Bois's well-mannered racial discourse, Countée Cullen, as a son-in-law, explodes Du Bois's eugenic, heterosexist family portrait. Du Bois does not

Countée Cullen and his ushers at his wedding to Yolande Du Bois, *Crisis*, June 1928. Among those in attendance were Langston Hughes, Arna Bontemps, and best man Harold Jackman.

blame Cullen for the marriage's dissolution, however. As both David Levering Lewis and Mason Stokes have pointed out, Du Bois's private correspondence with the poet indicates that it was Yolande, "the modern young colored woman," whom Du Bois held responsible for the failure of the picture-perfect marriage. In Lewis's words, Du Bois "consoled his son-in-law and excoriated his daughter."[89] In a letter to Cullen, Du Bois suggests that Yolande's sexual inexperience might be the cause of the marriage's early faltering; her first sexual experience, he writes, could not "have failed to have been unpleasant and disconcerting."[90] When it becomes clear that the marriage will not last, Du Bois frames his daughter as a burden he shares with his son-in-law, asking the poet to "keep" her "till Christmas if any way possible and then — God show us the way." A subsequent letter expresses Du Bois's keen disappointment in the failure of their union: "I had dreamed of fine things from this marriage."[91] Indeed, eugenic progeny would not be forthcoming from his daughter's alliance with Cullen, and Yolande Du Bois was never able to match the dutiful and extraordinary daughter that her father envisioned.[92] At the same time, Du Bois himself seemed unable to match his public feminist agenda (he consistently and staunchly supported women's suffrage, for example) with an equally feminist personal family story. But even more important, both his private and public politics, including his feminism, were shaped by his particular utopian, heterosexual vision of a world "remade" by the united intellectual, political, *and reproductive* efforts of first-rate men and women of color, the vision that he had painted, largely in purple, in the fictional *Dark Princess* and that his daughter and Countée Cullen could not reproduce for him in reality.[93]

That vision led W. E. B. Du Bois, like the character James Vayle in Nella Larsen's *Quicksand*, to worry about the intellectual and genetic quality not only of his own family but also of the race as a whole. He willingly collectivized all African Americans for purposes of political-numerical representation in *The Philadelphia Negro* ("eight million Americans are entitled to a capital letter");[94] but, as of the 1920s and 1930s, he wanted to be able to pick his relatives more carefully—at least when it came to the textual-photographic representation of the modern Negro family. This shifting racial-familial allegiance emplots a kind of cultural and political history of uplift, though not a neatly linear or a cleanly chronological one, from the turn of the century through 1930. Increasingly intraracial and eugenic, the uplift model of the 1920s and 1930s culminates in the photographic and textual representations of Du Bois's own family in the *Crisis*.[95] To his credit, the journal under his editorship was, in general, striving for racial and social equality while also attempting to navigate the increasingly unstable and complex terrain of modern, collective (racial, national, political, and gendered) forms of subjectivity. And certainly Du Bois was not alone in following, at least to a degree, a eugenic map of that terrain in the first few decades of the twentieth century. He was joined in eugenic discourse not only by other "race men" largely sympathetic to his political and social agenda and his leadership (such as James Weldon Johnson, as we have seen) but also by a number of his rivals.

Du Bois's greatest rival, Marcus Garvey, also subscribed to a version of eugenics, though one clearly incompatible with Du Bois's class-inflected version. As his organization's name, the Universal Negro Improvement Association, suggests, Garvey too sought a better black subject. As William A. Edwards argues, "There was an underlying assumption that Garvey shared with [Booker T.] Washington: Blacks were a fallen people."[96] And, like Du Bois, Garvey envisioned uplift as being achieved in part through an intraracial breeding project; however, quite unlike Du Bois, he emphasized color above all and class hardly at all. Garvey's 1924 "creed" for the UNIA appeared in his weekly Harlem-based newspaper *Negro World* and included the following tenets:

> The Universal Negro Improvement Association advocates the unity and blending of all Negroes into one strong, healthy race.
>
> It is against miscegenation and race suicide. . . .
>
> It believes in the purity of the Negro race and the purity of the white race.[97]

As historian Michele Mitchell argues, "homogenizing the race was part and parcel" of Garvey's ideology: "Garveyites inveighed that the race had to produce better children and more children" (316, 346). Du Bois repeatedly and vociferously refuted such bioracial politics of purity not only from Garvey but from all opponents, black or white, even when he endorsed cultural or economic segregation.[98]

As a result of his rigorous defense of the quality of the mulatto, critics have often ascribed to Du Bois a color-based intraracial elitism. But Du Bois's discussions of quality and color in the 1920s must be seen in the context of his refutation of "mainline" American and European eugenics—the most powerful and common version, a Stoddardian version that took the biological inferiority of the racially mixed as a given. Du Bois had quite literally been taught this lesson. In *Dusk of Dawn*, Du Bois recounts his experience as a graduate student in a classroom at the University of Berlin: "I can never forget that morning in the class of the great Heinrich von Treitschke in Berlin . . . his words rushed out in a flood: 'Mulattoes,' he thundered, 'are inferior.' I almost felt his eyes boring into me, although probably he had not noticed me. 'Sie fühlen sich niedriger!' 'Their actions show it,' he asserted. What contradiction could there be to that authoritative dictum?"[99] Du Bois took it upon himself to carefully and systematically contradict Treitschke's dictum as well as Stoddard's influential white supremacism and Garvey's powerful rhetoric of black racial purity. Particularly in a 1935 (unpublished) essay titled "Miscegenation,"[100] Du Bois explicitly challenged Stoddard (and Treitschke) regarding racial mixture and decline: "The decline of Rome was certainly social and economic rather than racial"; regarding the quality of mulattoes: "In general, the achievement of American mulattoes has been outstanding"; and regarding the results of racial hybridity on the American continent and in Africa: "In West Africa, the West Indies and South America, the racial mixture which is going on does not disturb the community and is not, therefore, a social problem."[101] In an equally direct 1920 assault on Garvey's politics of color, Du Bois asserted that "there is no doubt but what Garvey has sought to import to America and capitalize [sic] the antagonism between blacks and mulattoes in the West Indies. . . . [This antagonism] is absolutely repudiated by every thinking Negro. . . . American Negroes recognize no color line in or out of the race, and they will in the end punish the man who attempts to establish it."[102] Although Garvey was certainly his most effective and blunt rival (he responded to Du Bois's "A Lunatic or a Traitor" essay by calling the *Crisis* editor a "cross-breed Dutch-French-Negro" who deserved a "good horse whipping"),[103] and one whom he clearly found threatening,[104] Du Bois had rivals in other "race men" of the 1920s, who likewise endorsed a kind of bioelitism.

Self-styled radical socialist race leaders A. Philip Randolph and Chandler Owen explicitly aimed in the 1920s to provide an alternative to the Du Boisian model of politics and leadership. These polemicizing editors of the *Messenger* (in their words, the "only radical Negro magazine in America") sought to supplant Du Bois as the paradigmatic New Negro. Yet they, too, described their own fitness as modern race leaders in biological, even social Darwinist, terms, citing the "inability of the old crowd [represented by Du Bois] to *adapt itself to the changed conditions*, to recognize and accept the consequences of the sudden, rapid and violent social changes that are shaking the world."[105] The "New Crowd," they insisted, "must be composed of young men who are educated, radical and fearless"—in other words, just like themselves.[106] In the first three decades of the century, Randolph and Owen, like Du Bois, were trying to negotiate an uneasy balance between collectivity (race-wide solidarity and interracial equality) and selection (class identity and intraracial difference). For all of them, their quasibiological self-selection as racial leaders mediated between competing impulses toward racial solidarity on the one hand and individualist elitism on the other. Their selection processes promised collective racial improvement (political and social uplift) through individual action (being and reproducing the ideal "New Negro").

That tension between the collective subjectivity of "the Negro race" and the individual subjectivity of members of the Talented Tenth stands in doctrinal and ideological counterpoint to similar tensions in

Anglo-American modernism. White and black moderns alike had to confront and finesse competing tendencies toward collectivism and individualism.[107] For Du Bois and other modern black intellectuals, the inflection of race often served to translate collectivism into political radicalism, whereas for reactionary, white male modern writers, collectivism emerged as authoritarianism ("tradition," for Eliot; fascism, for Pound). On the other hand, for Du Bois's Talented Tenth, individualism frequently found expression in a singular kind of bourgeois success story—the story told by the individual "Men of the Month." For the white (male) moderns, individualism was seen as the artist's extreme subjectivity, or "individual talent," in Eliot's terms. To put it another way, for Eliot and Pound, the anti-individualism of high modernism arrived class-specific, and so logically corresponded with political and aesthetic reaction. But for black male writers of the 1920s and 1930s (who were always already "classed" by race), the collectivizing impulse logically corresponded with two different strands of political thought: one, a class-transcending, hence liberal, sometimes radically democratic or socialist politics; the other, a class-aspiring, bourgeois, materialist politics. The two strands were often intertwined in the text and photographs of Du Bois's *Crisis* (as well as of the *Messenger*).

In the 1920s at least, class-transcending intraracial politics surface only sporadically and contingently in Du Bois's work. Sometimes he includes all African Americans in his picture of the modern racial family; at other times, only a chosen few. In a kind of racial editorship, he attempts to formalize, both photographically and textually, that selection process. Who will escape "the bonds of medievalism" in order to represent the New Negro, the authentically modern Negro subject?[108] For Du Bois, the choice is clear. In 1928, at least, he ultimately chooses, not Claude McKay or Nella Larsen, but his *own family* to represent the eugenic future of the race. When Yolande Du Bois and Countée Cullen fail either to produce or reproduce his ideal family portrait, all that remains in his picture are the prodigal sons and not-so-dutiful daughters of a family *Crisis*.

DU BOIS'S FAMILY PORTRAIT, however problematic, must be understood against the period's backdrop of extraordinarily intense, legislated racism. As Gaines argues, black intellectuals' appropriation of racial theories in the modern era "says more about power, black vulnerability, and the centrality of race in the nation's political and cultural institutions than it does about the motives or complicity of black elites."[109] Even as they tailored a discourse of eugenics and "natural selection" to a project of intraracial uplift, black leaders of the 1920s and 1930s, including Garvey and Du Bois, could not help but be aware that mainline (white) American eugenics generally considered "Negroes" biologically and genetically inferior. Du Bois, in his Manifesto of the Second Pan-African Congress in September 1921 (also, ironically, the date of the Second International Congress of Eugenics), sustains his model of individual elitism while insisting on interracial equality: "No one denies great differences of gift, capacity and attainment among individuals of all races, but the voice of science, religion and practical politics is one in denying the God-appointed existence of super-races, or of races naturally and inevitably and eternally inferior."[110] But even if he and other writers of the Harlem Renaissance did believe, as David Levering Lewis suggests, that "they were, in truth, superior human material,"[111] America's Jim Crow laws did not respond to such intra- or extraracial differentiation. Lewis perhaps rightly points to a kind of naïveté in "using culture as a substitute for the economic and political arena," to use Ann Douglas's words.[112] Lewis, along with a number of other critics, has suggested that this naïveté resulted in the failure of the Harlem Renaissance writers to effect real political change. Granted, the African American intellectuals of the twenties and thirties may have in fact "failed," like Pound and Eliot, to fulfill their "promise to overcome a stultified society and make with the tools of art a new future;"[113] but, unlike the white modernists, from Ezra Pound to Havelock Ellis, they were simply making the most of the two national arenas relatively available to them: the aesthetic-cultural and the domestic-familial.[114] Eugenic discourse reveals the deep connections between the two.

Eugenics offered a means for narrowing the parameters of ideal, collective (particularly racial and national) subjectivities—not only in the public policy but also in the cultural production of the modern era. Thus in the 1920s W. E. B. Du Bois sought a better representational politics, wherein black cultural production would address what he viewed, in part at least, as a problem of racial reproduction. His frequent call for "positive" literary and photographic images correlates directly, then, with his 1926 call for more children among Negro families "of the better class." Likewise, anxiety about violations and aberrations within a national or racial "body" correlates with a white modernist drive for high aesthetic, formal standards. Cleanth Brooks in 1938 calls for "poetical fitness," and Eliot notes in 1942 that poets must avoid words that are "ugly" as a result of "foreignness or ill-breeding."[115] As Maud Ellman has pointed out, this "conceit [the ill-bred word] makes social and poetic harmony interchangeable."[116]

Granted, more "literal" expressions of eugenics, such as immigration restriction and compulsory sterilization statutes, carried a kind of power unavailable to the more metaphorical eugenics of writers of the 1920s; nevertheless, many intellectuals and artists (white and African American, reactionary and progressive) envisioned a better social and political future achieved through aesthetic and reproductive means. Their versions of that better future were, of course, quite different. Michael North argues that "it is quite easy to see a connection between [the modernist] aesthetic drive for reconciliation and authoritarian politics,"[117] but it is equally easy to see a connection between the modern African American male intellectuals' drive for positive (literary and photographic) racial representation and both democratic and aristocratic (or even *Dark Princess*'s "oligarchic") politics. In the words of Horkheimer and Adorno, "The claim of art is always ideology too."[118] Better still, in the words of Du Bois, "Thus all Art is propaganda and ever must be."[119] This often-quoted sentence appears in one of Du Bois's most famous essays, "Criteria of Negro Art," which was published in the 1926 Children's Number, interspersed with several pages of "prize baby" photos.[120] In Du Bois's uplift project of the 1920s, cultural production and reproduction could not be linked any more clearly.

It has to do with maintaining the very cleanliness of the tools, the health of the very matter of thought itself.—Ezra Pound, "The Serious Artist" (1913)

You can forward the "Bolo" to Joyce if you think it won't unhinge his somewhat sabbatarian mind.—Ezra Pound, letter to T. S. Eliot, January 1922

After the bachelor quarters of the last six years, as Leonard Woolf put it, "surrounded by curates, he was now surrounded by women. . . . He read Uncle Remus aloud to them."—Lyndall Gordon, *T. S. Eliot: An Imperfect Life* (1998)

CHAPTER TWO

T. S. Eliot's Strange Gods
Celibacy, Hierarchy, and Tradition

T. S. Eliot's sexual squeamishness has been well documented by his biographers and has long been accepted as conventional wisdom. By contrast, W. E. B. Du Bois's authoritative biographer David Levering Lewis has come under criticism for his forthright discussion of his subject's many extramarital affairs. Some reviewers have contended that this information is extraneous and that it unfairly airs a great man's dirty, irrelevant laundry; better, they say, to focus on Du Bois's social, intellectual, and political—that is, his public—work. A reviewer in the *Washington Post* suggests that "in reconstructing his subject's sub rosa life as an elegant rake, Lewis sometimes seems to transform old gossip into history. Even in cases where the documentation is scrupulous, the question 'Why is this important?' hangs in the air."[1] But sex in fact carried great importance for Du Bois's public, particularly his racial, agenda. As Claudia Tate has persuasively argued, Du Bois's erotic vision was in fact closely allied with his political vision. For Du Bois, she says, the "public satisfaction of racial equality is connected and somewhat analogous to the private pleasure of eroticism, for eros and polity are mutually signifying."[2] I would take this argument even further: the erotic and the reproductive stood at the core of Du Bois's social and political desires. In a 1922 *Crisis* editorial, he declared that, "practically, marriage must be a compromise and if the compromise is based on common sense and reasonable effort, it becomes the center of real resurrection and remaking of the world."[3] It is important to understand that Du Bois's own erotic freedom, his comfort with heterosexual liaisons, connects quite closely to his eugenic vision of world progress, particularly for people of color. His very sexual progressiveness permitted him to consider sexuality and reproduction as a viable means of *social* progress—that is, he was willing to explore the positive global implications of glorious, self-conscious heterosexual union, as his steamy 1928 novel, *Dark Princess*, clearly demonstrates. In Du Bois's erotic-political-novelistic vision, sex among quality people of color would help produce the elite leadership that would in turn "remake and resurrect the world." Just so, his African American hero produces a "messiah" through a liaison with an Indian princess.[4] Analogously, if quite differently, Eliot's conservative sexual politics also bear a direct relationship to his social and cultural agenda.

T. S. Eliot, too, certainly wished to "resurrect" (although not, as I will argue, to "remake") the world. But he equally certainly did not consider glorious heterosexual union the means of that resurrection—nor, for that matter, did he view the progeny of talented people of color as potential saviors for the world. Eliot preferred a far more traditional savior and, in general, a return to religious and cultural tradition quite unlike Du Bois's wholly secular agenda for racial, economic, and political progress—that is, a world remade. Similarly, Eliot's often-noted sexual prudery and discomfort with women are about as unlike Du Bois's ease with his own sexuality and his appreciation for women as can be imagined for the modern period—the age of the New Woman and of debates over free love and birth control. Ironically, Eliot's conservative sexual, social, and religious views are precisely what prevented him from embracing some of the period's most dangerous means of remaking the world—or purifying a modern waste land. He was at most a partial eugenicist, one solely in metaphorical and cultural terms, rather than the enthusiastic and thoroughgoing advocate that some contemporary criticism has labeled him.[5]

Indeed, some of the most prominent, and perhaps apparently least likely, American modernists resisted eugenic thinking (at least to some degree and in at least some of their writings). F. Scott Fitzgerald, for example, scoffed at the eugenic regulation of human passion; he rejected eugenics' inherent sexual utilitarianism and its ideals of human standardization. Hemingway, too, mocked eugenicists, but he mocked them for their assumption of their own superiority and for their fetishization of race and nation. Current critical views of a number of white American modernists as eugenics sympathizers, especially Eliot, may stem more from their troubling racial and class politics than from their explicit or enthusiastic embrace of eugenic thinking.[6] Granted, Eliot treated his racist, fantasized version of blackness as source material for experimental modernism, but in that he was far from alone; Stein and Joyce, among others, often filtered their literary innovations through a racial, and often a racist, lens. In Toni Morrison's words, white American writers have long been "playing in the dark."[7] Thus, Eliot's racial-aesthetic utilitarianism renders him a representative figure within Anglo-American aesthetic modernism, even as his prudery and his conservative religious views, if not his eugenic skepticism, render him distinctly nonrepresentative. In fact, to the degree that eugenics, relative sexual liberalism, and a desire for progress characterize the modern era, Du Bois—with his ideal of a simultaneously cultural and reproductive remaking of the world—may actually stand as a more "representative" modern thinker than Eliot.

If for Du Bois (black) uplift in the 1920s was closely allied with reproduction and concomitantly with heterosexuality, for Eliot modern (white) literary and cultural improvement was carefully disengaged from matters of sexuality, and in particular from the female body. Certainly Eliot was not alone among male modernist writers in believing that women were not as able as men to produce significant art or culture. Many male modernists consciously and explicitly sought to purge cultural works of the early twentieth century of the sentimentality and femininity they associated with romanticism.[8] As Colleen Lamos succinctly argues, while women in some modernist texts, like Wyndham Lewis's *Tarr*, "are mired in a primordial muck," they also, somewhat contradictorily, "represented, for Lewis, Eliot, Pound, Lawrence, and many other modernists, an effete, overly refined literary culture."[9] Indeed, a shared endorsement of a masculine literary cure bound Pound and Eliot throughout the years of high modernist literary experimentation. In April 1915, seven months after meeting Pound, Eliot wrote to him: "It might be pointed out again and again that literature has rights of its own which extend beyond Uplift and Recreation. Of course it is imprudent to sneer at the monopolisation of literature by women."[10] Twenty years later, Pound wrote to Eliot regarding *Criterion*: "It wd. be nice if you wd. reserve say 4 pages per issue to tell the reader honestly what is fit to read. Hen. Miller having done presumably the only book a man cd. read for pleasure and if not out Ulyssesing Joyce at least being infinitely more part of permanent literature than such ½ masted slime as the weakminded Woolf female, etc."[11] Such an explicitly masculine and even phallic rhetoric of literary fitness, far from being peripheral, is actually fundamental to Pound's and Eliot's aesthetic projects. But Eliot took the matter even further than Pound and the other male modernists; he *was* alone in seeking nearly full containment not just of women but of sexuality itself, both in his published writings and in much of his adult life (until his second marriage, at least). According to biographer Lyndall Gordon, Eliot took a vow of celibacy in March 1928 (perhaps not coincidentally, this was during his separation from his first wife, Vivien, and about six months after his conversion to Anglicanism), a vow that he apparently kept for decades.[12] At the same time, Eliot relegated salaciousness to his private correspondence with other male moderns, to his unpublished "Bolo" verses, and, in his published poetry, to the vernacular of Irish and lower-class characters. For Eliot, sex was apparently something that "others" did in the 1920s and 1930s. Tellingly, he was taking his celibacy vow just as Du Bois was writing and publishing his sexual-racial-political prescription in *Dark Princess*. In the 1928 novel, Du Bois's passionate hero, Matthew Towns, resembled Du Bois himself. Eliot, by contrast, regularly filtered sexual matters—as well as relatively simple intergender relations—through imaginary figures that he perceived to be quite unlike himself (like the black King Bolo and Cockney pub crawlers). Indeed, it is striking that during his 1940s residence at "The Shambles," as the only man in an all-women English guesthouse, a kind of war refuge, Eliot read Uncle Remus stories to the women who "surrounded him."[13] Eliot's imagined "others"—blacks, Jews, the Irish, and the working class—regularly served as repositories and conduits for his sexuality and ribaldry. For the majority of his life and writing career, Eliot sought to control or compartmentalize both—that is, both those "others" and sexuality; he was what Lamos cleverly terms "the straight man" of modernism.[14]

Because eugenics requires direct engagement with, as well as regulation of, sexuality and reproduction, that reluctance to permit sex and sexuality any role outside the marginalia of his life and writing (not to mention his "anglo-catholicism," famously and explicitly declared in 1928, at about the same time that Du Bois was "converting" more fully to socialism) precluded Eliot's being an enthusiastic eugenicist.[15] Granted, eugenic ideology did have some appeal for him, especially in the early 1920s, before his conversion. Donald Childs and Juan León have done extensive work regarding the influence of eugenics on Eliot; both consider him a eugenicist, focusing on the dysgenic imagery in his early 1920s poetry and on his period reviews of eugenic texts to make their case. Bringing what León terms Eliot's "eugenic anxiety" to bear on a reading of *The Waste Land* of 1922, we can indeed see emerge there a horrifying national landscape tainted by migration and immigration, by the Irishman and the Jew.[16] The poem conflates the "Phoenician Sailor" with the ironically named "Mr. Eugenides," thereby linking promiscuity and excessive fertility with the presumably Jewish "Smyrna merchant." Both traffic in the currents ("currants") that make up Lothrop Stoddard's "rising tide" of the racially, ethnically, and morally inferior. The poem's clear implication that the "one-eyed" sailor suffers from a syphilitic's blindness is of a piece with Eliot's persistent linkage, in several poems, of Irish and Jewish characters with atavistic promiscuity and venereal disease. In fact, "Sweeney Erect" (1920) seems to set up a fully populated, dysgenic nightmare-scape, featuring the promiscuous and devolved Sweeney:

(The lengthened shadow of a man
  Is history, said Emerson
Who had not seen the silhouette
  Of Sweeney straddled in the sun.)[17]

The dysgenic cast is complete with "the epileptic on the bed" who "curves backward, clutching at her sides," and the equally bestial prostitute "Doris," who "enters padding on broad feet." The multiplication and spread of such genetically flawed characters threatens to drag civilization back toward the dysgenic "protozoic slime" of "Burbank with a Baedeker: Bleistein with a Cigar" (1920). Indeed, the original beginning of *The Waste Land* (cut by Pound)—"London, the swarming life you kill and breed"—succinctly evokes the mainline eugenicists' central, paradoxical anxiety over the fecundity of an obviously less "fit" urban mass. As Stoddard put it in 1924: "In some ways, [during the last century] selection in the human race has almost ceased; in many ways it is actually reversed, that is, it results in the survival of the inferior rather than the superior."[18] In this view, modernity itself, especially the modern city, has produced an unnatural selection that breeds hordes of lesser beings, an overpopulated waste land.

But rather than establishing Eliot as a lifelong eugenicist, *The Waste Land* actually represented the peak of his engagement with such explicit and promiscuous, bodily and sexual, images of cultural decay and lower-class sexuality. After his verse of the early 1920s, Eliot moved steadily away from the carnal and steadily toward the spiritual, away from linguistic and temporal mixture and toward hierarchy and boundary (both social and literary). As Michael Levenson argues, Eliot "was in flight from *The Waste Land* as soon as he completed it."[19] We should not mistake Eliot's elitism (or his "royalism"), and not even his anti-Semitism or his racism or his anti-Irish beliefs, as constituting full-fledged eugenics; indeed, eugenics' inherent progressiveness and its explicit regulation of sexual matters stand quite at odds with Eliot's traditionalism, his ascetic tendencies, and his Anglo-Catholicism. Eliot might indeed have been willing to regulate social, linguistic, and aesthetic boundaries, and might have been willing to advance stringent criteria for art and culture, but he was not willing to regulate sex, to level social hierarchy, or to abandon spiritual solutions to national and social problems in favor of biological ones.

What is truly striking is not the fact that Eliot suffered from "eugenic anxiety," but the fact that a thinker so preoccupied by cultural decay, race, class, nationality, and gender should have such a mild form of that anxiety. In *Modernism and Eugenics*, Donald Childs argues, by contrast, that Eliot sustains a patently eugenic vision from the 1910s well into the 1940s. He cites Eliot's 1918 commentary on a Leonard Darwin *Eugenics Review* essay titled "Quality not Quantity," pointing to Eliot's assertion: "Darwin's 'articles always deserve attention' " (97). But that hardly constitutes a strong endorsement of Darwin's explicitly eugenic program. Childs argues further that Eliot was persuaded, even as late as the 1940s, that "a biological crisis was at hand," citing a passage in "The Idea of a Christian Society" (1939) wherein Eliot "alludes" to the "wave of terror of the consequences of depopulation" (95). But Childs misreads the passage; in it, Eliot in fact satirizes the eugenical alarmism that has resulted, he believes, from the inconsistencies and contingencies, "the disorder," of pagan "Liberalism": "The attitudes and

beliefs of Liberalism are destined to disappear, are already disappearing.
. . . Out of Liberalism itself come philosophies which deny it . . . those
who are most convinced of the necessity of *étatisme* as a control of some
activities of life, can be the loudest professors of libertarianism in others, and insist upon the preserves of 'private life' in which each man
may obey his own convictions or follow his own whim: while imper-
ceptibly this domain of 'private life' becomes smaller and smaller, and
may eventually disappear altogether. It is possible that a wave of terror
of the consequences of depopulation might lead to legislation having
the effect of compulsory breeding."[20] Here, Eliot makes quite clear his
distaste for eugenics as an expression of panicked liberal-statist policy.
Alert to the tensions between the collective and the individual good
inherent in eugenics and within the modern state itself, Eliot rejects
the messy and temporary, in his view, political formations that accompany eugenics (both liberalism and fascism) in favor of "a way of life
for a people"—that is, the "universal" and "permanent" culture of Christianity (14). Christianity, he believes, will protect the individual while
providing the consistent, orderly "collective temperament" (14), the
deep structure, necessary for a healthy society (18). "Without faith," he
warns, "we shall have regimentation and conformity, without respect
for the needs of the individual soul; the puritanism of a hygienic morality in the interest of efficiency; uniformity of opinion through propaganda, and art only encouraged when it flatters the official doctrines
of the time. To those who can imagine, and are therefore repelled by,
such a prospect, one can assert that the only possibility of control and
balance is a religious control and balance" (18–19). His clear prefer-
ence for *religious* rather than *population* control, and for the individual
over the state, saves Eliot not only from the mainline (nativist, white
supremacist, and elitist) eugenics of Lothrop Stoddard, but also from
the fascism of Pound.

While Eliot agreed, to some extent, with a eugenic cultural diagnosis—that modernity had become dangerously unnatural—it was his ostensibly nonpolitical, and explicitly antinationalist, prescription that
set him apart from most eugenicists and from many other modernists,
including the fascist Pound and the Irish nationalist Yeats. In "The
Idea of a Christian Society," Eliot observes: "What is more depressing
still is the thought that only fear or jealousy of foreign success can
alarm us about the health of our nation; that only through this anxiety can we see such things as depopulation, malnutrition, moral dete-

rioration, the decay of agriculture, as evils at all" (46). Eliot here employs a eugenic lexicon ("depopulation" was a popular period code word for the supposedly lower rate of reproduction among the upper classes) but explicitly rejects the nativism and nationalism that generally accompanied eugenic discourse. Coolidge, in his 1925 inaugural address had promoted just such "jealousy of foreign success," arguing that America's "most important problem is not to secure new advantages but to maintain those which we already possess."[21] Stoddard likewise raised a nativist alarm in 1924 about the quality of American "germplasm" (*Revolt*, 34): "In the United States conditions are no better than in Europe—in some respects they seem to be rather worse. . . . The American intellectual groups are much less fertile than European groups. The average number of children per married graduate of the leading American colleges like Harvard and Yale is about two, while among women's colleges it is about one and one-half" (111). Eliot's dismissal of Coolidgian rhetoric of national supremacy and Stoddardian bioelitist rhetoric of nativism suggests that we may not be able to develop a single model, or offer a single representative author, for modernist literature and politics. For example, Eliot challenges Walter Benn Michaels's recent, influential reading of 1920s American literature as largely nativist, modernist, and pluralist.[22] Eliot, in my argument, is a pluralist rather than a nativist, an elitist but not much of a eugenicist, and only in some ways a "typical" modernist. Even if, as Michael North argues, aesthetic modernism—represented in his argument by Pound, Yeats, and Eliot—sought "to overcome a stultified society and make with the tools of art a new future,"[23] the three authors' improved futures (their prescriptions) as well as their analyses of that stultification (their diagnoses) had little in common.

Unlike most writers and reformers of the 1920s and 1930s, including Pound and Yeats, Eliot prescribed Christianity—not biologism, reformism, nationalism, socialism, or fascism—as the means both to diagnose and to cure moral and social ills. This focus on a religious solution set Eliot apart not only from most other modernists but also from eugenics sympathizers across the political spectrum, from Havelock Ellis to Lothrop Stoddard. While Eliot shared their belief that modernity was marked by "unnaturalness," he did not identify, as they did, faulty human breeding—unnatural selection—as the primary source of that unnaturalness, nor did he advocate their scientific solution. For the most enthusiastic eugenicists, by contrast, science provided the only solution. A. E. Wiggam, a popular American journalist and self-appointed eugenics propagandist, proclaimed in his best-selling 1924 eugenics tract, *The New Decalogue of Science*, that "science alone can supply mankind with the true technology of the will of God," and he railed against the "biological ungodly."[24] For reactionary eugenicists like Wiggam, eugenics not only supplanted old religions; it *was* the new religion, and it offered the ideal scientific cure for a nation sickened by the conditions of modernity, particularly migration and immigration. It is simply unimaginable that the Anglican Eliot could ever have abided A. E. Wiggam's astonishing declaration: "Had Jesus been among us, he would have been president of the First Eugenics Congress."[25] In stark contrast to Wiggam's biological-religious enthusiasm stands Eliot's anti-eugenic declaration in "The Idea of a Christian Society": "We may say that religion, as distinguished from modern paganism, implies a life in conformity with nature. It may be observed that the natural life and the supernatural life have a conformity to each other which neither has with the mechanistic life: but so far has our notion of what is natural become distorted, that people who consider it 'unnatural' and therefore repugnant, that a person of either sex should elect a life of celibacy, consider it perfectly 'natural' that families should be limited to one or two children. It would be perhaps more natural, as well as in better conformity with the Will of God, if there were more celibates and if those who were married had larger families" (48). For Eliot, birth control (that is, the "mechanistic" regulation of sex) was "unnatural." In fact, any regulation of heterosexual marital sex, and therefore any form of eugenics, constituted an *unnatural* act that—far from offering a new, corrective, and scientific religion—actually signified the collective spiritual sickness of the period. At least a few religious thinkers of the period agreed. As Marouf Hasian has shown, Catholic writers in the 1920s and 1930s, while they did not always completely reject the premises of eugenics, did offer some of the period's rare challenges to state eugenic policies, particularly compulsory sterilization.[26] The above passage from "The Idea of a Christian Society" suggests that the only regulation of sex that Eliot accepted as natural (at least in 1939, when he was still keeping his vow) was celibacy, a lifestyle choice he viewed as a "higher form of devotional life" (47), a life lived only by the best, most conscious Christians. Eliot does not worry that those elites will fail to reproduce because, in his view, the paramount social problem is neither biological nor political but moral and spiritual. Just so, he cites the divorce of the ethical from everyday life in conjunction with the "mechanised, commercialised, urban way of life" as his greatest concern, but he does not look to Progressive Era legislation as a remedy (49). On the contrary, he dismisses the chimera of so-called progress as not "always integral" and advocates instead "reascending to origins" and "recover[ing] the sense of relation to nature and to God" to cure the ills of modernity (49). Eliot thereby re-spatializes modernity as lower than tradition, below (in quality and religiosity and naturalness) than the past.

This anti-Progressiveness perhaps more than anything makes Eliot a nonrepresentative modern thinker at the same time that it precludes his being a true eugenicist. Granted, Eliot does argue that his ideal, the "formation of a new Christian culture," will "involve radical changes," but it is clear that those changes will return society to a better, earlier, and more traditional form (10); again, he aims to resurrect, not to remake, the world. In other words, Eliot advocates cultural change in order to recover a prior order; by contrast, eugenics advocates across the political spectrum, including Du Bois, argue for social interventions and public policy to create a new, higher social order of the future. Stoddard, for example, advised a "series of constructive reforms" (*Revolt*, 230) that included "spreading contraceptive knowledge among the masses and thus mitigating as far as possible the evils of a racially destructive differential birth-rate" (119) and encouraging the superior to have more children (255). He further recommended that "habitual paupers should be prevented from having children" (243) through "segregation of the insane and feeble-minded in institutions" and "sterilization" (249). Oddly enough, Stoddard and Du Bois begin to sound more alike than do Eliot and Stoddard, as Stoddard dreams of a eugenic "neo-aristocracy," an "ideal of race perfection [that] combines and harmonizes into a higher synthesis the hitherto conflicting ideas of aristocracy and democracy" (263). Du Bois's *Dark Princess* similarly envisions a pool of "Talent" created from "the great Reservoir of All Men of All Races, of All Classes, of All Ages, of Both Sexes—this is real Aristocracy, real Democracy—the only path to that great and final Freedom which you so well call Divine Anarchy" (285). Eliot, while he agreed with the notion of an elite cultural leadership, never advocated the kinds of social and sexual intervention promoted by reactionary eugenicists like Stoddard—or, for that matter, liberal ones like Du Bois and Aldous Huxley.

Indeed, even in his period reviews of pro-eugenics texts—reviews on which both Childs and León rely so heavily to establish that Eliot was a eugenicist—Eliot often voiced either halfhearted support or outright skepticism regarding eugenic social policies. For example, Childs cites as evidence of Eliot's eugenics a 1927 essay in which Eliot "writes of the futurist John Rodker that he 'is up-to-the-minute, if anyone is; we feel sure that he knows all about hormones, W. H. R. Rivers, and the Mongol in our midst'" (90). Here Eliot is clearly referring to eugenicist F. G. Crookshank and his popular 1924 book, *The Mongol in Our Midst*, and is, just as clearly, mocking both Crookshank and Rodker for their biological earnestness and their sense of superiority. Eliot's spiritual solution challenges Rivers and Crookshank's vision of themselves as a kind of social-scientific priesthood bringing enlightenment, correction, and much-needed biological regulation to a deeply flawed modern world. Fitzgerald, too, lampooned eugenics for such self-righteousness. A well-known passage from *The Great Gatsby* (1925) portrays Tom Buchanan as an overheated buffoon spewing popularized eugenic clichés obviously gleaned from Stoddard's *Rising Tide of Color* (Buchanan misremembers the title and author as "*The Rise of the Coloured Empires* by this man Goddard").[27] Tom declares: "The idea is if we don't look out the white race will be utterly submerged. . . . It's up to us who are the dominant race to watch out or these other races will have control of things. . . . This idea is that we're Nordics . . . and we've produced all the things that go to make civilization—oh, science and art and all that. Do you see?" (14). Interestingly, Fitzgerald's eugenic satire here takes the form of class criticism; the crass Buchanan counts on his whiteness to bolster his social position. The narrator Nick, apparently far more sophisticated, merely "laughed aloud" at the sight of a limousine that passed them on their way into the city, carrying "three modish Negroes, two bucks and a girl," "as the yolks of their eyeballs rolled toward us in haughty rivalry" (55). Nick thinks, "Anything can happen now that we've slid over this bridge" (55). Claiming fearlessness of race rivalry even as he is patently racist, Nick welcomes crossing the "bridge" of race for the sake of a night of entertaining modern social experimentation. As I will argue, the modernist literary experiment itself often depended on such tangential, indirect experiences of blackness, accompanied by elitist and racist interpretations of the "other."

Anglo-American writers like Fitzgerald and Eliot repeatedly positioned themselves above the Tom Buchanans of the modern landscape. Fitzgerald's eugenic skepticism, like Eliot's, places the modernist author-critic in the truly superior position, above (or at least so Fitzgerald and Eliot thought) the racial and class anxieties of the period's resolutely middle-class eugenicists. The modernist men of letters saw themselves in a class of their own—a class distinguished by superiority of vision and taste and a *perceived* agility in crossing racial and class lines. Eliot and Fitzgerald poke fun at the white professional managerial class for whom eugenics functioned both as a kind of shared racial creed articulating their select status and as a state-administered policy ensuring their dominance. Ironically, then, it is precisely their (aesthetic) elitism, their self-selection of artists as cultural diagnosticians, that permits Eliot and Fitzgerald to satirize self-selecting, white, middle-class eugenicists. Eliot's own take on the middle class and its culture was most succinctly articulated in his 1923 "Marie Lloyd" essay: the middle classes, Eliot claims, have no such "expressive figure" as the dance hall singer Lloyd, for they are "morally corrupt."[28]

Fitzgerald also shared with Eliot a distaste for the regulation of sexuality implied by eugenics. However, unlike Eliot, his distaste did *not* stem from sexual prudery. On the contrary, eugenics's clinical nature and its interference with naturally robust and passionate sexual activity amused him, while the idea of choosing a mate according to eugenic criteria (rather than according to natural inclination) struck him as absurd. Fitzgerald's little noted book and lyrics for the musical *FIE! FIE! Fi-Fi!* (written in 1914 for the Princeton Triangle Club) energetically satirizes the eugenicist's instrumentalist view of sex. In a song titled "Love or Eugenics," the musical's two female leads (one with "no fashionable bustle but plenty of muscle," the other "a most popular, tipular, topular Maiden born to vex") sing the chorus in unison:

> Ladies, Here's a problem none of you can flee,
> Men, which would you like to come and pour you tea.
> Kisses that set your heart aflame, Or love from a prophylactic dame.
> Ladies, take your choice of what your style shall be.

The silly song pits the plain, muscled dame and her "ascetic verses" (Clover) against the "queen of the feminine sex" (Celeste), with the natural choice for men being obvious.[29] Fitzgerald's un-Eliotic but more typically modern and explicit sexual thinking, with its loosening of Victorian constraints, led him to mock and reject eugenics's programmatic, constrained approach to sex and reproduction. What real man, after all, would want a "prophylactic dame"? Rendering women more like men, leveling sexual difference, strikes Fitzgerald as quite unsexy. Eliot, too, rejected eugenic human leveling, but he focused, as one would expect, not on sexuality but on class and race.

The eugenicists' careful differentiation of the layers of humanity might have jibed with Eliot's understanding and valuing of social hierarchy, but its concomitant goal of leveling human quality—that is, of creating a plurality of certain kinds of modern subjects—conflicted with his desire to retain social distinctions. Any form of eugenics, be it of the right or the left, sought greater social and human uniformity. As the socialist Aldous Huxley put it: "We can't do much practical eugenics until we have more or less equalized the environmental opportunities of all classes and types—and this must be done by levelling up."[30] The right-wing Stoddard, by contrast, offered this version of uniformity: "The eugenic ideal is thus seen to be *an ever-perfecting super race* . . . cleansing itself *throughout* by elimination of its defects, and raising itself *throughout* by the cultivation of its qualities" (*Revolt*, 262; emphasis in the original).[31] Eliot, unlike both Huxley and Stoddard, argued that sustained racial and social distinctions sustain healthy culture; this cultural model matches, at least in part, the modernist pluralism Walter Benn Michaels has ascribed to the 1920s. But Eliot's version of pluralism does not manifest, as Michaels argues modernism in general does, a "new indifference to class" (53). Eliot is indifferent neither to race nor to class; a modernist hierarchy of race (or class, for that matter) never resolves into mere difference, as Michaels suggests it does ("In pluralism one prefers one's own race not because it is superior but because it is one's own," 67). Eliot, like Stoddard, does see his layer of the culture—determined by class, race, religion, gender, and intellect (Christian, white, literary, and male)—as superior. But that does not mean therefore that, like Stoddard or the liberal eugenicists, he wishes either to "eliminate" or to "uplift" the lower layers of culture. Eliot can be at once a pluralist and an elitist.

Much recent Eliot scholarship has emphasized his ambivalence regarding mass and working-class forms of culture.[32] And indeed, with his apparently competing interests in classical literary forms and dance halls, modern epic and vaudeville, Sanskrit and working-class African American and English speech, Arnoldian literary values and the values of the literary marketplace, Eliot seems the ideal figure to demonstrate modernist ambivalence and contradictoriness. But clarity, urgency, and diagnosis—not ambivalence and contradiction—generally characterize Eliot's critical and creative writings, as well as his relationship to, and participation in, the political, social, and aesthetic questions of modernism. For example, he often expresses, rather than ambivalence, a clear enjoyment of much working-class culture. As Barry Faulk puts it, "Eliot was clearly moved by the English popular."[33] And, as Faulk further argues, what Eliot feared was the ever-expanding consumption, in readily reproducible and available forms, of a lower-class culture that should remain, in his view, within national boundaries and outside systems of global commercialism and mechanical reproduction (605). Eliot contends in his famous 1922 eulogy for Marie Lloyd that the dance-hall singer and actress "represented and expressed that part of the English nation which has perhaps the greatest vitality and interest" (405). He despairs that "when every theatre has been replaced by 100 cinemas, when every musical instrument has been replaced by 100 gramophones, when very horse has been replaced by 100 cheap motor-cars, when electrical ingenuity has made it possible for every child to hear its bedtime stories from a loud speaker, when applied science has done everything possible with the materials on this earth to make life interesting, it will not be surprising if the population of the entire civilized world rapidly follows the fate of the Melanesians" [i.e., "dying from pure boredom"] (407–8). Eliot saw the dance hall as a bulwark against the mechanization of popular culture by movie theaters and the radio, just as he saw the perpetual separateness and vitality of the working-class as a bulwark against the standardization of the family and the society as a whole.

Eliot sustained a commitment to social division and hierarchy not just in the 1920s but throughout his career. As of his 1949 "Notes towards the Definition of Culture," Eliot still considered "the persistence of social classes" to be one of the "conditions for culture." And Eliot himself still resides at the cultural summit, where he can and should benefit from the bottom without at the same time raising the bottom to his level. "Error creeps in again and again," says Eliot,

> through our tendency to think of culture as group culture exclusively, the culture of the "cultured" classes and elites. We then proceed to think of the humbler part of society as having culture only

in so far as it participates in this superior and more conscious culture. To treat the "uneducated" mass of the population as we might treat some innocent tribe of savages to whom we are impelled to deliver the true faith, is to encourage them to neglect or despise that culture which they should possess and from which the more conscious part of culture draws vitality; and to aim to make everyone share in the appreciation of the fruits of the more conscious part of culture is to adulterate and cheapen what you give. For it is an essential condition of the preservation of the quality of culture of the minority, that it should continue to be a minority culture.[34]

Although Eliot seeks a pluralistic retention of "local and racial distinctions," he does so in the name of "world culture" (157) and "minority" culture (184). We must understand that for Eliot "minority" culture signifies that of "the best of the most advanced," not that of "the humbler parts of society." In other words, he does not use "minority," as we now generally do, to mean nonwhite racial or ethnic groups and their languages or cultural practices; by "minority," he means his own elite culture. "Local and racial" forms of culture, by contrast, serve mainly as sources of "vitality" for the conscious creators (like himself) of the higher, "minority" culture, who are thereby positioned as cultural arbiters for the society as a whole. Eliot thus explicitly rejects an Anglo-American version of "uplift" or cultural democracy ("to aim to make everyone share in the appreciation of the fruits of the more conscious part of culture") and aims instead to maintain a cultural hierarchy and therefore avoid the "degeneration" and "cheapening" of the "more conscious part of culture"—in other words, *his* part: "Shall I at least set my lands in order?"[35]

In order to ensure that the social order remains intact, Eliot will keep, not mass or popular culture (which must continue to flow upward), but the masses themselves, in their place. He views the literal mobility of others as a direct threat to the quality of all culture. As he puts it in "Notes towards the Definition of Culture": "On the whole, it would appear to be for the best that the great majority of human beings should go on living in the place in which they were born" (125). Of course, Eliot's own expatriatism imbues this edict with unintended irony. Clearly, he is prescribing immobility only for the majority, not for the elite minority. Expatriatism emerges, then, as an intellectual

commodity, with Eliot and other expatriate modernist writers possessing a surplus of mobility; while he himself, possessing the ultimately
mobile identity (a "metic," as he once put it) becomes the preeminent
modernist, reaching down into the lower levels of culture to sample
their wares.

In sum, Eliot grants the literary intellectual a privileged subjectivity that permits cultural diagnosis as well as prescription in order to
reestablish a social hierarchy whose sustenance and integrity depend
on a single religion. In "The Idea of a Christian Society," Eliot envisions a utopian Christian community to be administered by the intellectual elite: "It would be a society in which the natural end of man—
virtue and well-being in community—is acknowledged for all, and the
supernatural end—beatitude—for those who have the eyes to see it.
. . . It should not be necessary for the ordinary individual to be wholly
conscious of what elements are distinctly religious and Christian, and
what are merely social and identified with his religion by no logical
implication. . . . [The community's rulers] will be the consciously and
thoughtfully practising Christians, especially those of intellectual and
spiritual superiority" (27–28). An integrated and unified consciousness, like expatriatism, emerges for Eliot as an intellectual commodity bestowing qualities of natural leadership and superior vision. As he
puts it, "It is now the opinion of some of the most advanced minds that
some qualitative differences between individuals must still be recog-
nised, and that the superior individuals be formed into suitable groups
. . . the individuals composing them will be spoken of as 'leaders' "
("Notes," 108). Eliot, as just such a superior individual claims membership in an "international fraternity of men of letters . . . whose
business" it is "to maintain intellectual activity on the highest level"
("Notes," 95–96). The literary man, as possessor of the most intact
and enlightened consciousness, thereby becomes the guardian of culture, part of what Du Bois might term the "advance guard."[36] For Eliot,
as for a number of other modernists, writers and artists are distinguished by intellectual, phenomenological, and moral superiority;
they are therefore naturally in a position "to form the conscious mind
and the conscience of the nation" ("Idea," 34). Eliot's cultural elitism
here could easily have shaded into eugenic thinking. In his 1924 *Revolt
against Civilization*, Lothrop Stoddard observed that "civilization always
depends upon the qualities of the people who are the bearers of it" and
that superior civilizations contain within them "a relatively large num-

ber of very superior individuals, characterized by energy, ability, talent, or genius. It is this élite which leavens the group and initiates progress" (9–10). In this instance, it is only Stoddard's desire for progress that distances him from Eliot.

But Eliot cannot be considered the utter reactionary he is often reputed to be. Despite his patently elitist cultural model, Eliot consistently, if somewhat contradictorily, called for cultural motility along with a stable tradition and sustained class differences. He stated in *After Strange Gods* (his controversial 1933 lecture at the University of Virginia, published in book form in 1934) that while we must take care to preserve "tradition," we must also realize that tradition should be neither "immovable" nor "hostile to all change."[37] This cultural prescription of tradition coupled with change, class coupled with mixture, remains consistent in Eliot's critical writings from the 1910s through the 1940s. As he put the idea in "Notes towards the Definition of Culture" (1949), in potentially liberal-pluralist (if not particularly democratic and certainly not socialist) and anti-eugenic fashion: "The classes, while remaining distinct, should be able to mix freely" (123). Yet his fixation on tradition results in a far less liberal, even authoritarian view of culture and art. From "Tradition and the Individual Talent" (1919) to "The Function of Criticism" (1923) to *After Strange Gods* (1933), Eliot insisted that artists' new, "individual works of art" have significance "only in relation to" a tradition that may consist "of the literature of the world, of the literature of Europe, [or] of the literature of a single country."[38] Moreover, both creative and critical writers should have "a sense of tradition," should give "allegiance to something outside themselves," should listen to something other than an "inner voice" ("Function," 68, 70). In other words, artists and critics may produce the new, but they must at the same time listen to the tradition that precedes them, that lies "outside" them ("Function," 68). Eliot likens those writers who fail to heed tradition to those who "ride ten in a compartment to a football match at Swansea, listening to the inner voice, which breathes the eternal message of vanity, fear, and lust" ("Function," 71). If the cultural guardians of tradition fail in their mission, then, we might as well all be working class and therefore carnal. This 1923 image of train-riding football fans neatly returns us to Eliot's hardening, post–*Waste Land* views on mobility in relationship to culture and class as well as to his emerging desire (presaged in his 1928 conversion and articulated plainly in 1939) for a permanent, Christian "way of

life for a people" ("Idea," 14), a kind of collective "allegiance to something outside themselves," with religion playing the role for the society that tradition plays for the writer.

This call for steady allegiance to Christianity alone ultimately leads
Eliot to a clearly nonliberal and dangerous social prescription. Eliot
went on in his 1933 *After Strange Gods* lecture to praise the University of
Virginia for having "at least some recollection of a 'tradition,' such as
the influx of foreign populations has almost effaced in some parts of
the North."[39] He claimed that, in order to preserve and protect that
tradition and thus to revive "native culture" (*ASG* 16), "stability is obviously necessary. You are hardly likely to develop tradition except where
the bulk of the population is relatively so well off where it is that it has
no incentive or pressure to move about. The population should be homogeneous; where two or more cultures exist in the same place they are
likely either to be fiercely self-conscious or both to become adulterate.
What is still more important is unity of religious background; and reasons of race and religion combine to make any large number of free-
thinking Jews undesirable" (*ASG* 20). Eliot later claimed that in this,
perhaps the most troubling passage in any of his writing, he meant
nonbelieving Jews, explaining that he viewed nonbelievers of any faith
(Christianity and its denominations included) as equally undesirable.
In other words, he was simply giving an example (in "free-thinking
Jews") of the lack of allegiance to a tradition (here, a religious one),
the sort of allegiance to an external system that he had always posited as
vital for the continuation of a healthy culture. "Free-thinking Jews," in
this interpretation, had simply ceased listening to the external voice of
their religious tradition and were therefore placing the entire culture
at risk. Despite Eliot's revisionary analysis of it, the passage actually suggests that "unity" and "homogeneousness," rather than religious funda-
mentalism or adherence to tradition, stand as the primary prerequisites for the sustenance of a healthy tradition and culture. Jews, in this
view, will always be a threat to "native [Christian] culture." Modern heterogeneity—the instability of national boundaries, foreign immigration, and domestic migration, with their attendant racial, ethnic, and
class mixture—obviously frustrated Eliot's vision of a stable, unified,
yet stratified culture (especially in "the North").[40] Indeed, it is worth
remembering in this context that Eliot idealizes a "Christian," and not
a *Judeo-Christian*, "society." Anti-Semitism becomes a necessary corollary
to any project of Christian hegemony and homogeneity.[41] As Zygmunt

Bauman has argued, Jews represent for Eliot the disruption of "a total harmonious design"; it is such "admixing of resentment of 'the Other'" that "turns—at least potentially—into genocide."[42] At the same time, Eliot, in advocating immobility for the masses while in the Jim Crow South at an all-white university, is necessarily, even if implicitly, endorsing racial segregation along with religious intolerance.[43]

Thus it is in his analysis of the hazards for culture entailed by the mobility of "the bulk of the population," Eliot sounds most disturbingly like the white supremacist eugenicists of the period.[44] Indeed, Eliot was far from alone in his vision of cultural progress as dependent on a stable tradition and a homogeneous population. A. E. Wiggam, mouthpiece for the mainline eugenics movement in the United States, advanced a similarly dual, and potentially monstrous, recombination of Malthus and Gobineau, of progress and retrenchment: "Nations cannot progress to any high standards of social life, gentility and polish, nor to any ordered working of political institutions, without a homogeneous national mind, a common racial outlook, similar cultural traditions, common language and literature. . . . The ideal, therefore, of nationality which should be wrought into the fabric of all social thought, is that of a stable population in every nation, whether large or small, of very great homogeneity, constantly balanced between numbers and food supply, developing its national personality and slowly elevating the biological quality of its people by every eugenical agency."[45] It is just this national "homogeneity" and "stability" that Eliot was calling for in *After Strange Gods*. But whereas Wiggam seeks to eliminate heterogeneity as well as the biologically inferior in order to level the quality of the national population and culture, Eliot seeks cultural improvement through a return to a premigratory demographics, a restoration of hierarchy, an internalization of tradition, and, above all, a return to a Christian culture. In other words, although Eliot's and Wiggam's diagnoses are the same (breakdown in national and cultural unity), they offer different prescriptions. Certainly, Eliot and Wiggam agree with mainline eugenics' central tenet: that "all men are born unequal."[46] But even after race and religion have been appropriately compartmentalized and evaluated, men will still remain unequal—for Wiggam, that is where eugenics comes in; for Eliot, that is culture as it should be.

On the other hand, Eliot does want to improve and promote the highest level of culture, and, in that, he begins to sound again rather like a eugenicist. Indeed, in "Notes towards the Definition of Culture," Eliot endorses and prescribes the propagation of elites as a cultural cure: "I have suggested elsewhere that a growing weakness of our culture has been the increasing isolation of élites from each other, so that the political, the philosophical, the artistic, the scientific, are separated to the great loss of each of them, not merely through the arrest of any general circulation of ideas, but through the lack of those contacts and mutual influences at a less conscious level, which are perhaps even more important than ideas. The problem of the formation, preservation and development of the élites is therefore also the problem of the formation, preservation and development of *the* élite" (110). In other words, we must be sure to continue to breed ("develop") outstanding individuals ("the élites") who, en masse, form a single superior elite group ("*the* élite"). But Eliot does not become a literal eugenicist here: he is talking about a kind of asexual (or possibly homosocial) procreation of a group. This nonbiological, clearly metaphorical notion of breeding among elites is perfectly consistent with Eliot's consistently noncorporeal (that is, cultural) version of eugenic rhetoric. He wishes to encourage mingling and figurative propagation among the culturally superior. We find A. E. Wiggam declaring in 1923 a similar sentiment—that in the "building of nations, schools, churches, industry, law and order, a high-born godly race is everything, absolutely everything."[47] Eliot's "international fraternity of [white, Christian] men of letters," constitutes his version of Wiggam's "high-born godly race," a kind of race of writers.

A more literal form of race also does significant cultural work for Eliot, as it does for many other Anglo-American modernist writers. As Laura Doyle has argued, race "shapes modernist fiction's very practice."[48] Just so, Eliot's often ugly use of race and class—his troubling representations of working-class, Irish, and African American characters and speech—renders him vulnerable to accusations of eugenic thinking. But racism and elitism do not necessarily translate into eugenics; Eliot in fact found great cultural use for some racial and social "others," at least as he perceived them, and he certainly did not seek their elimination. A number of critics have pointed to Eliot's fascination with, and ambivalence toward, the language of the working class, of the Irish, and of black people.[49] But ambivalence does not offer the best description of Eliot's use of their language. Yes, he included the street speech of lower-class Londoners in the published version of *The*

Waste Land and representations of an imagined black vernacular in earlier drafts, but that inclusion was not therefore ambivalent. Eliot could easily sustain interest and use—even approval—without direct contact or public engagement (he wrote no elegy for Ethel Waters), as long as those "others" remained in their literal places and continued to serve their aesthetic function for the cultural elite. For Eliot, black people and the working class served as vehicles to express sexual desire as well as sexual disgust; their actual presence in the modern landscape was not nearly as important as their imagined role in his discourse. He used Uncle Remus stories to filter his social contacts with the ladies at "The Shambles." In his correspondence, he sketched and rhymed about the hypersexual black character King Bolo. In other words, black male characters attenuated his discomfort with women and expressed his sexual, scatological, and puerile ribaldry. Eliot's bizarre female counterpart to the King Bolo character—"King Bolo's big black bassturd kween"—compactly expressed such sexualized and racialized fiction-making by means of a semantically impossible, linguistically promiscuous disordering of size, color, breeding, gender, and social status. Likewise, his Cockney vernacular in *The Waste Land*—"It's them pills I took, to bring it off, she said"—engages matters of uncontrolled sexuality and (sometimes controlled) fertility—where Eliot's standard English poetic voice cannot. Here, Eliot moves closer to his fellow modernists and offers a more truly "representative" model for white modernist literary experimentation. Yes, Eliot is foisting his sexual expressiveness onto black and working-class characters in a decidedly personal solution to his own repressions and anxieties. But, particularly in his imagined version of black speech, he is also offering typically modernist social and literary misspelling masked as vernacular—with both misspelling and promiscuity rendered safe (depersonalized and aestheticized) by its being channeled through that "other" language.

Significantly, Eliot shared his invented black speech with fellow (male) modernists, most often in his correspondence with Pound, but also with James Joyce, among others. Thus Eliot's racialism should not be seen as identical to his anti-Semitism. Anthony Julius rightly points out Eliot's "aesthetic commitment to anti-Semitism" rather than his commitment to Jewishness.[50] That is, in his writing Eliot did not promote Jewish speech and cultural practices as sources of social or literary vitality; he framed them instead as cultural contaminants, as disrupters of social order—and that is true whether such anti-Semitism is

Eliot's own (as Anthony Julius and others have argued) or his characters' (as Craig Raine has argued). By contrast, blackness and black
speech (however fantastic and implicitly racist)—rather than explicit
antiblack racism—did function not only as cohesive source material
for Eliot but also as a male modernist lingua franca.

Eliot's relationship to black language is analogous to his relationship
to his black characters. Dialect, at least as he imagines it, functions as
an expressive vehicle for otherwise repressed passions and for modernist literary experimentation. For many white moderns, black people represented the exceptional and the extraordinary in both fright-
ening and useful ways. Stoddard, in his analysis of racial mixture in
the Caribbean argued that among the region's "many racial elements,
one easily outweighs all the rest put together. Everywhere Negroes swarm
—and breed."[51] "Negro blood," he believed, with "the tenacity of its emotional qualities," "accounts in large part for the notoriously unstable
characteristics displayed by the truly mongrelised populations" of Latin
America and the West Indies. According to Stoddard, "The Negro's
outstanding quality is great animal vitality," leading to "intense emo-
tionalism" and "extreme fecundity."[52] Eliot exploits this ultimate "oth-
erness," this perceived impassioned nature of blackness, especially in
his representations of dialect. Michael North argues, by contrast, that
"for Eliot, black dialect is a flaw, a speech impediment that clogs his
language and blocks his attempts to link his own individual talent with
tradition."[53] But just like Pound, Eliot finds his imagined version of
black dialect (as opposed to actual speech by actual black people) to be
both incorrect and enabling; as North argues of Pound, Eliot too uses
his "assumption of a black voice to remake the English language" in
distinctly and self-conscious modern ways.[54]

That Eliot included working-class and black speech in his private
correspondence with Ezra Pound, Scofield Thayer, and Conrad Aiken
throughout the 1910s and 1920s does not mean, then, that Eliot embraced blackness and working classness in their "raw" states. His perception and his use of that rawness are more important than the imagined working-class and black voices that sound in his published and
unpublished writings. North rightly argues that Eliot was "a writer for
whom conventional racial boundaries were necessary to avoid moral
chaos and disintegration."[55] Equally important, those boundaries were
necessary to avoid aesthetic degradation. Eliot accepted Pound's excision of black vernacular from *The Waste Land*; he confined scatology and

linguistic blackface largely to his not-to-be-published poetic oeuvre and his letters with other male moderns.[56] Contained and controlled via a private, male modernist, literary-experimental alembic, lower-class, black, and popular culture (unlike Jewishness—which was, for Eliot, a quite real and disturbing presence in modern life) becomes salutary for his "international fraternity of men of letters."[57] Eliot, or the male modernist poet figure in general, patrols racial and aesthetic boundaries. He is the linguistic and cultural expatriate who can safely and productively cross lines of dialect, race, and nation. In Eric Lott's words (from a somewhat different context), Eliot performed "a simultaneous drawing up and crossing of racial boundaries."[58] Or, as Eliot himself put it in a 1921 letter, "I have got used to being a foreigner everywhere."[59]

Critics and biographers have often concluded from that statement, as well as from others, that Eliot was anxious about his own unstable identity. In an infamous passage from his correspondence with Herbert Read, Eliot wrote in 1928 that he wanted "to write an essay about the point of view of an American who wasn't an American, because he was born in the South and went to school in New England as a small boy with a nigger drawl, but who wasn't a Southerner because his people were northerners in a border state and looked down on all southerners and Virginians, and who so was never anything anywhere."[60] Michael North argues that this letter shows that "Eliot felt himself to be just such an adulterate mixture" and that he possessed a "fear of that placelessness, that lack of identity."[61] On the contrary, his ostensibly mixed identity is precisely what constitutes Eliot's literary desire—he *wants* to write the essay. Eliot is neither afraid of nor ambivalent about "placelessness" or "lack of identity" or blackness (at least as he understands it); once he has transcribed black speech (he thinks) within his writing, his valuation and his enjoyment of it are precisely what distinguishes him and Pound as the best and wittiest of the moderns. In a 1915 letter to Pound, he jokes:

> I fear that King Bolo and his Big Black Kween will never burst into print. I understand that Priapism, and Narcissism, etc. are not approved of, and even so innocent a rhyme as
>
> . . . pulled her stockings off
> With a frightful cry of "Hauptbahnhof!!"
>
> is considered decadent."[62]

Eliot and Pound are the bad and the best boys of modernism here. Eliot's "racial masquerade"[63] in conjunction with his expatriatism lend him special imaginative, poetic, editorial, linguistic, and evaluative powers. That is, his flexible citizenship and his exploitation of invented black speech offer Eliot, ironically enough, a secure and stable identity as the modern-ist of modern writers—and as modernism's ultimate editor.

In a 1921 letter to James Joyce evaluating the manuscripts of the "Circe," "Eumaeus," and "Oxen of the Sun" episodes in *Ulysses*, the American-English Eliot conspired with his Irish counterpart in a kind of high white modernist blackface routine: "Only, in detail, I object to one or two phrases of Elijah: 'ring up' is English, 'call up' the American; 'trunk line,' if applied to the telephone service, is English, the American is, if I remember, 'long distance.' I don't quite like the wording of the coon transformation of Elijah, either, but I cannot suggest any detailed alteration. But otherwise, I have nothing but admiration; in fact, I wish for my own sake, that I had not read it."[64] The tone of this letter suggests that Eliot is coyly proud of his international and ostensible interracial expertise (though it has its limits); it constitutes that which elevates him above even Joyce, who can claim only Irishness (certainly not literary experimentalism or knowledge of tradition and the classics) as a distinction from Eliot. Thus an invented form of African American language (along with American slang) is both a shared "dirty secret," just as Michael North suggests,[65] and the fundamental ingredient in Eliot's private-to-public cultural tonic.

The manipulation and application of popular, lower-class, and, especially, black cultural forms for the purposes of modern literary craft —signified by the appalling term "coon transformation"—represent Eliot's implicit cultural prescription during the 1910s–30s, a prescription later rendered explicit in "Notes towards the Definition of Culture," when he speaks of the need to sustain the lower forms of "culture . . . from which the more conscious part of culture draws vitality" (184). Contemporary critics, while decrying the obvious racism and puerility of the King Bolo verse, have largely overlooked the formal importance of an imaginary blackness, particularly in Eliot's work, but also more generally in modernist writing. It's as if Eliot is saying to Joyce, let's put on a "coon show," one that other white modern writers can join. Indeed, the passage in *Ulysses* to which Eliot alludes, the "coon transformation of Elijah," bears a striking resemblance to Stein's "Melanctha"[66] (which I will discuss at length in the following chapter):

ELIJAH

(In rolled up shirtsleeves, black in the face, shouts at the top of his voice, his arms uplifted.) Big brother up there, Mr President, you hear what I done just been saying to you. Certainly, I sort of believe strong in you, Mr President. I certainly am thinking now Miss Higgins and Miss Ricketts got religion way inside them. Certainly seems to me I don't never see no wusser scared female than the way you been, Miss Florry, just now as I done seed you. Mr President, you come long and help me save our sisters dear. *(He winks at his audience.)* Our Mr President, he twig a whole lot and he ain't saying anything.[67]

Eliot needed black culture—along with lower-class culture—to remain intact below in order to perform his "transformations," his higher modernist cultural work above. Steady racial and class distinctions were as important as Christianity in Eliot's post—*Waste Land* vision of an ongoing, vital culture administered by himself and Pound and Joyce and his whole "international fraternity."

But not all prominent Anglo-American modernists took as seriously as Eliot and Joyce the function of racial difference in modernist literary innovation and cultural improvement. Hemingway, for one, understood and parodied the habitual modern linkage of race and writing in his 1926 novel, *The Torrents of Spring: A Romantic Novel in Honor of the Passing of a Great Race.* In it, he lampoons even metaphorical uses of race for cultural or personal improvement projects. The novel follows two peripatetic white male protagonists, Scripps O'Neil and Yogi Johnson, as they encounter Negroes and Indians, buxom white waitresses and Indian squaws, in an absurd search for passion, renewal, and virility in the frozen American North. As the novel's title suggests, Hemingway simultaneously satirizes the racialism of Madison Grant's influential *The Passing of the Great Race* (1916) and modernist writers' mannered styles, thereby exposing and discrediting that overplayed link between race and writing, particularly in the 1920s.[68] For example, in two efficient paragraphs, Hemingway dispatches Sherwood Anderson, Huysman, and Stein, as well as their cherished beliefs in racial and national character. Yogi Johnson, accompanied by two Indians who have befriended him —"Red men and white men walking together. Something had brought them together. Was it the war? Was it fate? Was it accident? Or was it just chance?"—is pondering his situation:

> He was a white man, but he knew when he had enough. After all, the white race might not always be supreme. This Moslem revolt. Unrest in the East. Trouble in the West. Things looked black in the South. Now this condition of things in the North. Where was it taking him? Where did it all lead? Would it help him to want a woman? Would spring ever come? Was it worth while after all? He wondered.
>
> The three of them striding along the frozen streets of Petoskey. Going somewhere now. En route. Huysmans wrote that. It would be interesting to read French. Must try it sometime. There was a street in Paris named after Huysmans. Right around the corner from where Gertrude Stein lived. Ah, there was a woman! Where were her experiments in words leading her? What was at the bottom of it? All that in Paris. Ah, Paris. How far it was to Paris now. Paris in the morning. Paris in the evening. Paris at night. Paris in the morning again. Paris at noon, perhaps. Why not? Yogi Johnson striding on. His mind never still.[69]

Stein's notion of "bottom character," along with her repetitive style, are the primary targets in this passage that appears in the last section of the novel, titled "The Passing of a Great Race and the Making and Marring of Americans." Indeed, Stein's hypnotic family epic, *The Making of Americans*, had finally been published the year before *Torrents of Spring*.[70] But a more general modernist tendency to produce writing that hinges on white expatriate modernist pretension (even his own) gets hit by Hemingway's broadside as well.

Eliot, on the other hand, took quite seriously from the 1920s through the 1940s the possibility of a cultural cure administered by a great international race of writers tapping into the cultures of races and classes below them. This metaphorical brand of eugenics focused on propagating the literary elite, who in turn would control the quality of art and patrol the boundaries of culture. Eliot begins "Notes towards the Definition of Culture" with an *Oxford English Dictionary* definition of "definition": "I. The setting of bounds; limitation (rare)—1483." His epigraph aptly describes Eliot's political and aesthetic aims (as well as his own rare talent for the setting of bounds) not just in the 1940s, but almost from the start of his literary career. Just as the *Crisis* delivered Du Bois's literary, visual, political, and biological view of an ever-improving

African American race, the *Criterion* helped to deliver Eliot's view of an ever-improving religious society articulated through high-quality writing and administered by a literary elite. He and Vivien, together in the founding of the periodical, demurred when it was suggested that the title of the *Criterion* was meant to evoke some notion of measurement or evaluation,[71] but in a 1922 letter to John Quinn, Eliot explains: "I have gone on the principle [in starting *Criterion*] of trying to secure the best people of each generation and type . . . and my theory is that the best of the most advanced writing of our time (which of course means a very small number of writers) will really appear to better advantage among the really respectable and serious writers of the older type than among their own third-rate and vulgar imitators."[72] Eliot, in his essay "The Music of Poetry" (1942), starkly renders the literary-social purification project to be administered by this "international fraternity." He argues that there are words which are "ugly" because they are "not fitted for the company in which they find themselves," and that "there are words which are ugly because of foreignness or ill-breeding."[73] "Not all words are equally rich and well-connected," Eliot explains; therefore, "it is part of the business of the poet to dispose the richer among the poorer, at the right points."[74] Eliot's Darwinian conceit is not accidental. The poet's authority establishes proper *semantic-social* order; he administers a metaphorically eugenic linguistic-cultural hierarchy—but not a biological one.

Eliot apparently came closest to being a literal, biological eugenicist in his private, not his professional, life. According to Donald Childs, Eliot applied eugenic analysis to his first marriage, unconvinced that he himself represented eugenic material (once again, quite unlike Du Bois). As Childs puts it, "The potentially dysgenical dimension of both his own and his wife's health problems seems to have led [Eliot] to question whether or not they should have children."[75] Eliot may indeed have had doubts about the quality of his own (and his unstable and sickly wife Vivien's) germplasm, but he had no doubts about his greatness as a writer and critic. He functioned as an arbiter and editor of Anglo-American modernism in much the same way that Du Bois functioned as arbiter and editor of the Harlem Renaissance. But Eliot's editorial policy—to the degree that it was eugenic—was more metaphorical than literal, and certainly less overtly eugenic than Du Bois's editorship of the *Crisis*. Tom and Viv might not have been appropriate parents in their own estimation, but they surely produced a fine periodical together, one that served the function, in Eliot's words, of bringing together "a small number of intelligent persons . . . aware of the necessity to harmonize the interests, and therefore to harmonize first the ideas, of the civilized countries of Western Europe" in order to "further formation" of "the European tradition."[76] Eliot's modernist "cure" had more to do with improving civilization through literary and religious rather than biological and racial means. Indeed, for Eliot the bodily itself (along with the secular in general) represented part of the problem, and improved aesthetics and spirituality were his specifically authorial—that is, his public and published—solution. Eliot's literary experimentalism, his troubling racial, ethnic, and class politics, and his belief in the nearly priestly power of the artist can be considered, to a degree, "representative" of white modernism. Eliot's willingness to use racial and social others, and especially his much-debated anti-Semitism, "were," as Juan León puts it, "far less an anomaly than a characteristic of his age."[77] On the other hand, Eliot's asceticism and his religious prescription for cultural improvement are far less characteristic of the period and of modernist writers in general. As a result, we find that Eliot and Pound meet on the grounds of aesthetic improvement and Uncle Remus (Ol' Possum and Br'er Rabbit corresponded over many years via a particularly fantastic form of black vernacular), but that they part ways on the grounds of religion and sex and politics. Pound found Eliot's Christianity confounding and his prudery amusing, even as he admired Eliot's verse above that of all other modernists. In his review of *After Strange Gods*, Pound termed Eliot's Christian solution an "irrelevance."[78] What Pound failed to understand was the intimate relationship among Eliot's strange gods—celibacy, hierarchy, and tradition—a relationship that measures Eliot's distance from the era's Progressiveness, from its characteristic eugenic discourse, and even from his fellow modernists.

Many kinds of all these women were strong to bear many children.
—Gertrude Stein, *The Making of Americans* (1925)

As there are in medicine the art of diagnosis and the art of cure, so in the arts, so in particular the arts of poetry and of literature, there is the art of diagnosis and there is the art of cure.—Ezra Pound, "The Serious Artist" (1913)

CHAPTER THREE

The Making and Delivering of Americans in Gertrude Stein's Early Writings, 1903–1925

Quite unlike T. S. Eliot, Gertrude Stein took women and the middle class to be legitimate subjects for innovative literary modernism. She declares in *The Making of Americans*: "I have it, this interest in ordinary middle class existence, in simple firm ordinary middle class traditions, in sordid material unaspiring visions, in a repeating, common, decent enough kind of living, with no fine kind of fancy ways inside us, no excitements to surprise us, no new ways of being bad or good to win us."[1] Her experimental literary style, characterized by ongoing repetition with slight variations, mirrors the very "monotonous middle class tradition" (34) she unashamedly embraced in her earliest writings, from 1903 to 1911. In *The Making of Americans*, written between 1906 and 1908 and finally published in 1925, Stein was creating, quite explicitly, not "an ordinary kind of novel with a plot and conversations to amuse you, but a record of decent family progress," thereby correlating an extraordinary type of writing (her incantatory repetitions) with a most "ordinary" type of "existence" (American middle classness) (34—35). At the same time, Stein wrote, sometimes obliquely but always centrally, about women and their bodies. Together, *Fernhurst*, *Q.E.D*, *Three Lives*, and *The Making of Americans* suggest that Stein herself was a "Student of the Nature of Woman," the original subtitle of *Fernhurst*, a novella based on a real-life academic love triangle. Women were not only appropriate literary subjects for Stein; they were her preferred site for the exploration and exposition of distinctively modern and national forms of identity and literary subjectivity.

At the beginning of *Fernhurst*, the narrator says, "I wonder if the new woman will ever relearn the fundamental facts of sex. Will she not see that college standards are of little worth in actual labor."[2] From the beginning, then, Stein linked modernity, womanliness, sex, and labor in a kind of repeating play on words; the New Woman's labor for Stein always carried a double meaning: women were, at bottom, responsible for the "making of Americans." For Stein herself, such reproduction was solely literary, but for at least some of her characters it was often literal. She conflated the two kinds of "labor," literary and literal, in a 1925 letter to Carl Van Vechten about her experience of readying *The Making of Americans* for publication nearly fifteen years after she had begun writing it: "there he is the eldest son, *Three Lives* being the eldest but a daughter, and ainé as I call him has been a bother, we will hope now that his travaux and all is nicely done and that he will make the future easy for his parents, anyway there we are and you are his god father so you're responsible at least for his religion and morals, poor dear ainé."[3] We can only assume that Alice B. Toklas is the book's other parent, as she and Stein had cooperated in the demanding task of proofreading and delivering the completed manuscript, which ran to more than 900 pages. For Stein, modern women together were "strong to bear many children" and thus to create (here in a decidedly nonheterosexual context) a national "record of decent family progress." However, at least according to her early writings, only certain types of women were fit to produce a new literary future; others were fit to produce children— that is, a literal future. Stein thus seemed to concur with Margaret Sanger and W. E. B. Du Bois, both of whom explicitly articulated the contradiction between achieving authentic New Womanhood and reproducing the race. Sanger argued: "If women in fortunate circumstances gave ear to the demand of masculine 'race-suicide' fantasies they could within a few years be down to the condition of their sisters who lack time to cultivate their talents and intellects. A vigorous, intelligent, fruitfully cultured motherhood is all but impossible if no restriction is placed by that motherhood upon the number of children."[4] Du Bois likewise observed: "Only at the sacrifice of intelligence and the chance to do their best work can the majority of modern women bear children."[5] In Stein's early writings, middle-class (often lesbian) "new" women perform cultural production, whereas heterosexual, working-class, and African American women—and sometimes ordinary middle-class white women—traffic in more literal forms of labor and production.

Bryn Mawr is the setting for *Fernhurst*, written in 1904 or 1905.[6] In it, Stein sets up several alternative types of "new" women, though all are white, college-educated, middle class, and childless—English professor Miss Bruce, who is intellectual, physically awkward, shy, and gentle; Mrs. Redfern, wife of philosophy professor Philip Redfern, who is "blond eager good-looking" (10–11); and Miss Thornton, dean of the college, who combines "a genuine belief in liberty and honor and a disinterested devotion for the uplifting of the race with an instinct for domination and a persistent indifference to any consideration but expediency in the actual task of working out her ideal" (17–18). Miss Thornton's "ideal" is the New Woman; "bred" in her is "the conviction . . . of the value to the world of women's labor in all fields of work" (16). She is dean of a women's college: "so now the future of the race to the extent of five hundred young women every four years was in Helen Thornton's hands" (17).[7] Stein's tone here may be gently ironic, but Miss Thornton's production of New Women launches Stein's own career of producing literary newness. Like Stein herself, *Fernhurst*'s title character, Philip Redfern, is "filled with an interest in the nature of marriage and the meaning of women" (23); he falls in love with Miss Bruce, thus choosing an intellectual partnership over a conventional marriage, to the detriment of his career. But, for Stein, the meaning of college-educated or literary women lay not so much in "the nature of marriage" or in their literal reproductive capacity, but in their role as reproducers of modern national subjectivity outside marriage and outside conventional social and sexual narratives.

Indeed, Stein explored, instead of the nature of marriage, the nature of lesbian desire in her 1903 novella *Q.E.D.* In that work, the main characters are again "college bred women" caught in another love triangle, this time a lesbian one based on Stein's own experience with a fellow student, May Bookstaver, whom she met while pursuing medical studies at Johns Hopkins. *Q.E.D.*'s three women characters "were distinctly American but each one at the same time bore definitely the stamp of one of the older civilisations, incomplete and frustrated in this American version but always insistent" (54). Mabel Neathe, rival to Adele for Helen Thomas's affections, displays New England rigidity on the outside but inside has "a nature of the tropics" (55). As a number of critics have noted and as I will discuss at greater length, Stein here darkens, even racializes, desire (and not in this instance alone) and so moves closer to Eliot and other Anglo-American modernists in their sexual-literary use of "others."[8] At the same time, Stein's New and New World women of *Fernhurst* and *Q.E.D.*, even while they "bore the stamp of one of the older civilisations," were not positioned as literal breeders in the way that her immigrant and African American characters would be in *Three Lives*, begun in 1905.[9] The characters in *Q.E.D.*, while clearly sexual beings, spend far more time analyzing and discussing their relationships than engaging in physical or sexual intimacy. The *Q.E.D.* character closest to a stand-in for Stein herself, Adele, declares, "I always did thank God I wasn't born a woman" (58), and she has trouble abandoning herself to the passion she feels for Helen Thomas. Adele thinks, as she is contemplating sex with Helen, "I once thought I knew something about women" (62). In this instance, Stein appears to share with Eliot some antifeminism, or at least some squeamishness about women's bodies and sexuality. Both Catherine Stimpson and Steven Meyer have argued that Stein felt such squeamishness, noting that she failed, seemingly almost on purpose, several clinical rotations during her last year at Johns Hopkins, including her obstetrical rotation.[10] But we must note that Adele does eventually succumb to her passion for Helen, even if the relationship, like Stein's own with May Bookstaver, eventually ends miserably; moreover, Stein herself eventually finds a long-lasting passion with Alice B. Toklas. Even more important for my argument, Stein's consistent willingness to experiment literarily on and with women characters, including working-class, immigrant, and African American women, sets her quite apart from many other modernists, especially Eliot and Pound. In other words, Stein always applied herself to the research, if not the clinical aspects, of both her education and her modernist experimentation regarding women. In *Q.E.D.*, Helen in fact comments despairingly on Adele's decidedly clinical approach: "Helen gave way utterly. 'I tried to be adequate to your experiments' she said at last 'but you had no mercy. You were not content until you had dissected out every nerve in my body and left it quite exposed and it was too much, too much. You should give your subjects occasional respite even in the ardor of research'" (82). Like Redfern and Adele, Stein consistently and willingly touched the (female) body in the context of her research and writing.

Perhaps because of her sustained engagement in her work and life with women, with the female body—that is, perhaps because of her literary feminism and her lesbianism, Gertrude Stein has often been granted an exemption from the troubling politics readily assigned to other modernist U.S. writers. A number of critics have looked to her as a kind of avant-garde antidote to Pound and Eliot.[11] And she might seem "naturally" to represent an alternative to their brand of modernism. But, as John Whittier-Ferguson has recently argued, such a literary-historical approach begins with two faulty premises: one, that "political beliefs and aesthetic practices correspond" and, two, that "'politics' is a practice that begins and ends with a forthright assertion of one's identity."[12] Similarly, Jaime Hovey has pointed out that while Stein "rendered lesbian sexuality intelligible," she simultaneously engaged in a rhetoric of primitivism and in "deterministic racial stereotypes."[13] Overall, many of Stein's formal innovations do disrupt received notions of the literary, even of the modern—but that formal radicalism does not always or necessarily translate into social or political radicalism. Stein in fact participates quite resoundingly in a problematic modernist conflation of national, ethnic, and racial identity with literary subjectivity and experiment. As I discussed in the previous chapter, Eliot wrote explicitly and offensively of "coon transformation" in his literary conversations with Joyce, but Stein, too, used an imagined form of blackness, including an invented form of black vernacular, in order to advance her aesthetic project. Lorna Smedman argues that the use of "racialized words and tropes of dark and light in Stein's early work was probably prompted by her aesthetic concerns with similarity and difference at the level of the signifier and an anxiety about the effects of binary categorization, rather than any overt desire on her part to comment, one way or the other, about racism."[14] Even if it is true that Stein was merely abstracting racial rhetoric for literary-experimental ends, she nonetheless constructs and depends on an imagined field of blackness—both in her characters and her language—in order to conduct that experimentation. As Laura Doyle argues of the work of Stein and other Anglo-American writers, race "shapes modernist fiction's very practice."[15] Such literary-racial shaping brings Stein quite close to Eliot, who explicitly positioned lower-class and black cultural practices as source material for high modernist experimentation. On the other hand, Stein must still be seen as wholly unlike Eliot in her very real concern for modern women and their material conditions—that is, their bodily realities. When Stein's medical training, literary experimentalism, gynocentrism, and racialist imagination converge, as they do in *Three Lives*, the result is a highly complex, politically unstable examination of alternative forms of subjectivity articulated specifically via women characters. When Stein writes from the early 1900s through the 1920s of women's "making of Americans," she also (perhaps inevitably) participates in Progressive Era discourses and developments surrounding the (literary and literal) production of modern national subjects, including the New Woman, eugenics, and the emergence of obstetrics as a medical specialty.

Unlike her earlier texts, *Fernhurst*, *Q.E.D.*, and *The Making of Americans*, *Three Lives* insists on the legitimacy of working-class, black, and ethnic immigrant American women as literary subjects. But it also relies on dangerous racial and cultural stereotypes to describe them. *Three Lives* challenges, in clearly feminist terms, oppressive, modern-male-authored medical and literary models, yet it treats the black female body as the object of an authoritative and relentless literary-medical gaze. In sum, *Three Lives* worries about conventional literary and medical treatments of laboring (in both senses) female bodies, but it also worries about the presence and proliferation of those bodies in the modern, urban United States. It is this racially and ethnically inflected, and literary, medicalization of her subjects that discloses the eugenic anxiety attending Stein's participation in a modern, Poundian, "diagnosis and cure" aesthetic model (set forth in the second epigraph of this chapter).[16] Put more simply, the book's literary-medical experimentation engages racialist and eugenic, along with feminist, thinking. One biographer observes that Stein can "seem not to be an artist at all, but a scientist elaborately constructing metaphors in a laboratory of words."[17] Many kinds of women entered Stein's literary laboratory, especially in *Three Lives*, but not all survived her experiments.

Three Lives consists of stories about the lives, illnesses, hospitalizations, and deaths of three women: two immigrant German domestic servants, Anna and Lena, and one "mulatto" woman, Melanctha. Stein's first published book, *Three Lives* (1909) carries out many of her characteristically unconventional literary experiments, especially her use of rhythmic repetition and vernacular speech. Stein doubted that the book, with its unconventional protagonists and literary techniques, would reach a wide readership. As James Mellow notes, Stein once wrote that her "very simple and very vulgar" characters would not "interest the great American public."[18] Stein might have been right that her protagonists did not at first seem compelling, or at least conventional, subjects for high modernist literary experiment. Anna, a housekeeper modeled after Stein's own immigrant housekeeper during her medical school days in Baltimore, is a domineering yet not particularly articulate woman. The narrator periodically reminds us that "Anna led an arduous and troubled life."[19] Melanctha, an unstable and "melancholy" mulatto woman, is characterized chiefly by her vague desires: "Melanctha did not know what it was she so badly wanted" (93). Finally, Lena, a pathologically passive servant, is relentlessly characterized by the narrator as "gentle" and "patient." All three women eventually become ill and die. Anna, worn down by constant labor and anxiety, dies in the hospital after an operation. Melanctha contracts tuberculosis and dies "in a home for consumptives" (236). Lena dies in the hospital while giving birth to her fourth baby (280).

Stein began writing *Three Lives* shortly after abandoning her study of medicine in 1902, and the book unquestionably reflects Stein's experiences among the poor, largely African American and immigrant urban population for whom she provided care during her clinical rotations at Johns Hopkins. Set in Bridgepoint, a thinly veiled Baltimore, the book effectively blends medical documentation and literary experimentation; William Carlos Williams once aptly described "Melanctha" as a "thrilling clinical record."[20] And, indeed, Stein was writing *Three Lives* just as the "individual folder system for maintaining records" was "replacing the single, continuous record book that had been the mainstay of many institutions."[21] She was, then, both witnessing and contributing to new forms of medical and literary discourse. Her original title for *Three Lives*, *Three Histories*, suggests that the three lives might well function as fictional medical histories, as charts.[22] Generic hybrids, they occupy a discursive space between modern medical and literary authority—partaking of and, at times, resisting both. Suggestively, as physician-author, Stein frequently exerts the greatest clinical authority precisely where she appears most formally experimental, with African American and immigrant women the subjects, perhaps victims, of some of her most radical early experiments.

In *Three Lives*, Stein's very denomination of immigrant and black heroines, however progressive in terms of white modernists' construction of literary subjectivity, becomes imbricated with their medicalization, indeed their pathologization. First, "The Good Anna" and "The Gentle Lena," the first and third of the three stories/lives, are conjoined by their titles to their diagnoses. Anna's goodness and Lena's gentleness stand for the laboring and the passivity that eventually lead to their deaths. "Melanctha," by contrast, remains conspicuously unmodified, as if to suggest that her essential racial identity, her "melan" (with its dual connotations of *blackness/melanin* and *melancholy*), is her pathology. Just so, it is Melanctha's racial and psychological makeup that apparently leads to her death. Second, Stein's experimental narrative chronology, what she termed a "continuous present," links *Three Lives* at once with literary-formal radicalism and with clinical authority. Just like medical charts, the three lives consist of encounters that are narrated retrospectively but are also informed by the present that invariably distinguishes the clinical relationship. Medical charts document a series of face-to-face encounters which, by definition, take place in the present. Conventionally written shortly after the clinical encounter, the chart, with its always present-tense verbs, encompasses the patient's past experiences along with the most recent encounter. To put this another way, only through an accumulation of recorded clinical observations made in the (continuous) presence of the patient can a medical chart be constructed. This temporal correspondence to a chart suggests a medical source for the Steinian literary technique of a "prolonged" or "continuous present."[23] For example, the narrator of "The Good Anna" assesses the title character's physical and emotional states in precise clinical terms: "At this time, Anna, about twenty-seven years of age, was not yet all thin and worn. The sharp bony edges and corners of her head and face were still rounded out with flesh, but already the temper and the humor showed sharply in her clear blue eyes, and the thinning was begun about the lower jaw, that was so often strained with the upward pressure of resolve. Today, alone there in the carriage, she was all stiff and yet all trembling with the sore effort of decision and revolt" (21–22). In this passage, the narrator acts as diagnostician, noting "temper" and "humor" like a medieval physician. At the same time, the tension in the passage (bodily and grammatical) between "Today" and the past verb tense ("was") matches the temporal dynamic of medical case histories. Admittedly, Stein's narrator here actually possesses temporal authority and knowledge beyond those of the physician. In its awareness of what *will* come to pass ("Anna was . . . not yet all thin and worn"), the narrative voice mirrors Stein's selection of literary over medical authority in her career. Literary authority actually grants Stein greater power; as author, she can manipulate the present and the future of characters in a way that Stein as physician certainly would never have been able to with her patients.

Yet Stein still finds modern medical-narrative models useful for her literary innovations in *Three Lives*. Stein's modernist narrative experiment offered new ways to establish character just as the chart offered physicians a new clinical genre through which to describe (even construct) the individual patient.[24] The narrator of Anna's history introduces her as "a small, spare german woman at this time about forty years of age" (5). Anna "presents," then, with the potential (medical) problems of gender, age, and ethnicity. Moreover, like each of the three lives, "The Good Anna" ends (as ongoing medical histories eventually must) with the death of the patient. In "The Death of the Good Anna," the final section of Anna's story, physician and narrator together command and oversee her death, first linguistically—"the doctor said she simply could not live on so"—then literally: "In a few days they had Anna ready. Then they did the operation, and then the good Anna with her strong, strained, worn-out body died" (77–78). Such careful attention to, and recording of, Anna's condition apparently establishes the text's participation in a classically Foucauldian model of medically authoritative discourse, wherein "doctor and patient are caught up in ever greater proximity."[25] Harriet Chessman, noting that increasing proximity between Anna and the narrator, has pointed out that they "share . . . narrative space."[26] But in "The Good Anna," character-patient and narrator-doctor actually merge into a dialectical narrative even more intimate than free indirect discourse. As a result, Stein seems initially to depend on but ultimately subverts a clinical gaze in "The Good Anna." For example, in the following passage, the subjectivities of narrator and character converge: "To Anna alone there in the carriage . . . the warmth, the slowness, the jolting over stones, the steaming from the horses, the cries of men and animals and birds, and the new life all around were simply maddening. 'Baby! if you don't lie still,

I think I kill you. I can't stand any more like this' " (21). The bodily experience here is shared by Anna and the narrator, while Anna's angry speech to her dog follows without break from the charting of her "simply maddened" emotional state. By sharing narrative space with Anna in this instance, the narrator temporarily relinquishes a diagnostic stance so as to see through the character's eyes. Stein's narrative technique thus destabilizes the power relations encoded in a potentially oppressive clinical encounter, while it establishes mutually constitutive relationships between physician and patient and between narrator and character. Stein's sympathy for immigrant, working-class women and their bodily realities leads her to a literary merging of perspectives that in turn mirrors her own relinquishment of medical authority and her selection of women as paradigmatic modern subjects.

But Stein reinvokes that authority, at least to a degree, in the second of the three lives, "Melanctha." Here Stein projects her ambivalence about the exertion of medical-literary authority onto racialized female bodies as either sites of resistance (as with the half-white Melanctha) or of clinical inscription (as with Melanctha's "black" friend Rose Johnson). Without a titular diagnosis beyond her identity as tragic mulatto, Melanctha presents the narrator with questions, but no answers: "Why did the subtle, intelligent, attractive, half white girl Melanctha Herbert love and do for and demean herself in service to this coarse, decent, sullen, ordinary, black childish Rose, and why was this immoral, promiscuous, shiftless Rose married, and that's not so common either, to a good man of the negroes, while Melanctha with her white blood and attraction and desire for a right position had not yet been really married" (83). The narrator explains that Melanctha "always loved too hard and much too often" and "was always full with mystery and subtle movements and denials and vague distrusts and complicated disillusions" (86). It is just her "complex, desiring" (83) nature that resists the text's impulse to fix Melanctha either temporally ("always") or diagnostically ("too").

As female patient/subject, Melanctha frustrates the diagnostic efforts of both the narrator and her physician-lover, Jeff Campbell.[27] The narrator's diagnostic impulse is associated with a (male) medical desire to know, to circumscribe and describe Melanctha: "Some man would learn a good deal about her in the talk, never altogether truly, for Melanctha all her life did not know how to tell a story wholly. . . . Melanctha never could remember right" (97). Jeff Campbell later concurs with the narrator's diagnosis: "You certainly Melanctha, you ain't got down deep loyal feeling, true inside you, and when you ain't just that moment *quick with feeling,* then you certainly ain't got anything more there to keep you. . . . You certainly Melanctha, never can remember right, when it comes to what you have done and what you think happens to you" (179, emphasis added). Jeff acts at once as internist and obstetrician by assessing Melanctha's "inside" as pathologically non-impregnated ("ain't . . . quick"). Analogously, the narrator has already told us that Melanctha cannot reproduce experience via normal narrative production ("for Melanctha all her life did not know how to tell a story wholly"). As Marianne DeKoven has suggested, in "Melanctha," "race, class, and childbirth figure together in the disruption of traditional narrative form."[28]

Melanctha, by insisting on her own version of the narrative, challenges the ostensibly normative clinical and narrative diagnoses imposed by both the narrator and Jeff Campbell. As a result, both encounter "trouble with Melanctha's meaning" (127). Janice Doane has pointed out that Melanctha is "incapable of assimilation into [her] own narrative history."[29] She will not fully ("altogether truly") reveal herself to either a medical or a narrative gaze. She replies to Jeff's assessment: "You remember right, because you don't remember nothing till you get home with your thinking everything over, but I certainly don't think much ever of that kind of way of remembering right, Jeff Campbell. I certainly do call it remembering right Jeff Campbell to remember right just when it happens to you, so you have a right kind of feeling" (180). In this passage, "Melanctha," as story, rejects Jeff's diagnostic "remembering" as a kind of Wordsworthian poetics (conventional literary memory).[30] Melanctha, as character, likewise rejects his universalized prescriptions: "Melanctha did not feel the same as he did about being good and regular in life, and not having excitements all the time, which was the way that Jefferson Campbell wanted that *everybody should be*" (113, emphasis added). Melanctha (along with "Melanctha") thereby devalues the traditional sort of storytelling performed by (male) physicians and narrators.

Despite that feminist challenge to conventional institutional (literary and medical) memory, Stein fails to divest herself fully of a potentially oppressive medical gaze, along with its documentation of pathology, particularly in the racially "other." "Melanctha" offers a version of blackness that presents with clear symptoms, and thus re-presents an all too familiar diagnostic field. The "very black" Rose Johnson was "careless and was lazy," and she "had the simple, promiscuous unmorality of the black people" (82). Rose's "white training" had "only made for habits, not for nature" (82). Melanctha, by contrast, was "a graceful, pale yellow, intelligent, attractive negress" who "had been half made with real white blood" (82). The narrator here uses a spectrum of essentialized racial biology to perform differential diagnoses for Rose and Melanctha. "Melanctha" describes "naturally" complex mulattoes and fully legible black characters, thus participating quite resoundingly in the (unreconstructed) racialism of its day.[31] Just as in Eliot's Bolo verse, here pure blackness represents unleashed sexuality and pure vitality.

Also like Eliot, Stein associates racial mixture with morbidity. The narrator describes Melanctha as "pale yellow and mysterious and a little pleasant like her mother," while "the real power in Melanctha's nature came through her robust and unpleasant and very unendurable black father" (86). Stein here racializes the model of genetic individual identity she had advanced in *The Making of Americans*: "So now we begin again this history of us and always we must keep in us the knowledge of the men and women and parents and grandparents who came together and mixed up to make us and we must always have in us a lively sense of these mothers and these fathers, of how they lived and married and then they had us and we came to be inside us in us" (67). At the same time, in describing Melanctha's "nature," Stein also sounds more than a bit like the eugenicist Lothrop Stoddard, who confidently observed that in "ethnic crosses, the negro strikingly displays his prepotency, for black blood, once entering a human stock, seems never really bred out again."[32] But, in a classic eugenical paradox, it is Melanctha's white blood, with its own "prepotency," that complicates (elevates) her nature and establishes her as the tragic mulatto, "with her white blood and attraction and desire for a right position. . . . Sometimes the thought of how all her world was made, filled the complex, desiring Melanctha with despair" (83). Stoddard similarly describes the genetically determined fate of mulattoes: "These unhappy beings, every cell of whose bodies is a battle-ground of jarring heredities, express their souls in acts of hectic violence and aimless instability" (120).

Melanctha's "aimless instability" corresponds to her inability to fulfill the marriage plot: she cannot, finally, live happily ever after. Her "wandering" (Stein's euphemism for Melanctha's sexual experimentation) leads in the end to her death and the termination of her story. Unlike the lesbianism of the characters in *Q.E.D.*, Melanctha's straying from racial, sexual, and narrative normativity ultimately translates into pathology, both literal and literary. Non-middle-class, non-college-educated, nonwhite women apparently cannot survive outside the marriage plot in Stein's early work. Just so, after her final wandering with Jem Richards does not result in marriage ("Jem Richards never could want to marry any girl while he had trouble," 221), Melanctha runs out of story. But the narrative does not permit her even the fallen heroine's conventional ending: "But Melanctha Herbert never really killed herself because she was so blue, though often she thought this would be really the best way for her to do. Melanctha never killed herself, she only got a bad fever and went into the hospital where they took good care of her and cured her" (235). Although the hospital initially cures Melanctha (unlike Anna and Lena), her pathology persists. Melanctha's fate is determined not by medical intervention, but by her own pathological, hybrid identity. In the end, as with the good Anna, the doctors must pronounce Melanctha's death: "Melanctha went back to the hospital, and there the Doctor told her she had the consumption, and before long she would surely die" (236).

In contrast to the tragic and sickly mulatto figures in "Melanctha," the "sullen, childish, cowardly, black" (222) Rose Johnson thrives explicitly by *not* wandering.[33] Unlike Melanctha, Rose "had the sense for decent comfort, Rose had strong the sense for proper conduct, Rose had the sense to get straight always what she wanted, and she always knew what was the best thing she needed, and always Rose got what she wanted" (214). Rose, who "was a real black negress" (82), does not stray from racial normativity. Thus she can fulfill the marriage plot, for, as the narrator informs us, Rose is "married, and that's not so common either, to a good man of the negroes" (83). As products of miscegenation (an inviable mixture for this version of eugenics), the "tragic" mulattoes in *Three Lives* apparently have access neither to Rose's well-aimed stability nor to her unmixed vitality.

Just as "Melanctha" assigns an essential unfitness to mulattoes, "The Good Anna" and "The Gentle Lena" essentialize the laboring immigrant ("german") character. For Stein's immigrant characters, class, along with ethnicity, forms part of their pathology. "The Good Anna" meticulously identifies all its working-class characters according to ethnicity: Lizzie, "a pretty, cheerful irish girl" (6); Molly, "born in America of german parents" (6); and, extraordinarily specifically, Anna herself, who "was of solid, lower middle-class south german stock" (17). In contrast to such precise ethnic identification, the narrative's description of the employing class suggests that they are racially and ethnically unmarked. Miss Mathilda, Anna's employer (generally considered a stand-in for Stein herself), apparently possesses neither race nor nationality; she is, simply, "a large and careless woman" (14). According to the narrator, "Anna's superiors always must be these large helpless women, or be men, for none others could give themselves to be made so comfortable and free" (18). The socio-anatomical hierarchy here is clear: the "small, spare german" Anna naturally serves the "large" and "helpless."

"The Gentle Lena," too, constructs an immigrant apparently biologically fit for servitude. Lena's life story begins like the others, with an authoritative assessment: "Lena was patient, gentle, sweet, and german. She had been a servant for four years and liked it very well" (239). As in "The Good Anna," the tone here matches that of a medical history. The narrator continues, describing Lena, precisely, as "a brown and pleasant creature, brown as blonde races often have them brown, brown not with the yellow or red or the chocolate brown of sun burned countries, but brown with the clear color laid flat on the light toned skin beneath, the plain, spare brown that makes it right to have been made with hazel eyes" (240–41). Not only Lena's plain brownness, but her very anatomy (like Anna's) reflects a working-class destiny: "Lena had the flat chest, straight back and forward falling shoulders of the patient and enduring working woman" (241). Indeed, the "gentle Lena" embodies the eugenicist's paradoxical anxiety: like all the less genetically "worthy" European immigrants, her reproductive success signals the unnatural selection that, according to eugenicists, characterized modernity.[34] Lothrop Stoddard asserted that the "white race divides into three main sub-species—the Nordics, the Alpines, and the Mediterraneans" (162), with "no question that the Nordic is far and away the most valuable type" (162). But, he claimed, the "cramped factory and the crowded city" have "weeded out the big, blond Nordic . . . whereas the little brunet Mediterranean, in particular, [has] adapted himself to the operative's bench or the clerk's stool, prospered—and reproduced his kind" (164–65). Lena embodies his fertile "little brunet Mediterranean," one who, despite her relative unfitness and inferiority to Nordics, repeatedly "reproduces her kind." When viewed through the

lens of its ethnic and racial typing, *Three Lives* thus emerges less as a progressive feminist text and more as an anxiously eugenic one.

Three Lives paints an urban landscape populated by "mysterious mulattoes," "careless Negroes," and immigrant servants—characters who
are, to Stein, racially and culturally "other." Of course, as my prior chapters have shown, Stein was not alone in her representation of modern
urban space as overpopulated by the racial and ethnic other. The 1910s
and 1920s witnessed a kind of cultural consensus that the United
States needed to protect and improve its national stock by correcting
for the unnatural selection that its urbanization and modernity had
produced. As the prominent U.S. eugenicist Harry Laughlin put it in
1914, if "America is to escape the doom of nations generally, it must
breed good Americans."[35] Unprecedented levels of immigration to the
United States between 1880 and 1920 represent perhaps the clearest
stimulus for the period's eugenic thinking. Roughly 28 million immigrants came to the United States during that time.[36] Along with this
massive foreign immigration, the period witnessed dramatic levels of
domestic migration as well. Between 1890 and 1920, over 1.2 million
African Americans migrated from the southern to the northern United
States.[37] At the same time, medical and public health professionals (who
were observing, treating, and regulating the new arrivals) were emerging in large numbers.[38]

The changing population profile of the United States, along with
advances in medical knowledge (such as the acceptance of germ theory), called for new strategies on the part of the new health and social
service professionals. Among these "members of the new social control professions," as Nicole Rafter terms them, middle-class imagin-
ings about the reproductive capacities of the newly mobile—along with
a very real concern about their suffering—promoted positive public
health (as well as disturbing eugenic) measures designed to aid (but
also to contain) the urban poor.[39] For example, in the first decade of
the twentieth century in the United States, plumbing and sanitation in
many cities were being improved, but the nation's first compulsory sterilization laws (along with increasingly restrictive immigration acts)
were also being passed. Literary critic T. Hugh Crawford identifies in
William Carlos Williams's poetry just such a tension between progressive compassion for the poor and reactionary desires for both literal and
figurative urban purification. As Crawford puts it, the "doctor cannot
have both cleanliness and contact simultaneously."[40] Some doctors

chose cleanliness over contact; eugenics historian Daniel Kevles notes that the foremost eugenic "enthusiasts" in the United States "tended to be well-to-do rather than rich, and many were professionals—physicians, social workers, clerics, writers, and numerous professors, notably in the biological and social sciences."[41] This specifically medical version of eugenic anxiety was perhaps nowhere more clearly expressed than in the field of obstetrics.

Modern obstetrics was "born" in the late 1800s (when Stein was attending Johns Hopkins Medical School), but the first modern U.S. obstetricians, unlike other new medical specialists, encountered competition from a well-established lay tradition. As one medical historian describes it, the "decade from about 1908 began the contest between the increasingly self-conscious obstetrical specialist and his adversaries, the midwife and her advocates. . . . The result [was] the complete defeat of the United States' variety of midwife and the essential triumph of a 'single standard of obstetrics.' "[42] As evidenced by the proliferation during the 1910s in medical journals of physician-authored articles with titles such as "Control of Midwives" and "The Elimination of the Midwife," many obstetricians were waging an overt economic and professional war on midwifery.[43] We must realize that the medical profession's suppression of midwifery between 1900 and 1924 in the United States correlates directly with the period's (eugenic) restrictions on immigration. As exclusionary measures, both disclose the intense and complex struggle that was taking place over the nature of modern American nativity (with both its figurative-national and literal-birth meanings)—that is, the "making of Americans." A 1916 physicians' forum on midwifery printed in the *Journal of the American Medical Association* quotes Dr. J. M. Baldy, who asserts that the United States "contains several groups of foreigners who have been accustomed to the midwife, and until immigration ceases and these peoples have evolved into Americans, the midwife will be demanded."[44] Here, assimilation—authentic national subjectivity—is associated with a higher degree of both evolution and medical-obstetrical professionalism. Indeed, as Richard Wertz and Dorothy Wertz have pointed out, by the late nineteenth century, midwives in U.S. cities were disproportionately immigrants.[45] Thus immigration restriction was equally effective as a restriction of midwifery. In 1910, 50 percent of all births in the United States were reported by midwives, and, as medical historian Frances Kobrin observes, "the percentage for large cities was often higher," because midwives were consulted primarily by African American and immigrant women, who were concentrated in urban population centers, and who "usually shared race, nationality and language" with their midwives.[46] But the percentage of midwife-attended births dropped over the following three decades (along with immigration levels), until midwifery was all but eradicated by the 1940s.[47]

Three Lives registers both structurally and thematically the period's national anxieties over the imagined fecundity of immigrant and non-white women and the control of their births, but the book's politics surrounding these matters are not simple.[48] *Three Lives* does assign a central role to African American and immigrant women's fertility, but the text's competing and complementary ideologies—eugenics, racialism, and feminism—complicate its representation of that fertility. "Melanctha," for example, depends, at a structural level, on childbirth. The story begins with, and in the end returns to, Rose Johnson's delivery. The birth represents the temporal touchstone within the narrative's continuous present; it provides the parentheses between which Melanctha's story unfolds. "Melanctha" in fact begins with a sentence that makes grammatical sense only from an obstetrical point of view: "Rose Johnson made it very hard to bring her baby to its birth" (81). The following passage suggests that the absence of Melanctha (and her "white blood") quite literally leads to death for Rose's baby: "The child though it was healthy after it was born, did not live long. Rose Johnson was careless and negligent and selfish, and when Melanctha had to leave for a few days, the baby died. Rose Johnson had liked the baby well enough and perhaps just forgot it for awhile, anyway the child was dead and Rose and Sam her husband were sorry but then these things came so often in the negro world in Bridgepoint, that neither of them thought about it very long" (81). Here, the inadequacy of "negro" memory is associated with morbidity, even mortality. The text seems to suggest that the black (non-mulatto) community pathologically lacks conventional literary-medical memory. In an inversion of a statistically based model of public health, the high incidence of "negro" infant mortality ("these things came so often") *actually prevents* documentation and inscription of memory within the "negro" community ("neither of them thought about it very long"). Therefore, from the public health professional's point of view, as from the obstetrician's, Rose and her fertility are difficult to regulate and record.

Indeed, each of the stories emerges out of a preoccupation with fertility and its failed regulation. The good Anna represents the absence of desire and the urge to suppress sexuality and reproduction. Anna even "had high ideals for canine chastity and discipline," so "she always took great care to seclude the bad dogs from each other when she had to leave the house" (4–5). And, significantly, Mrs. Lehntman's adoption of a baby boy temporarily estranges Anna from her friend (36–37). But, despite Anna's attempts to curb others' familial and sexual desires, her dog Peter does impregnate a neighbor's dog, and Mrs. Lehntman does keep the baby. In Anna's immigrant community, as in the "negro" community in "Melanctha," fertility is difficult to regulate. That suggests why the fecundity of the nonnative, the poor, and the working class constituted the primary target of the nation's eugenic policies of immigration restriction and compulsory sterilization. On the other hand, *Three Lives* does not advance a thoroughgoing version of such mainline eugenic ideology. White supremacist and nativist eugenicists of the period, such as Lothrop Stoddard and Harry Laughlin, worried primarily about the toll of immigrant, poor, and nonwhite reproduction on the national body.[49] Stein, by contrast, worries about the particular toll of labor—both manual and reproductive—on immigrant (if not black) women's bodies. This double meaning of labor for working-class women forms the core of the text of *Three Lives*. As a result, Stein's reservations about medical and eugenic prescriptions emerge as feminist, although not antiracist, in all three women's lives, particularly in "The Good Anna."

Stein represents in "The Good Anna" an alternative, (immigrant) woman-authored model of medical care in an allegory of the obstetrician-midwife contest that was taking place at the time of its publication at around the turn of the century in the United States. In "The Good Anna," the presumably immigrant Mrs. Lehntman, who is "the romance in Anna's life" (24), is also a midwife. The narrator describes her practice as a benevolent women's refuge: "Mrs. Lehntman in her work loved best to deliver young girls who were in trouble. She would take these into her own house and care for them in secret, till they could guiltlessly go home or back to work" (24). So Mrs. Lehntman provides absolution as well as deliverance; her intervention actually removes "guilt." But, as the following passage suggests, Mrs. Lehntman's female idyll is disrupted by a male physician in a narrative reenactment of the actual institutional contest then taking place between the native U.S. doctor and the immigrant midwife:

Anna did not fail to see that Mrs. Lehntman had something on her mind that was new. What was it? What was it that disturbed Mrs. Lehntman so? . . .

Through the fog and dust and work and furnishing in the new house, and through the disturbed mind of Mrs. Lehntman, there loomed up to Anna's sight a *man*, a *new doctor* that Mrs. Lehntman knew. (50, emphasis added)

According to this passage, the advent of the male medical professional obscures, at least partially, the woman's diagnostic gaze. Anna is never quite clear about the trouble the doctor causes Mrs. Lehntman: he was "a mystery that Anna had not the strength just then to vigorously break down" (50). But Anna knows that he "was too certainly an evil as well as a mysterious man, and he had power over the widow and midwife, Mrs. Lehntman" (58).

Anna's worries may well be justified on a literal, bodily level. As one historian of the advance of obstetrics observes, "Rather than making childbirth safer, physicians in the 1920s and 1930s . . . were responsible for maintaining high rates of maternal mortality."[50] Moreover, despite the "widely held medical opinion" that in the United States the use of midwives by poor women was responsible for the relatively high rate of maternal mortality in the early decades of the century, the lowest maternal mortality figures in the 1910s and 1920s were "frequently found in cities with the highest percentage of births attended by midwives."[51] "The Good Anna," as obstetrical allegory, suggests that Stein resists modern medical authority as a result of its potentially dangerous treatment of the female body, as well as its displacement of the female medical expert.[52] In other words, assimilation to a national, professionalized (medical) narrative could prove lethal to the immigrant, working-class female subject.

Lena, in the last of the three lives, enacts that fatal assimilationist narrative, but she simultaneously enacts the eugenicist's anxious story about the fecundity of working-class, immigrant women. Admittedly, Stein invites the reader to think of the overly "gentle" Lena as a passive victim, rather than as one of the mainline eugenicist's "swarming, prolific aliens,"[53] who demographically and genetically victimize the employing class. Lena actually emerges as a relatively appealing and sympathetic character. The narrator observes "the rarer strain there was in Lena" (246). This "strain" (with its associations of lineage, ancestry, genetic trait) engenders Lena's heroine status along with reader sympathy. Semantically, then, she possesses a quasi-biological uniqueness that, ironically, helps bring about her tragic ending. Lena stands as a kind of maladaptive mutation in both Germany and the United States. She is never quite *fit* for her family (or nation) of origin or affiliation: "Lena did not like her german life very well. It was not the hard work but the roughness that disturbed her" (246). This "rarer strain" that makes Lena "not an important daughter in the family" also makes her worthy of readerly and narrative attention. We care about Lena in a way that we can't care about her brutish cousin Mathilda, who "was an overgrown, slow, flabby, blonde, stupid, fat girl, just beginning as a woman; thick in her speech and dull and simple in her mind" (248). Lena, by contrast, is "dreamy," "not there," and possessed of a "rarer feeling" (245, 241).

Yet the degree to which Lena behaves as a normal "german" determines her fitness, if not as a heroine, then as a domestic laborer in a U.S. family (and therefore her survival as an immigrant). Sometimes, Lena behaves like a model immigrant domestic: "Lena's german patience held no suffering. . . . She stood in the hallway every morning a long time in her unexpectant and unsuffering german patience calling to the young ones to get up" (239–40). Although Lena's "german patience" here forestalls suffering in her domestic labor, it cannot save her from the suffering that accompanies obstetrical labor. Lena's fate is biologically determined as much by *re*production as by production. Stein may inscribe Lena as quasi-biologically special in a minor way, but, as a fertile immigrant female, she cannot rise above her dual role as laborer. Gentle Lena's interminable labor is assured when she agrees to a marriage arranged by her domineering aunt: "'I do whatever you tell me it's right for me to do. I marry Herman Kreder, if you want me'. . . . And so for Lena Mainz the match was made" (253). With that final declarative sentence, Lena's fate is not only determined, but overdetermined, by the combined weight of her "rarer strain," her class, and her gender.

For Lena, marriage signals the beginning of the end. She and her new husband move in with his parents, "and Lena began soon with [their move] to look careless and dirty, and to be more *lifeless* with it" (270, emphasis added). Lena's first pregnancy accelerates her decline: "Poor Lena was not feeling any joy to have a baby. . . . She was scared and lifeless, and sure that every minute she would die" (277). With each successive pregnancy, "Lena was always more and more lifeless and Herman now mostly never thought about her" (280). The "only things Herman ever really cared for were his babies. . . . He more and more took all the care of their three children" (279–80). All that remains for the unfit and "lifeless" Lena is labor; and, as the "good german cook" explains, "That's the only way a german girl can make things come out right Lena" (274). Lena ultimately dies in childbirth, leaving Herman "very well content" and "always alone now with his three good, gentle children" (281). Their children thus carry both the dominant german "good" (Anna) and "gentle" (Lena) traits, with no hint of Lena's recessive and maladaptive "rarer strain." The narrative does, then, "come out right," with only the fittest surviving to live happily ever after.

Paradoxically, although the children's dominant strains of "goodness" and "gentleness" may indeed be adaptive for tolerating domestic labor, those traits may, in the end, lead (like their mother's "rarer strain") to premature mortality. The only old immigrant in the book is the far from gentle "Old Katy," with her "uncouth and aged peasant hide" (9). Within the textual world of *Three Lives*, the niche occupied by the immigrant domestic laborer is itself associated with premature morbidity; goodness and gentleness simply serve to accelerate the process. Good, gentle workers like Anna and Lena die in labor. And yet we are never sure what exactly kills these immigrant women. After she marries and has her babies, "patient" Lena promptly becomes "lifeless": "Then there was to come to them, a fourth baby. Lena went to the hospital nearby to have the baby. Lena seemed to be going to have trouble with it. When the baby came out at last, it was like its mother lifeless. While it was coming, Lena had grown very pale and sicker. When it was all over Lena had died, too, and nobody knew just how it had happened to her" (280). As Jayne Walker puts it, Stein's "discourse effectively blurs the moment of passage from figurative to literal lifelessness."[54] "The Good Anna," too, ends with neither an explicit cause of death nor even a clear-cut diagnosis: "Then they did the operation, and then the good Anna with her strong, strained, worn-out body died" (78). This narrative gap, like an unfilled blank on a medical chart, undermines the medical-statistical containment of patient Lena and good Anna. Stein thus exploits poetic, rather than medical, license to reveal the inadequacy of conventional modern treatments of women patients/characters. Lena is rendered lifeless by the U.S. literary-medical prescription: the hospital (and, presumably, the obstetrician), in conjunction with the marriage plot, kills the female patient. Apparently, conformity to the narrative of the laboring, assimilating immigrant kills both Anna and Lena: domestic work for Anna; obstetrical labor for Lena.

The Stein who literally (or perhaps literarily) kills the good Anna and the gentle Lena clearly has reservations about the beneficence, at least for immigrant women, of both literal and literary operations. Along with their immigrant, laboring status, Anna's goodness and Lena's gentleness ensure that they will survive neither Stein's literary experimentation nor more conventional plotting. Just so, the "mulatto" Melanctha dies despite her resistance to traditional inscriptions and prescriptions, whereas her "black" friend Rose Johnson chooses and survives both the marriage plot and childbirth. Both the working-class immigrant and the racial hybrid thereby emerge in *Three Lives* as essentially unfit for long-term survival either as patients or as modernist literary subjects. Lena's rarer strain does suggest, however, that she might have been able to survive, given access to less conventional—that is, more feminist and egalitarian—plots and medicine.

According to Stein's other writings from the early 1900s through the 1920s, a rarer strain compels only the immigrant or mulatto woman to enact a tragic drama of gender- and class-specific "unfitness." Stein's own rarer strain marks her as a genius. As she declares in *Everybody's Autobiography*: "I know that I am the most important writer writing today."[55] Stein, along with the heroines of *Three Lives*, may fail to conform to racial, sexual, or cultural norms of early-twentieth-century America; but, unlike them, she, along with the characters of *Q.E.D.*, is *not* selected against as a result. As middle-class, college-educated "new" women, they have the requisite access to unconventional literary and social forms. Indeed, Stein herself conceives of and delivers those forms. Thus, immigrant servants and black women may perform literal labor, but Stein's authentically "new" women will provide the literary and cultural labor for modernist literary and social experimentation in the early twentieth century.

For her longest literary experiment, Stein turned not just to the middle class but also to her own family in the epic novel *The Making of Americans*, written between 1903 and 1911 and finally published in 1925. As Donald Gallup points out, Stein began the book "quite simply as the story of [her] own family, but it soon developed into 'the history of everybody the family knew and then it became the history of every kind and of every individual being.' "[56] The book centers on two families, the Dehnings and the Herslands, modeled after Stein's cousins. Julia Dehning, the heroine of *The Making of Americans*, is a decidedly middle class, even bourgeois example of the New Woman, one who "had so strongly in her, the new illusions and the theories and new movements that the spirit of her generation had taught to her" (18). In a kind of self-selection process, Stein chooses her own family, along with its resolute middle classness and Americanness, to represent modern national subjectivity and to function as an appropriate vehicle for her particular brand of literary innovation. Repetition characterizes both. Stein delights in a middle class that "is sordid material unillusioned unaspiring and always monotonous for it is always there and to be always repeated" (34), because it lends itself so well to her method of fully describing, of fully containing individuals by means of repetition mixed with an accrual of slight variations. Stein requires and relishes a "slow history" (67) in order to express the whole of a human character. As the narrator in *The Making of Americans* puts it: "There is then now and here the loving repetition, this is then, now and here, a description of the loving of repetition and then there will be a description of all the kinds of ways there can be seen to be kinds of men and women. Then there will be realised the complete history of every one, the fundamental character of every one, the bottom nature in them, the mixtures in them, the strength and weakness of everything they have inside them, the flavor of them, the meaning in them, the being in them, and then you have a whole history of each one" (290). As much as Stein, through her narrator, delights in repetition—"the loving there is in me for repeating"—and believes that it permits a whole description and understanding of the individual, even she admits that "it is often irritating to listen to the repeating" (291). Certainly Stein's style lends itself readily to satire, as Hemingway's novel *The Torrents of Spring* (1926) demonstrates. In the final section of the novel, called "The Passing of a Great Race and the Making and Marring of Americans," her former ally mercilessly lampoons Stein's mannered style: "He repeated the phrase to himself. My woman. My woman. You are my woman. She is my woman. It is my woman. My woman. But somehow he was not satisfied. Somewhere, somehow, there must be something else. Something else. My woman. The words were a little hollow now."[57] But for Stein, repetition was satisfying as a sign of the achievement of comfortable modern middle-class identity and as a literary mode for the representation of that identity: "This is a solid happy satisfaction to any one who has it in them to love repeating and completed understanding" (293). Stein herself might not have literally made Americans, but she could count on the Herslands and Dehnings to carry on the family line. Stein was indeed optimistic about the middle-class characters who survive and thrive within one of her earliest "laboratories of words" and about the repetition that makes them *her* Americans. Crucially, Stein's repetition is, as Steven Meyer argues, "*repetition with a difference*,"[58] and so results in a story of "decent family progress" (34).

But for some kinds of characters, Stein's repetition proved fatal. The immigrant domestics Anna and Lena and the mulatto Melanctha did not have access to healthy modern subjectivity, to white middle-class New Womanhood. Stein seems alert to the ways that conventional narratives and medicine may harm immigrant working-class women. But, in Melanctha's case, Stein posits a mulatto individual apparently unfit to survive, to tell a sustained story, or to produce progeny—as a result of her mixed racial "nature," not, apparently, as a result of her environment. As I will argue in the following chapter, a number of African American women writers of the 1910s and 1920s were also writing new kinds of literature at the intersection of race, gender, class, and reproduction—and, like Stein, they also used repetition to analyze and articulate that intersection. But their repetition was not an optimistic Steinian literary-experimental one, but one that mirrored the relentless, ongoing racism of the modern United States. In their antilynching dramas, writers such as Angelina Weld Grimké, Georgia Douglas Johnson, and Mary Burrill were just as committed as Stein to women as legitimate and powerful literary subjects, but they were equally committed to exposing the ways that New Negro women (unlike white New Women), however fit or middle class, faced an environment that consistently and virulently selected against them. Instead of underscoring the "bottom nature" of African American women or their families, repetition in the antilynching dramas signals a national pathology of racial oppression that worked, across generations, to block African Americans' access to secure middle-class subjectivity and thus to "a record of decent family progress."

I think the loveliest thing of all the lovely things in the world is just being a mother!—Angelina Weld Grimké, *Rachel* (1916)

Nothing lies nearer the heart of the colored woman than the children. —Mary Church Terrell, "Lynching from a Negro's Point of View" (1904)

On March 9, 1892, there were lynched in this same city [Memphis] three of the best specimens of young since-the-war Afro-American manhood. —Ida B. Wells, *On Lynching: Southern Horrors* (1892)

Agnes Milton had taken a pillow off of my bed and smothered her child. —Angelina Weld Grimké, "The Closing Door" (1919)

This is not a story to pass on.—Toni Morrison, *Beloved* (1987)

CHAPTER FOUR

Blessed Are the Barren
Lynching, Reproduction, and the Drama
of New Negro Womanhood, 1916–1930

African American women have, from the start, been vulnerable in their reproductive lives. Contemporary theorists, historians, and novelists —as well as nineteenth-century slave narrators and abolitionists—have repeatedly examined and analyzed that vulnerability. Hortense Spillers succinctly argues that, in a context of slavery, "the customary lexis of sexuality, including 'reproduction,' 'motherhood,' 'pleasure,' and 'desire,'" is "thrown into unrelieved crisis."[1] In her 1861 *Incidents in the Life of a Slave Girl*, Harriet Jacobs experienced and clearly understood that crisis, explaining that even had she been granted permission by her master to marry her free black lover, their children would have had to "'follow the condition of the mother.' What a terrible blight that would be on the heart of a free, intelligent father!"[2] At first, Jacobs's focus in this passage on her lover's emotional state, rather than her own, might seem misplaced. But we must take into account, as did she, the complexities both of her particular situation as a fertile black slave woman in love with a free black man—and of the intertwining of race, gender, and reproduction within a slave economy. Gendered and raced experiences of parenthood within such an economy call for precise analyses like Jacobs's. She points out (radically, for her time) that white women in slave-holding families did sometimes quite willingly bear children by their male slaves, but that those children were treated differently than children born to black women impregnated by white men:[3] "In such cases [white mother and black father] the infant is smothered, or sent where it is never seen by any who know its history. But if the white parent is the *father*, instead of the mother, the offspring are unblushingly reared for the market" (52). Frederick Douglass offered a similarly cogent analysis of the capitalist, patriarchal, and white supremacist dynamics underpinning such reproductive and sexual politics, an analysis that has yet to be improved on: "Slaveholders have ordained, and by law established, that the children of slave women shall in all cases follow the condition of their mothers; and this is done too obviously to administer to their own lusts, and make a gratification of their wicked desires profitable as well as pleasurable; for in this cunning arrangement, the slaveholder, in cases not a few, sustains to his slaves the double relation of master and father."[4] Douglass, like Jacobs, offers his own family's history as an example of such politics of race, sex, and capital. In speaking of his grandmother, Douglass explained: "She had been the source of all his wealth; she had peopled his plantation with slaves; she had become a great grandmother in his service."[5] In other words, black slave women become the lineal vehicles for the production of white wealth in the form of their children, regardless of the identity of the father. Thus the domestic-familial space that mid-nineteenth-century white, middle-class social ideologies viewed as private and sanctified was anything but that for unfree African Americans. As Hazel Carby has shown, conventional constructions of womanhood, domesticity, and motherhood were not designed to fit black women in the nineteenth century.[6] Jacobs could not possibly locate secure subjectivity through maternity: "There was a dark cloud over my enjoyment," she says of her infant son; "I could never forget that he was a slave. Sometimes I wished that he might die in infancy" (62). Indeed, according to Angeletta Gourdine, black infanticide in the context of slavery becomes "paradoxically an ultimate protection of life."[7]

But the end of slavery did not mean that motherhood and fertility became substantially less vulnerable or troubled states for black women.

Likewise, the trope of an African American woman's wishing for her children's death did not disappear with emancipation.[8] Long before Toni Morrison recovered the tragic history of Margaret Garner in *Beloved* (1987), African American women characters began again, as of the 1910s and 1920s, to imagine and even hope for their children's deaths, with lynching's emergence as the paradigmatic modern form of the oppression of black people in this country—what Jacqueline Goldsby terms "*the* image that compresses the horrific brutality of America's racial history with regard to African-Americans into a singular act."[9] The return of the nineteenth-century trope of black women's choosing childlessness—or, even more grim, committing infanticide—in response to lynching suggests that childbearing becomes a renewed site of trauma for African Americans in the late nineteenth and early twentieth centuries. With at least 5,125 lynchings taking place in the United States between 1882 and 1939,[10] such repeated acts, *across generations*, of ultimate home invasion threw into relief the impossibility of treating even the post-emancipatory black home as a refuge, or modern versions of domesticity and childbearing as effective "allegories of political desire," to use Claudia Tate's apt phrase.[11] However, while Mary Church Terrell famously and persuasively argued that lynching was "the aftermath of slavery,"[12] it is important to note that it was not therefore identical with slavery. Lynching functions as a specifically modern means of racial terrorism—quite distinct from slavery. As a kind of extra-institutional complement to *Plessy v. Ferguson*, lynching served on a local, familial level to block African Americans' from achieving full citizenship and secure middle-class subjectivity. African American women writers responded to this new, modern form of racial-domestic violence by stretching literary form to—and beyond—its limits in order to enact their protests against it and against a modernity that permitted it.

The cross-generational trauma of lynching was represented by women writers of the Harlem Renaissance through what I would term "allegories of domestic and political protest," in a genre invented by New Negro women writers during the 1910s: antilynching drama. Angelina Weld Grimké, Georgia Douglas Johnson, Alice Dunbar Nelson, Mary Burrill, and Myrtle Livingston all wrote antilynching plays between 1916 and 1930. Significantly, Grimké also repeatedly wrote on the subject of birth control and maternity for black women, often within her antilynching plays and short stories. Gloria Hull has observed of Grimké: "Lynching and the sorrow of having children are the dual

themes of the drama and fiction that she produced before the Renaissance heyday, so much so that even a radical partisan wonders about
her absolute fixation upon these subjects."[13] Grimké did in fact return
again and again to those two subjects — lynching and maternity — to the
dismay of both Hull and Tate; the latter has observed that "had it not
been for Grimké's obsession with rendering lynching . . . and . . . pa-
thetic repudiations of motherhood, her writing might have had a
broader creative plateau on which to develop."[14]

But Grimké was not alone in her "fixation," her "obsession," and the
repetition Hull and Tate note constitutes not so much an aesthetic failing as a stark literary-formal and performative protest. Indeed, the three
most compelling — and interrelated — features of New Negro women's
nearly compulsive representations of lynching are, one, their psychoanalytic underpinnings (note the critics' own terms: "fixation," "obsession"); two, their function as specifically modern and literary forms
of protest; and, three, their linkage of lynching and black motherhood as
symbolic and literal — that is, as psychosocial — structures. Whereas
most analyses of lynching — both period and contemporary — have emphasized white women's and black men's (and sometimes white men's)
sexuality, it is the sexuality and reproductive lives of modern black
women that centrally concern Grimké and all of the other antilynching dramatists; neither their writings nor lynching itself can be understood apart from those concerns.[15] As we have begun to acknowledge
the centrality of lynching in twentieth-century U.S. psychosocial and
political history, there has been developing a body of scholarship on
lynching and on lynching protest. A number of historians have acknowledged the central role black women played, especially through
their club work, in agitation against lynching and for the Dyer bill (never
passed), which was to have designated lynching a federal crime.[16] But,
so far, there has been relatively little literary-critical scholarship on
black women's antilynching plays of the 1910s and 1920s, works that
represent perhaps the period's clearest and most literal enactments of
protest, not only against lynching, but also against the intense institutionalized and ritualized forms of racism and sexism that shaped modern black women's lives, especially their reproductive lives.[17]

The antilynching plays offer a scathing indictment of an entire racist, morally inverse modern social order, a social order in which the
best black women repeatedly renounce motherhood as a result of the
repeated lynching of the best black men. In her notes about the process

of writing and revising her best-known work, *Rachel* (1916), Angelina Weld Grimké declared: "I drew my characters, then, deliberately from the best type of colored people."[18] In addition to *Rachel*, Grimké's short stories "Goldie" and "The Closing Door," Mary Burrill's play *Aftermath* (1919), Myrtle Livingston's play "For Unborn Children" (1926), and Georgia Douglas Johnson's plays *A Sunday Morning in the South* (1925) and *Safe* (1929) all represent the finest sons, brothers, and husbands as becoming victims of lynch mobs. Conversely, much New Negro women's writing, in particular Nella Larsen's novel *Quicksand* (1928) and Mary Burrill's play "They That Sit in Darkness" (1919), represents "Old Negro" women of the South as not only rural and unsophisticated but also disproportionately fertile and prolific. In the context of antilynching fiction and drama, repetition thus is not an individual psychological response or symptom and certainly not a writerly error; it is a shared representation of the social symptoms of a modern lynching culture that perversely selects against the "fittest," generation after generation. As a result, antilynching dramas, indeed a wide range of New Negro women's writings, use and rely on the vocabulary of such characteristically modern discourses as psychoanalysis and eugenics, even as they challenge their "truth," their applicability to the lives of modern African Americans. According to Grimké, Burrill, Livingston, Douglas Johnson, and Larsen, the New Negro Renaissance—a movement whose very title signified the birth of newly fit, modern African American subjects—could not be sustained in the modern United States. The project of creating improved black subjectivity (the intraracial uplift of the Harlem Renaissance) and the counterweight of lynching (the simultaneous interracial enforcement of white supremacy) combined to produce modern African American and mixed race characters who are made crazy, again and again, by dominant social formations that select against them. All the antilynching dramas and stories register, through their repetitions and ruptures of literary form, the damage to individual and collective black subjectivities and psyches rendered by such unnatural selection.

As I argued in chapter I, racial uplift in the 1910s and 1920s was, for "race men" such as W. E. B. Du Bois and James Weldon Johnson, clearly intertwined with eugenics. In a feminist analysis, Du Bois argued that "only at the sacrifice of intelligence and the chance to do their best work can the majority of modern women bear children,"[19] but as a eugenicist Du Bois insisted that Negro "families of the better class" should have more children.[20] New Negro women thus faced the paradoxical duties of simultaneously being and reproducing the New Negro. Of course, one could argue that black women had, from the start in the Americas, been treated as functional reproducers in a way that, if not explicitly eugenic, was certainly unrelated to "pleasure" and "desire."[21] Black slave women were positioned as "breeders" whose children would by law follow their mother's condition and thus expand their master's property. Because of that specific history surrounding their reproductive and sexual lives, modern African American women were positioned quite differently than were white women in relationship to the discourses and debates of the 1910s and 1920s surrounding New Womanhood, free love, and birth control. As Michele Mitchell concisely argues, "Stereotypes concerning black sexual appetites kept many aspiring and elite race members from engaging in" the period's "social emancipations" regarding sexuality.[22] But eugenics, on the other hand, affected the meaning of childbearing for all modern women; regardless of race, all became potential vehicles of national and racial improvement during the peak years of American eugenics (not coincidentally, also the era of antilynching drama).

The scientific notion of breeding better human beings did not emerge explicitly until the end of the nineteenth century and was not fully articulated by American and English social scientists until the early twentieth century. Astonishingly widespread and accepted by many activists and intellectuals of a variety of political outlooks and across racial lines, eugenics inevitably left its mark on the thought and discourse of modern African American women as well. But they were far more likely to resist its allure. A number of New Negro women writers and activists, although generally in favor of black women's access to and voluntary use of birth control,[23] expressed suspicion about the scientific or social regulation of reproduction (not surprisingly, given the legacy of slavery's politics of fertility), while they offered in their antilynching writings a remarkable challenge to the period's competing and complementary discourses of white supremacy, eugenics, psychoanalysis, and bourgeois racial uplift.[24] Writers like Grimké and Burrill were clearly protesting interracial oppression, as were Harriet Jacobs and Frederick Douglass in the nineteenth century, but they were protesting, as well, a specifically modern intraracial and gendered oppression—that is, African American ideologies of uplift that emphasized black women's domestic and reproductive value. For example, in

Nella Larsen's *Quicksand*, when James Vayle, the ex-fiancé of protagonist Helga Crane, insists that she have children in order to improve the race, she replies: "I, for one, do not intend to contribute any to the cause." In just this way, Larsen, Grimké, and a number of other early-twentieth-century African American women writers rejected the role of breeder both literally and literarily, supplementing their "express explicit and unreserved racial protest," as Tate puts it,[25] with feminist protest against the regulation or restriction of black women's bodies and lineages by men of any color. And they regularly linked the two—racial protest and feminist protest—through their repeated representations of lynching in relation to reproduction.

For Grimké, Burrill, Douglas Johnson, and Livingston, lynching represented a kind of extract of racial oppression that violently performed a moral and juridical inversion at the same time that it dramatically revealed the wholly ideological, gendered, and racially determined nature of much of the period's ways of knowing modernity itself. In condemning lynching, they implicitly challenged the fundamentally modern discourses of eugenics and psychoanalysis, discourses that emerged out of and described a crazy-making social order that at once permitted lynching and promoted the breeding of better human beings. Thus, if nineteenth century African American writers had had to reconstruct womanhood,[26] early-twentieth-century African American writers had to reconstruct modernity itself. Their first task was to expose that inversion within the modern social order, and, for many of them, a focus on lynching did just that. There is, for example, a deeply troubled and troubling passage in James Weldon Johnson's 1911 *Autobiography of an Ex-Coloured Man*, a passage that makes sense only in the context of such an inversion. Johnson's nameless mulatto narrator has decided not to pass for white—although he can—and has traveled south on his mission to collect Negro spirituals in order to reinterpret them as classical music. In the countryside outside Macon, Georgia, he witnesses a lynching. He describes his response to the savage scene: "I walked a short distance away and sat down in order to clear my dazed mind. A great wave of humiliation and shame swept over me. Shame that I belonged to a race that could be so dealt with; and shame for my country."[27] Feeling "as weak as a man who had lost blood," the narrator decides at this moment to abandon his Negro identity and his musical mission—that is, to lose specifically his black blood, in order to pass as white. What was "driving me out of the Negro race," he explains, is "shame" (499). Although the logical response to witnessing a lynching would seem to be shame at his whiteness, the narrator is in fact ashamed "at being identified with a people that could with impunity be treated worse than animals" (499). The inverted psychological response of the narrator mirrors the inversion of legal and moral order embodied in the practice—indeed the "brutal public ritual" and performance—that is lynching;[28] the modern mixed-race individual cannot interiorize a justice that fits the crime, because the individual mind and its internal sense of justice is sacrificed to the collective immorality of an institutionally condoned racial vigilantism.

By exploring the intersection of lynching and reproduction, Angelina Weld Grimké, Mary Burrill, Georgia Douglas Johnson, and Myrtle A. Smith Livingston add another layer to James Weldon Johnson's "inversion" analysis of white supremacy and racial terrorism, one that relates directly to black women's sexuality and fertility. Indeed, it is not coincidental that two of Grimké's lynching/motherhood stories were published in the *Birth Control Review*: "The Closing Door" in 1919 and "Goldie" in 1920. Grimké's exposure and exploration of the psychological impossibility of healthy black motherhood in the 1910s and 1920s at once marks her as a modern thinker and her characters as highly civilized—and explicitly raced and gendered—discontents who repeatedly challenge and complicate the era's most prominent social and scientific discourses. Both Carolivia Herron and Claudia Tate have analyzed Grimké's own psyche in relationship to her thematics of frustrated black maternity, linking Grimké's apparent lesbianism with her choice never to marry or have children.[29] But such psychoanalysis of the author may not be as productive as analysis of the ways that her characters and plots are, in turn, analyzing their own social milieu.

Grimké's antilynching play *Rachel*, including its setting, characters, speech, plot, and structure, enacts an especially clear "allegory of domestic and political protest," with ellipses, pauses, silences, repressions, and repetitions working as literary signifiers of familial trauma and of social dissent against an unjust modern social order. *Rachel* was first produced in Washington, D.C., in 1916; it takes place entirely within the top-floor flat of the allegorically named Lovings,[30] an African American family—Rachel, the daughter; Tom, the son; Mrs. Loving, the mother; and Jimmy, a neighbor boy adopted by Rachel. The other main character, John Strong, is Tom's friend and Rachel's eventual suitor. The play traces how Rachel eventually breaks down after being, at the beginning of the play, a high-spirited teen whose primary goal in life is to become a mother: "I think the loveliest thing of all the lovely things in the world is just being a mother!"[31] Rachel and Tom's sentimentalized and apparently happy domestic life is disrupted, almost from the start, by their mother's confession that, ten years earlier to the day, their father and older half brother had been lynched. By play's end, with repeated instances of racial discrimination afflicting each of the characters, an adult Rachel hysterically renounces marriage to John Strong and childbearing in general, refusing to bring any more black children into the world to suffer as her family has.

The play's investment (or, more precisely, disinvestment) in eugenic thinking emerges early on. Four years after their mother's confession, on the anniversary of their father's and brother's death, Tom bitterly considers the family's current situation: "Rachel is a graduate in Domestic Science; she was high in her class; most of the girls below her in rank have positions in the schools. I'm an electrical engineer—and I've tried steadily for several months—to practice my profession. It seems our educations aren't of much use to us: we aren't allowed to make good—because our skins are dark. (pauses) In the South today, there are white men [he is referring to the men who lynched his father and half brother]—(controls himself) They have everything; . . . With ability, they may become anything; and all this will be true of their children's children after them. . . . Our hands are clean;—theirs are red with blood —red with the blood of a noble man—and a boy. They're nothing but low, cowardly, bestial murderers. The scum of the earth shall succeed" (49). Lynching represents, then, a most unnatural form of selection, one designed to reinforce white supremacy and sustain black powerlessness, regardless of the quality and education of either whites or blacks. "Low" whites can murder "noble" blacks, and the result—that the lynchers, the worst of humanity, will "succeed"—is decidedly dysgenic for both races. Grimké's play thereby exposes the ways that social Darwinist and eugenic thinking is at best irrelevant, and at worst both morally and scientifically backward—given the racial injustice, white hegemony, and racial terrorism of the 1910s and 1920s. At the same time, Tom's barely controlled speech—with its dashes, pauses, and ellipses—reflects lynching's damage to modern individual and collective subjectivities and psyches as well as the concomitant ruptures and "fixations" in the play's language and structure.

The lynching that had taken place before the beginning of the play's action stands as the original traumatic and dysgenic event in the Loving family. In recounting the events that led up to the lynching, Mrs. Loving describes their father to Rachel and Tom as "a man among men," a "big-bodied-big-souled" man who "was utterly fearless" (40). Outraged at a lynching by whites ("a mob of the respectable people in the town") of an innocent black man, their father had "published a most terrific denunciation of that lynch mob" and stood by his denunciation, despite death threats (40). As a result, a lynch mob came to their house.[32] Mrs. Loving describes the scene: "We were not asleep—your father and I. They broke down the door and made their way to our bedroom. Your father kissed me—and took up his revolver. It was always loaded. They broke down the door. . . . (pauses) Your father was finally overpowered and dragged out. In the hall—my little seventeen-year-old George tried to rescue him. . . . It ended in their dragging them both out. My little George—was—a man!" (41). This highly suggestive scene shows the absolute termination of one lineage: George was Mrs. Loving's only child from a prior marriage (as she explains, when she married Mr. Loving, she was a widow and her son George by her first marriage was seven). But her odd reference to their not being asleep, though it may simply suggest the Lovings' apprehension, could also suggest that the lynch mob was interrupting love-making; as such, they may have been interrupting another lineage as well, forcing Mr. Loving to substitute violent resistance/gun/"revolver" for reproduction/phallus/"loving" in a kind of socially compelled "choice" of Thanatos over Eros. Indeed, as the play figures it, to be a "man among men" constituted a death wish for African American men in the United States in the South in the 1910s and 1920s.

Lynchers are repeatedly represented (not only in Grimké's plays but also in nearly all black women's antilynching stories and dramas of the 1910s and 1920s) as victimizing the very best black men and fathers[33]—and as leading the very best black women and mothers to choose, or at least to consider, childlessness or infanticide. Tom, the young son/brother in Georgia Douglas Johnson's A Sunday Morning in the South, announces his plan to fight lynching: "I mean to go to night school and git a little book learning so I can do something to help—help change the laws . . . make em strong" (105). The energetic and promising Tom is, of course, eventually lynched, falsely accused of raping a white girl. Lynching represents, then, not just a weak but an inverted legal (and moral) order that leads in turn to inversions of other orders: eugenic, maternal, familial, psychological, and so on. Perhaps worst of all, in its very unnaturalness, lynching leads to unnatural selection: not only through its direct annihilation of the best African Americans by whites, but also through the reaction of self-annihilation by the best African Americans—at least as represented in much modern black women's drama and fiction.[34]

In the 1910s and 1920s, that perverse social order showed little promise of improvement for African Americans. Jim Crow was the law of the land, and what Kirk Fuoss describes chillingly as the "peak years of lynching" stretched from 1880 to 1935.[35] The repetitiveness that Hull and Tate note should be viewed, therefore, not as an aesthetic or thematic failing but as a necessary corrective to, and protest against, the repeated, cross-generational performance of lynching itself. As Tate herself has observed, in another context, "Unremitting racial trauma demands an unending supply of stories."[36] Thus, inasmuch as lynching constituted a protracted form of terrorism taking place generation after generation in a kind of "lynching cycle,"[37] lynching protest, too, lent itself to repeated performance and so to drama.

The representation of such ultimate, and repeated, familial and racial trauma necessarily stretches literary form itself. The performance of lynching forms the play as it deforms conventional dramatic form. Indeed, the cyclical/generational nature of racial oppression in general, and of lynching in particular, is often represented and commented on explicitly within the antilynching plays. In Grimké's *Rachel*, when Rachel brings home a neighbor child she has befriended and will eventually adopt, Mrs. Loving cries out: "Rachel, he is the image of my boy—my George!" Such reimaging and reimagining, mirrored by repetitions, dashes, and pauses, constitute lynching's psychological and literary representational forms. Indeed, the play's plot and action are, throughout, structured according to the anniversaries of that original lynching of George and Mr. Loving. Analogously, again and again, tragic African American heroines of antilynching fiction and drama observe that to bear children, especially boy children, is to provide fodder for lynchers' insatiable, ongoing appetite for racial violence. As a result, in terms of classical theories of drama, there can be no catharsis in lynching plays for the characters,[38] for African American playwrights, or for their audiences.[39] As Andrew Ford convincingly defines it, "Tragic *katharsis* would be the specific form of ["pleasing and relaxing emotional"] response that attends the arousal of our emotions of pity and fear in an environment made safe by the fact that the tragic spectacle is only an imitation of the suffering."[40] We must realize that these plays offer, instead of an "imitation," a *representation* of a profoundly unsafe and ongoing social reality. As long as performances of lynching continue, antilynching dramas must also repeat the representation of lynching in a perpetual absence of release or purgation.

The repetition among and within antilynching plays subverts not only conventional theories of drama, but also conventional psychoanalytic (both Freudian and Lacanian) theories regarding trauma and its aftermath, theories that owe much to the notion of catharsis and to classical drama in general.[41] As Cathy Caruth concisely explains, "In its general definition, trauma is described as the response to an unexpected or overwhelming violent event or events that are not fully grasped as they occur, but return later in repeated flashbacks, nightmares, and other repetitive phenomena."[42] Thus, according to psychoanalytic theory, repetition results from the inability to have expected or the failure to have fully known the original trauma. Without full knowledge and understanding, the traumatized individual repeatedly returns—in dreams, nightmares, or flashbacks—to the original traumatic experience (96). But modern African American playwrights, along with their characters and audiences, did in fact "fully grasp" lynching because it was an external, predictable, often-repeated form of violent trauma that, in certain ways, was not only fully known but fully expected.

As William Storm has noted, black women's plays of the modern era generally "featured domestic situations in which mothers and children were prominent, with the husband either deceased or absent," and with "the event of a lynching . . . significant in the . . . action" so frequently that these elements may be considered "conventions."[43] But among the conventions of the antilynching plays is not simply the absent husband but the male—be it husband, father, son, or brother—whose return home has been delayed. When black men are late in these plays, lynching stands as the most feared and the most logical explanation. In Myrtle Livingston's 1926 play, "For Unborn Children," the grandmother, "a gentle, well-bred old lady" from "a refined family [of Negro descent], evidently of the middle class," worries about her past-due grandson, crying, "it's awful for him to keep us in this terrible suspense!"[44] Likewise, in Georgia Douglas Johnson's play *Safe* (1929), Liza, the pregnant wife of the hero John, and her mother, Mandy, repeat in a kind of unbearably anxious refrain: "I wonder where John is—," "He oughter been back here before now," "John ain't back," "Oh, where is John? Where is John?"[45] Although John is not lynched in the play, another black man is, and the entire family, including Liza, can hear the "hoarse laughter" of the lynch mob outside (113). Immediately after the lynching has taken place, Liza gives birth, then strangles her newborn son. The doctor in attendance reports that "she kept muttering over and over again: 'Now he's safe—safe from the lynchers! Safe!'" (113). Men's lateness in the plays thus brings with it a gruesome doubled suspense— a dramatic kind that lends itself particularly well to the stage and the temporality of performance, reinforced by a literal and horrifying tension. Given this second sense of "suspense" within the plays—black men may be attacked and hung by white mobs at any time for any reason—Liza's and Mandy's repetitiveness and Liza's hysterical infanticide, like Rachel's "convulsive laughter" as John Strong kisses her at the end of Grimké's play, cannot be understood as conventional hysterical responses of the modern stage. "Hysteria," as Elin Diamond argues, "in effect created the performance text for dramatic modernism."[46] But the abnormal symptoms here are not Liza's or Mandy's or Rachel's, but the modern lynching culture's. As Anne Cheng cogently argues in *The Melancholy of Race*, "The psychical experience of [racial] grief . . . is not separate from the realms of society or law but is the very place where the law and society are processed."[47] Yet the women in antilynching plays cannot truly be considered melancholic or neurotic individual subjects; the allegorical names of Grimké's characters—the Lovings, John Strong—suggest that Rachel and her family represent, not diagnosable bourgeois modern individuals, but model modern African Americans afflicted, indeed annihilated, by racism. Rachel and her family, just like Liza and her family, cannot afford the luxury of personal, highly contingent neuroses; they must contend with the external, racialized pathologies of the modern United States—and as long as the lynching culture's symptoms persist, so will the need for the antilynching plays and their representations of black women's hysteria, compulsive repetition, and infanticide.

The antilynching plays written and produced between 1916 and 1930 thus depend on, while they also complicate, a then-emerging popular vocabulary of psychoanalysis, just as they both depend on and complicate the even more popular modern vocabulary of eugenics. In a compelling analysis of contemporary "feminist theory and practice in theatre and film,"[48] Barbara Freedman has argued that a truly fem-

"RACHEL"

The Drama Committee
of the District of Columbia Branch
of the N. A. A. C. P.
—PRESENTS—

"RACHEL"

A Race Play in Three Acts by
Angelina Grimke
under direction of
NATHANIEL GUY
AT
Myrtilla Miner Normal School
Friday Eve., March 3rd and
Sat. Eve., March 4th, 8 P. M.

Tickets   -   75 and 50 Cts.
Tickets on Sale at Gray and Grays Drug Store 12th & U
Sts. N. W. after February 1st from 6 to 8 o'clock P. M.
All Seats Reserved.

PRINTED BY MURRAY BROS.

Playbill from a performance of Angelina Weld Grimké's *Rachel* in 1916. Courtesy of Angelina Weld Grimké Papers, Manuscript Division, Moorland-Spingarn Research Center, Howard University.

inist conjuncture of "feminism, psychoanalysis, and theatre" is one that will "reflect and effect change" (60); to do so, it must "insert a difference in our construction of the subject and so . . . make a difference," in part by undoing "the figuration of difference as [a] binary opposition" that is articulated through "phallocentric vocabulary" (56–57). But New Negro women playwrights disrupt not only "phallocentric vocabulary" but also white supremacist ideology, and they do so by means of a combination of difference (a black female central subject) and sameness (repetition). Grimké and Douglas Johnson neither believe in nor rely on a "binary opposition" of black and white; but they and their characters must nevertheless contend with that ongoing opposition as it was encoded in the 1920 U.S. census, in Jim Crow, and most especially in lynching. To put this more bluntly, the "castration" that is imagined by Freudians and Lacanians—and challenged by the white feminist psychoanalytic theory described by Freedman (58)—was not imaginary for African Americans between 1880 and 1930. They were fully conscious of both maintained "difference" and sustained punishment for that difference (a penalty that was anything but metaphorical). In response, antilynching dramatists offered sustained protest, with their repetitions serving to diagnose the nation rather than black women.

Grimké wrote a number of lynching plays and stories, and she also drafted several complete versions of *Rachel*, each with a different title.[49] Her notes about this revision process suggest the intentional use of literary form to offer a psychosocial analysis of lynching centered on black women. For example, she explains that, in revising the passage in which Mrs. Loving decides to tell Rachel and Tom about the lynching of their father and stepbrother,

> I have changed from "I believe it to be my duty." to this:
> MRS. LOVING.
> "Yes.—I see *now* it is—my duty."[50]

Indeed, over the course of several rewritings of the play, Grimké repeatedly revised Mrs. Loving's story of the lynching and her decision to tell that story—in this instance by adding dashes and a time frame ("*now*") which together express the elisions, silences, and pauses symptomatic of past trauma and of the process of telling and retelling that trauma in the present. But it is perhaps her revision of the play's title that is most provocative, particularly in the context of New Negro womanhood and reproduction. Her next to last title for the play, *Blessed Are the Barren*, suggests that choosing not to have children becomes a positive action for African American women under the consistently hostile conditions of modernity. Lynching renders the feminist psychoanalytic project of re-centering and performing femininity in general, and mother-child relations in particular, irrelevant and impossible for modern black mothers: *blessed are the barren*. Grimké's repetition is thus not so much with a difference, as Lacanian theory would have it, but repetition with a depressing, even hysteria-producing sameness. She and the other antilynching dramatists, were, therefore, "fixated" on lynching and maternity for good reason.

In the antilynching plays of Grimké, Burrill, and Douglas Johnson, black female protagonists repeatedly perform their maternal renunciations and infanticides. Because of this repeated juxtaposition of lynching and "barrenness," there emerges an obvious thematic link between lynching and infanticide/sterility. But the repetition also points to an even deeper structural (and literary-formal) connection between lynching and reproduction. First, modern representations of black infanticide necessarily refer to a long legacy of crisis surrounding African American women's reproductive lives, registering the unrelieved pressures on black female fertility even after the end of slavery. But there is, as well, a specifically modern dimension to the barrenness in the antilynching plays. Black women's repeatedly traumatic experiences surrounding childbearing stands in symbolic correspondence to black men's being lynched in the modern era; each is a gendered, generational oppression produced by white supremacy and patriarchy. As long as black women are not free both to control and to express their sexuality and fertility, they will be oppressed; as long as black men are at risk of being lynched, they will be oppressed. At the intersection of these oppressions reside black children, male and female, who must, generation after generation, contend with an unjust social order. Modern African American women's antilynching plays understand and protest that still-living political economy of race and reproduction.

But the dramas of New Negro women challenged not only white-dominated social forms and discourses; there was an intraracial politics of reproduction being challenged as well. Indeed, many New Negro men were trying to set an agenda for black reproduction and thus to establish control over modern black women's fertility. In an often overlooked passage in Nella Larsen's *Quicksand*, Helga Crane's ex-fiancé, James Vayle, urges her to breed:

> James was aghast. "But Helga! Good heavens! Don't you see that if we—I mean people like us—don't have children, the others will still have. That's one of the things that's the matter with us. The race is sterile at the top. Few, very few Negroes of the better class have children, and each generation has to struggle again with the obstacles of the preceding ones, lack of money, education, and background. I feel very strongly about this. We're the ones who must have the children if the race is to get anywhere."
>
> "Well, I for one don't intend to contribute any to the cause."[51]

James Vayle had his real-life counterpart in male race leaders such as W. E. B. Du Bois, who cautioned in a 1926 *Crisis*: "There are to be sure not enough children in the families of the better class."[52] E. Franklin Frazier concurred, arguing: "The whole social system in the South favors the propagation of the least socially desirable (in a civilized environment) among Negroes. The less energetic and resourceful fit easily into the *rôle* the white man has assigned the Negro, while the more energetic and resourceful leave or often fail to reproduce."[53] Although Du Bois and Frazier are not speaking explicitly either to or about middle-class black women—that is, New Negro women—their (pregnant) presence is necessarily implicit. Here lies the deep structural link between lynching and black women's reproductive lives, regardless of class. If the essence of racial and gender oppression for African American men is the lynching cycle, for black women the essence of their oppression is the cycle of repeated childbirth within a racist and lynching nation; in other words, childbirth for modern black women is intimately connected to both gender and racial oppression (just as lynching is intimately connected to both gender and racial oppression for black men). First, black women bear the children who will surely suffer from some form of racism, if not lynching; second, repeated childbirth will just as surely prevent the women themselves from attaining true modernity in the form of middle classness, independence, and "New Negro" status.[54]

This bleak inter- and intraracial economy of fertility and lynching, sexism and racism, reproduction and tragedy, is one that not only the antilynching plays, but an even wider range of modern African American women's writing expresses. Trouble seems inevitably to result from New Negro women's having children. In Nella Larsen's novel *Quicksand*, protagonist Helga Crane, despite her early declaration—"Well, I for one don't intend to contribute any [children] to the cause"—ends up dying as a result of repeated childbirth. As the last line of the novel states: "And hardly had she left her bed and become able to walk again without pain, hardly had the children returned from the homes of the neighbors, when she began to have her fifth child" (135). The ending's inconclusiveness (suspense) points to the endless, cyclical nature of the New Negro woman's dying in and from childbirth. By contrast, *Quicksand* represents other women—those who might be termed "Old Negro" —as less at risk from the repeated childbirth that is lethal for the modern, urbane Helga Crane. From her first pregnancy, Helga never fits her final identity as rural southern pastor's wife and serial reproducer. Nauseous and weak, she wonders, "How . . . did other women, other mothers, manage?"

> "Tain't nothin', nothin' at al, chile," said one, Sary Jones, who, as Helga knew, had had six children in about as many years. "Yuh all takes it too ha'd. Jes remembah et's natu'al fo' a 'oman to hab chillluns an' don' fret so."
> "But," protested Helga, "I'm always so tired and half sick. That can't be natural." (125)

The passage suggests that childbearing comes as naturally as dialect to the southern, rural African American woman, whereas multiple childbirth is unnatural for the modern, New Negro woman. Linguistic "primitiveness" and fertility are thereby linked via an economy of geo-racial family politics. Sary functions almost as Helga's contemporary ancestor; she resides in a still agrarian, premigration African American history. In other words, Sary's incomplete diction—with the apostrophe as signifier—discloses her necessarily inadequate subjectivity in any authentically modern setting. She represents the rural and premodern, just as Helga (along with her complete command of standard English) represents the urban, the alienated: that is to say, the modern and the paradoxically unfit—another kind of unnatural selection. Middle-class, New Negro women like Helga were in fact far less likely to die from childbearing than were their working-class and poor sisters. Historian Michele Mitchell points out that while African American women's overall fertility rate saw a decrease "beginning with the end of Reconstruction and lasting until at least 1930," middle-class northern women were likely to bear fewer children than women in the "agricultural South."[55] Indeed, many of the prominent women of the Harlem Renaissance remained childless, including Hurston, Larsen, and Grimké. This is not to say, however, that middle-class black women writers were wholly unsympathetic to the plight of poor and working-class, or of southern and rural, fertile women.

Like Helga Crane, Mrs. Malinda Jasper in Mary Burrill's short play "They That Sit in Darkness" (published in the *Birth Control Review*'s special "Negro Number" in September 1919),[56] becomes a victim of repeated childbirth. Mrs. Jasper is the mother of a poor black family "in a small country town in the South in our own day" (5). She suffers from a "weak heart" (7) and is having difficulty recovering from the birth of her most recent child just a week earlier, yet she continues to work at her laundry business. At the same time, her daughter Lindy is packing a trunk in preparation for attending Tuskegee, her tuition having been sponsored by a northern white philanthropist. Mrs. Jasper's husband Jim never appears in the play; we are told that he works from before the children wake in the morning until after they are asleep at night. Besides members of the Jasper family, the only other significant character is Miss Elizabeth Shaw, a visiting nurse—social worker who provides milk for the new baby, along with health advice for Malinda Jasper.[57] Miss Shaw admonishes Mrs. Jasper for going back to work so soon after the delivery: "You will have to stop working so hard. Just see how exhausted you are from this heavy work! . . . I heard the doctor tell you very definitely that this baby had left your heart *weaker than ever*, and that you *must* give up this laundry work" (7). Mrs. Jasper replies with a dose of reality: "'deed, Miss 'Liz'beth, we needs dis money whut wid all dese chillern" (7). We then discover that in addition to the seven Jasper children left at home, two other children have died and one daughter who "warn't right in de haid" was impregnated by a white employer (rape, or at the very least coercion, is implied) and ran way. Not only that, but Mary Ellen, one of the seven left at home, has tuberculosis. As Miss Shaw puts it, "Well, Malinda, you certainly have your share of trouble!" (7). But what distinguishes this potentially eugenic drama from the thoroughly elitist and eugenic writings of most white women birth control and sterilization advocates is its profound sympathy for Mrs. Jasper, along with its awareness of the shortcomings of Miss Shaw's advice. When Mrs. Jasper wonders "what sin we done that Gawd punish me and Jim lak dis," Miss Shaw replies: "God is not punishing you, Malinda, you are punishing yourselves by having children every year. . . . You must be careful!" Malinda answers: "*Be keerful*! Dat's all you nu'ses say! . . . You got'a be tellin' me sumpin' better'n dat, Mis' Liz'beth!"[58] Miss Shaw's reply gets to the heart of the matter and the title of the play: "I wish to God it were lawful for me to do so! My heart goes out to you poor people that sit in darkness, having, year after year, children that you are physically too weak to bring into the world — children that you are unable not only to educate but even to clothe and feed. Malinda, when I took my oath as nurse, I swore to abide by the laws of the state, and the law forbids my telling you what you have a right to know!" (7). Soon after this exchange, Mrs. Jasper's heart condition suddenly worsens; she dies, and, as a result, her daughter Lindy realizes that she must abandon her plan of attending Tuskegee in order to take her mother's place in caring for the rest of the children.

This play's complex attitudes toward poor and working-class fertility are neither wholly progressive nor wholly elitist. Clearly, poor people's "troubles" cannot be neatly resolved by birth control, as Miss Shaw's vague admonition and explanation imply. To paraphrase Dorothy Roberts, there are distinct dangers in promoting reduced reproduction as *the* means to social justice or economic equality.[59] Moreover, like Nella Larsen's *Quicksand*, Burrill's play problematically juxtaposes the standard English diction and unmarried, childless state of the professional Miss Shaw with the dialect and hyperfertility of the working-class Mrs. Jasper, seeming to lend support to Du Bois's view that "there are to be sure not enough children in the families of the better class." On the other hand, there is no suggestion in this play that the Jaspers — or the poor in general — are naturally inferior; indeed, Lindy seems clearly on the road to upward mobility as she packs her bag. Unlike Nella Larsen's "Sary Jones," Mrs. Jasper does not survive, yet she has an acute awareness of her own plight, along with a desire to change it. With education and family planning, Burrill seems to be arguing, Mrs. Jasper, like all African Americans regardless of class, can be uplifted, can become "New" Negroes; their problems stem from social conditions (including a perverse legal system that prevents the dissemination of birth control information to those who most need it), not their nature.[60] Birth control in this context offers a way out of the oppressive burdens of poverty and therefore a way up the social ladder. Indeed, knowledge of birth control corresponds with professional, middle-class status in Burrill's play: the ability to control female fertility, a commodity already possessed by Miss Shaw, is desperately needed by Mrs. Jasper. As Roberts puts it: "White eugenicists promoted birth control as a way of preserving an oppressive social structure; Blacks promoted birth control as a way of toppling it."[61] Even modern black club women, some of whom were prone to an elitism that could shade into eugenic thinking,[62] adopted "Lifting as We Climb" as their motto, connoting a belief in the improvability of all black women; there is no natural inferiority, then, just socially produced inferiority. This is elitist, to be sure, but not hereditarian.

As all the antilynching plays demonstrate, modern African American women knew, if anyone did, that the modern United States was not a meritocracy. Grimké's *Rachel* is fundamentally about the inability of the most educated and talented black people to rise professionally to the level of their abilities and the attendant inability of the fittest black people to reproduce happily and successfully. It makes perfect sense that New Negro women writers would not view poverty or racial violence solely as the lot of the unworthy or the naturally inferior.[63] Social Darwinism could only be true given prior social, economic, educational, and professional equality; African Americans were quite clear that such equality did not obtain in the modern United States. As I will discuss in the following chapter, New (white) Women birth control advocates and eugenics field workers, by contrast, viewed poverty, feeblemindedness, and tuberculosis, among a host of other conditions, as the natural states of lower-class dysgenic white folks; sterilization was therefore deemed a natural prescription. "Blessed" barrenness and sterility carry a wholly different valence in the writings of modern black women: they are the particular burdens of female blackness, a modern prescription issued by a sick lynching culture.

If not children, then, what can the New Negro woman pass on? In the absence of literal progeny, Grimké and Burrill pass on the tragedies of black motherhood, the drama of an African American family history that includes lynching. Repeatedly, their black women characters choose what to tell and when to do so, thereby intervening in and rewriting what Hortense Spillers calls "an American grammar" founded on the captivity and mutilation of African American men's and women's bodies (261–62). In Grimké's *Rachel*, Mrs. Loving holds on to her knowledge of the lynching of her second husband and her son from a prior marriage until her children, Rachel and Tom, are themselves of an age when they are likely to be lynched or to begin producing children. In Mary Burrill's antilynching play *Aftermath* (1919), plot, suspense, and characterization all flow from the withholding of the truth of lynching by Millie, a young African American woman.[64] A "slender brown girl of sixteen," Millie cannot bear to write to her brother John, who is away at war, about the lynching of their father. John unexpectedly returns home, soon discovers that Millie has been hiding the real reason for their father's absence, and begs her to reveal the truth, crying, "Come, Millie, for God's sake don' keep me in this su'pense!" (90). In response, Millie ends one form of suspense—explaining that "them w'ite devils came in heah an' dragged him—. . . . They burnt him down by the big gum tree!"—only to create another: the play ends with John's rushing out of the family cabin to exact revenge on his father's lynchers. Readers and audiences know that John, too, will surely be lynched, although the ending keeps us nominally "in suspense," with the son's lynching perpetually about to be performed.

Contemporary African American women continue to pass on such almost unbearable stories of lynching and infanticide, suspense and barrenness, loving and burning. That is, they are repeatedly relating the repetitive trauma within modern African American history. In her essay "Traumatic Awakenings," Cathy Caruth revisits Freud's well-known analysis of a bereaved father's dream—a dream that awakens him—of his dead child standing by his bed and saying, "Father, don't you see I'm burning?" As the father is dreaming, the child's corpse, lying in the next room, has in reality been lit afire by an overturned candle. Caruth argues that both Freud's analysis of this dream and Lacan's later revision of that analysis fall short: "The full implications of such a transmission [the dead child's speaking to the father in his dream] will only be fully grasped, I think, when we come to understand how, through the act of survival, the repeated failure to have seen in time—in itself a pure repetition compulsion—can be transformed by, and transmuted into, the imperative of a speaking that awakens others" (103). Caruth believes that the father's dream, along with its embedded message from the burning child and the resultant awakening of the father, represents the "ethical burden of . . . survival" (103). Repetitive performance, then, "transmits the ethical imperative of an awakening that has yet to occur" (104). To put this plainly, in the aftermath of traumatic loss, the father bears the burden of awakening, telling, and acting. The difference between the father's dream and the nightmare of lynching is that the father need not expect the death and burning of his children, or of his children's children, to occur again and again in his family history. The mothers, sisters, and daughters in *Rachel*, *Aftermath*, "For Unborn Children," *Safe*, and *A Sunday Morning in the South* repeatedly do in fact "see in time," but can do nothing to stop the burning, even though they have been awake all along. As Karla Holloway argues, "For black women, the kind of stress Lacan associates with the unconscious is not buried at all."[65] The "ethical imperative" to be awake and to tell is one that Grimké, Burrill, Livingston, and Douglas Johnson—to be followed by Toni Morrison and Michon Boston and Suzan-Lori Parks[66] —willingly accept, again and again, as they pass on a story that is, in the final words of *Beloved*, not to be passed on.

Committed to Bedford [Bedford Hills New York State Reformatory for Women] from town of Saugerties [N.Y.] on charge of impairing the morals of her children, Sept. 1912. She is a tall, big-boned girl with an abundance of dark brown hair, prominent masculine features, and large, conspicious [sic] teeth, black with tartar. To talk with her in the first days of her stay in Bedford one can get not the slightest idea why she was sent here. She asks frequently if she can go out tomorrow and offers me a crate of berries if I will take her away. . . . She tests 7 years by the Binet.—Notes of V. P. Robinson, eugenics field worker (c. 1914–17)

On account of this mental immaturity he should never have been allowed to become a father. It would have been a great economy for the community to have prevented his feeble-minded and criminalistic brood, by taking him into custody as a boy and keeping him segregated and at farm work all his life long. —Mary Storer Kostir, *The Family of Sam Sixty* (1916)

CHAPTER FIVE

New White Women
The U.S. Eugenic Family Studies
Field Workers, 1910–1918

Scholars have begun to challenge the notion that the "New Woman" represented a thoroughly socially progressive and feminist icon.[1] As quite a few historians have recently observed, nearly all feminist activism of the late 1800s to early 1900s was intertwined with the social purity movement and often with eugenics.[2] Literary critic Angelique Richardson argues persuasively that the New Woman, once placed "securely in her historical context," often emerges as having "perpetuate[d]" the mainstream elitism, gender essentialism, and biological determinism of her day.[3] Historian Gail Bederman ably demonstrates that even model New Woman Charlotte Perkins Gilman advanced a "feminism [that] was inextricably rooted in the white supremacism of 'civilization.' "[4] Similarly, Dana Seitler has recently focused on the "coterminous ideologies of feminism and eugenics that [Gilman] engages."[5] Of course, then, as now, activist women occupied a range of political positions—some women reformers advocated what contemporary scholars readily acknowledge to be reactionary, racist, and elitist versions of "social purity"; others promoted what were then quite progressive versions of social and labor reform. Kathryn Kish Sklar suggests that at least some middle-class women reformers of the Progressive Era sometimes "transcended their own class interests."[6] But very few advocated anything resembling contemporary challenges to class, gender, or racial distinctions, and it is perhaps unreasonable to expect them to have done so.[7] Indeed, some New Women did not even endorse women's suffrage.[8] Others willingly (and, in some cases, consciously and enthusiastically) established their professional freedom directly on the revocation of the bodily freedom of poor and working-class people.[9]

The many field workers for the U.S. eugenic family studies of the 1910s and 1920s are compelling, and largely neglected, New (white) Women whose professional and social mobility depended on, indeed could be defined by, the enforced immobilization of others, both women and men.[10] The field workers traveled throughout the United States collecting genetically incriminating data about supposedly dysgenic, feebleminded rural white families—data that could then justify the compulsory institutionalization or sterilization of as many family members as possible.[11] These workers were newly mobile, college-educated women—some professionals, some volunteers, but all clearly social reformers—even if the objective of their reform was not at all "progressive" according to present-day definitions, or even in comparison with other women's reform agenda of their day. Unlike more liberal women reformers who were generally committed to the protection and support of poor mothers and children, the eugenics field workers were committed to their confinement or elimination. Despite the appalling nature of their politics, however, the field workers must still be considered New Women. In fact, they are in some ways paradigmatic New Women, whose work demands a new, more precise taxonomy and analysis of the "New Woman" and, indeed, of the "Progressive Era" in general.[12] More reactionary paternalists than progressive maternalists,[13] the eugenics field workers help buttress the view that the 1910s and 1920s were an era of radical, but sometimes quite regressive and dangerous, reform enacted by women.

Cultural historians have in the past decade generally relied on the concepts of maternalism and professionalization to describe women's activism of the 1910s and 1920s, but the field workers' explicit project —to protect the nation's germplasm by institutionalizing and sterilizing dysgenic poor and working-class women and men—cannot be fully accounted for by either model. Scholars acknowledge that even the more socially progressive reformers, such as the settlement house workers, also benefited from constraints (albeit lesser ones) on others —generally immigrants, migrants, the poor, and the working class.[14] To explain this phenomenon, scholars have begun to focus on the problematic maternalism of many professional women reformers between 1890 and 1920, arguing that to promote social welfare policies founded on an idealization of bourgeois motherhood was also effectively to consign other, poorer women to more restrictive, and generally quite unrealistic, gender roles.[15] As Robyn Muncy observes, "In an era when constructions of gender would certainly not allow women any authority over men, those women who did gain authority wielded it over other women, and in many cases, used it not to liberate but to restrict their sisters" (122).[16] Thus the "female dominion" that historians agree was instrumental in the creation of the welfare state ironically enough rendered many women even less free to pursue activities outside the private, domestic sphere. It was for the sake of their own professionalization that women reformers relied on a maternalism that did not always serve the interests of other women. As Muncy points out, "turn-of-the-century women searching for professional niches" soon realized "that their male counterparts were much more willing to cede professional territory, to acknowledge the female right to expertise in instances where women and children were the only clients" (xv). But because women and children were *not* their "only clients"—and because many were volunteers—the eugenics field workers complicate the maternalist-professionalization model. The field workers collected data on and exerted power over men as well as women. That expanded clientele in turn permitted them to exceed the feminine, domestic sphere and to participate in the period's emergent and shifting discourses surrounding labor, social science, and medicine—that is, the "male dominion."

It was also in part because of their reactionary politics that the eugenics field workers were able not only to enter the male dominion but also to sidestep, at least to a degree,[17] the tangled interplay of professionalism and maternalism that plagued their more progressive sisters in reform. The idea that progressive women reformers had to finesse conflict between their professional ambitions and their often egalitarian ideals has become a focal point, indeed a commonplace, in much recent feminist scholarship concerning the reform era. As Muncy vividly puts it, even the most progressive reformers were "encouraged to blame their nonprofessional sisters for all children's ills" and "to shorten the leash that tied most women to home and children" (xv).[18] The eugenics field workers, by contrast, did not seek to protect poor women and their children or to level class differences; their aim was to protect the middle and upper classes from overpropagation by poor, nonproductive, and feebleminded men and women, as well as to maintain class differences. Therefore, unlike the socially progressive women reformers, the eugenics field workers occupied a "professional niche" quite compatible with their reform ideals; unhampered by social progressiveness, they were free to pursue their reactionary work apparently without ideological conflict between politics and profession.[19]

THE FIELD WORKERS' primary work was the collection of data for the white family studies that formed the rhetorical and scientific centerpiece of the mainline, conservative eugenics movement in the United States during the 1910s and 1920s (the most famous such study was Henry Herbert Goddard's 1912 *The Kallikak Family*).[20] While most of the directors and credited authors of these studies were men—usually sociologists and physicians affiliated with the United States Eugenics Record Office in Cold Spring Harbor, New York, the foremost eugenics institution in the nation in the 1910s and 1920s—the vast majority of the field workers who collected the data were college-educated women trained in biology, sociology, or social work. These field workers, all of whom were white, identified and documented the feebleminded members of supposedly inbred, generally rural, poor or working-class, usually white families—with the ultimate goal of reducing the families' fertility by institutionalization and sterilization. Occasionally, some families or family members in the studies are described as being of mixed race (as in Arthur Estabrook's 1926 study, *Mongrel Virginians*) or as having "bred" with other races. The studies invariably treated both whites' willingness to breed with other races as well as the resultant racial hybridity as a priori evidence of the families' genetic inferiority. But the organizers of the studies for the most part did not worry very much about the nonwhite dysgenic; for the eugenicists associated with the Eugenics Record Office (ERO), there was no urgency

to establish the lesser genetic quality of nonwhite Americans, particularly black Americans. Their brand of eugenics took white supremacy
as a given; they therefore concentrated on establishing, rather than an
interracial hierarchy, an intraracial one. Indeed, the overall project of
the family studies can be seen as a refinement and purification of a
white Americanness so thoroughly parsed that "Scotch-English blood"
generally occupied the top tier.[21]

Sociologist and historian Nicole Rafter has identified fifteen such
studies of rural, predominantly white families that were published in
the United States between 1877 and 1926. James Trent points out that
a family study was published as late as 1936.[22] Many of the studies were
written for a lay audience; several of them became best sellers. The
most widely read of the studies and the ones that remain the best-known
today are Robert Dugdale's *The Jukes* (1877), which was the first in the
genre, Henry Herbert Goddard's *The Kallikak Family* (1912), and Arthur
Estabrook's *Mongrel Virginians: The Win Tribe* (1926). But the published studies represent only a small fraction of the total number of studies conducted. Rafter's 1988 book, *White Trash*, as important and insightful as
it is, does not take into account the hundreds of additional, unpublished studies of "defective" families conducted by the ERO between
1910 and 1918, with the peak of family study research and publication
occurring between 1915 and 1917. Both the timing and the sheer number of the studies testify to the urgent, overdetermined nature of their
mission—one that could be bluntly summed up as "think nationally,
sterilize locally."

A wide range of political, economic, and social circumstances converged to create a national climate congenial for the widespread study
of dysgenic U.S. families in the 1910s and 1920s. Eugenic discourse,
with the family studies as its distinctive genre, accommodated and recorded collective U.S. class and racial anxieties resulting from World
War I, unrest among colonized peoples, class rebellion and revolution, labor organization and unionism, suffragist activism and mili-
tancy, the fluctuation of national and racial boundaries, widespread
immigration and migration, urbanization, industrialization, and economic uncertainty (the eugenics movement in the United States was,
in a sense, bracketed by the depression of 1893 and the Great Depression).[23] Indeed, a crucial, but underemphasized, context for the rise
of eugenics in the United States was the prevailing national perception

that a new, increasingly global form of economy had arisen—one that required new, more competitive kinds of American labor and of American laborers and their management.

Scholars' recent reliance on maternalist and progressiveness-versus-professionalization models to understand the reform era has led both to the relative neglect of such broader (though still gendered) class and labor issues embedded in the U.S. eugenics movement and to the marginalization of reactionary (professional and volunteer) women reformers like the eugenics field workers. Granted, the family studies in particular, as well as eugenic discourse in general, call—and call loudly —for both the feminist and the new historical critical perspectives that underlie the maternalist and professionalization models.[24] First, the field workers were limited both professionally and personally by the period's restrictive notions of gender; women simply did not have equal access to, or equal power within, male-dominated professions. As Rafter succinctly puts it, because the field workers were permitted to collect data but rarely to function as directors or authors, the family studies were "simultaneously advancing and segregating women in science."[25] Second, the disciplinary aspects of the studies' aims—diagnosis, involuntary institutionalization, and compulsory sterilization—are clear, as is eugenics's imbrication with the period's professionalization of medicine and the social sciences. Rafter has argued persuasively that the eugenic family studies "promised to further the interests of an emergent professional class," including the college-educated white women who made up the vast majority of the studies' field workers.[26] But neither a professionalization–new historical paradigm nor a maternalist-feminist one, nor their combination, can fully account for the field workers, or for the content and conduct of the eugenic family studies of the 1910s and 1920s.

To begin with, the studies' conservative, hereditarian eugenics effectively derailed a thoroughgoing maternalism. With nature favored over nurture in explanations of human behavior, fathers attain a (genetic) status equal to that of mothers. Just so, while the ERO and its field workers certainly worried about the sexuality and potential maternity of feebleminded and immoral women, they worried as well about the sexuality and potential paternity of feebleminded, criminal, and destitute men. Thus, Shawn Michelle Wallace's compelling insight that "racialized discourses in the postbellum era situated white middle-class mothers at the locus of biological inheritance"[27] is only partly valid; the class-based, intraracial eugenics typical of the 1910s and 1920s sought both to encourage middle-class women to select carefully the fathers of their children and to discourage the fertility of dysgenic lower-class women *and* men. First, as eugenics historian Mark Haller has shown, just as many men as women were compulsorily sterilized for eugenic reasons in the United States between 1909 and 1930; in some states, more men than women were sterilized in this period.[28] And it perhaps goes without saying that these procedures were performed predominantly on the incarcerated and on the poor and the working class.[29] Second, the studies were not conducted solely by professionals. During the 1910s and 1920s, many "volunteer collaborators," lacking a direct professional stake in the matter, willingly submitted to the ERO documentation of the feebleminded in their communities. Finally, the emergence of new forms of labor control and methods of production (especially scientific management and the assembly line in the 1910s, at precisely the same time that family study activity reached its peak) represents a crucial historical and economic context for understanding the extraordinary pervasiveness of eugenic thinking during the reform era. Efficiency became a byword both in production and reproduction in the United States in the 1910s and 1920s, and the family studies appeared to hold the promise of increasing America's economic and human efficiency. As Calvin Coolidge put it in his 1925 inaugural address: "The very stability of our society rests upon production and conservation."[30]

Most eugenics advocates, regardless of their political orientation, acknowledged that "positive eugenics," the promotion of births among the genetically desirable (generally from the middle/professional classes), had to remain voluntary, even purely theoretical.[31] But "negative eugenics," the prevention of births among those designated genetically toxic (generally from the poor and the working class), was not only widely endorsed but also actively practiced in the United States as early as the 1870s and 1880s, even before the term "eugenics" entered common parlance.[32] While the endorsement of negative eugenics was widespread among reformers of the day across the political spectrum of the United States, the eugenics field workers, both professionals and volunteers, were unique in their central role, as women, in the enactment of negative eugenic practices on poor and working-class women and men. This activist role, however unsavory, played by some New Women suggests that we must attend more closely to the complex economic and social patterns of the reform era in general and of the U.S. eugenics movement in particular.

THE EUGENICISTS responsible for the ERO's family studies—both male supervisors and female field workers—certainly had motivations beyond what Rafter terms "professional self-interest."[33] They truly believed in the scientific, national, social, political, and economic righteousness of their work; they considered themselves reformers, even progressives—not that they would be seen as such today. In their promotional materials, U.S. eugenics organizations often referred to eugenics as a charity that would end charities.[34] Not surprisingly, many well-to-do Americans, professionals and nonprofessionals alike, responded favorably to such rhetorical tactics. Eugenics activities in the United States during the 1910s and 1920s (including the family studies, as well as the passage of state compulsory sterilization statutes) were made possible by a collaboration between members of the middle/professional/managerial class and members of the upper/wealthy/entrepreneurial class. What Jeffrey Weeks has said of the eugenics movement in Britain can thus be applied to the U.S. movement as well: "There is undoubtedly an emphasis in eugenics on the social importance of the middle-class expert. . . . But we cannot explain eugenics simply in these class reductionist terms, because though eugenics ideas may have had a class-specific origin, they were presented as a strategy for the whole ruling class to adopt, and support was gained from outside the professional classes, just as opposition to eugenics came from within it."[35] For example, the Eugenics Record Office at Cold Spring Harbor was founded in 1910 by Charles Davenport, holder of a Ph.D. in zoology and perhaps the nation's most prominent eugenicist, with funding from Mary Harriman, widow of the railroad tycoon E. H. Harriman. John D. Rockefeller and the Carnegie Institution were early ERO sponsors as well.[36] That such a synergistic, cross-class private collaboration would have public policy effects was, perhaps, inevitable.

The ERO, under the supervision of founder-director Charles Davenport and superintendent Harry Laughlin, developed an ingenious method for insinuating its privately funded eugenic ideology into the state apparatus. First, the ERO trained eugenics field workers during annual summer courses, conducted between 1910 and 1924. Some workers were then sent out across the country to conduct field work directly for the ERO by collecting data for the family studies or by administering "fitter family" contests at state and county fairs.[37] The rest were assigned to various state institutions such as mental hospitals, colonies for the epileptic and feebleminded, reformatories for juvenile male criminals, and homes for delinquent girls. The ERO agreed to pay the institutional field workers' salaries for a year, during which time only the workers' "expenses [were to be] paid by various States."[38] The ERO hoped that, after the initial year, the institutions would voluntarily add the eugenics field workers to their payroll.[39] In the 1910s, at least half of the institutions did in fact elect to keep the workers on staff. The *Eugenical News*, a bulletin published by the ERO for its staff and field workers, regularly published news of such permanent appointments of the field workers by the state institutions where they had been installed for the one-year "introductory trials."[40] Individual professional ambition was certainly being served by such a policy—at the same time, widely held, but nonetheless private, eugenic beliefs were also being publicized, institutionalized, and nationalized.

There was significant nonprofessional participation in the U.S. family studies as well. Hundreds of "volunteer collaborators" obtained family study kits from the ERO that included "Brief Instructions on How to Make a Eugenical Study of a Family," along with "family pedigree charts" and "individual [genetic trait] analysis" cards.[41] Private citizen-volunteers sometimes submitted information about eugenic families known to them (usually their own); but most submitted to the ERO unsolicited, informal assessments of the dysgenic in their communities, as is shown by a letter from Ida M. Mellen to Harry Laughlin, superintendent of the ERO, written in 1912: "I have been trying for some months to find out just why the child of my charwoman is feebleminded,—aside from the obvious fact that the woman herself is 'cracked' on religion. By getting one fact at a time I have finally drawn out about all that seems possible, and herewith enclose you the account and chart. I do not know that it is worth anything, but send it in any event, for, in a general way, it shows a relationship between religious insanity, violent temper &c., and feeblemindedness."[42] This letter attests to the class dialectic engendered by the family studies, a dialectic more complex than a professionalization model allows. Ida Mellen had attended the ERO summer course in 1912, but she did not become a field worker (she became secretary of the New York Aquarium) and therefore would not reap direct professional benefits from the data she submitted

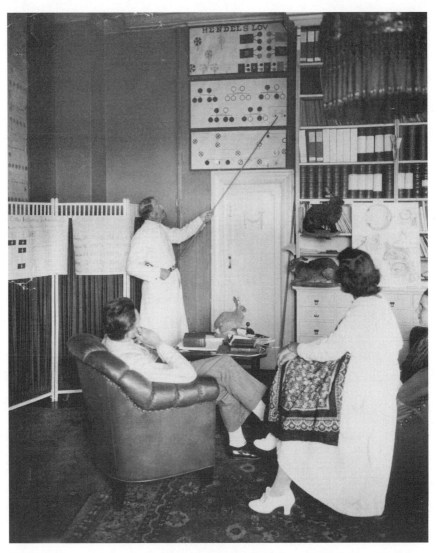

Field worker training at the Eugenics Record Office, Cold Spring Harbor, New York, 1910s. Courtesy of the American Philosophical Society.

about her feebleminded maid.[43] The letter provides clear evidence of the complex and disturbing interclass (as well as intragender) politics of the conservative eugenics movement in the United States. Quite a few women and men of the middle and upper classes volunteered to expose and document the feebleminded who worked in their homes or lived in their communities. During the 1910s, as many "volunteer collaborators" as professional field workers submitted information to the

ERO about what they perceived to be the often alarming genetic makeup of American families.[44]

Granted, the professionalization model does work to the extent that the professional field workers' individual careers were obviously being advanced by the family studies. Some of the workers' ambitions were even quite explicitly established on the backs of the "feebleminded"—most often those whom they knew personally. Bernice Reed, a volunteer collaborator attending New Hampshire College with hopes of a professional future, wrote to Charles Davenport in 1916 about her knowledge of "a low grade rural family" in the "small country town" in New Hampshire where she "used to live." According to Reed, the males in the family "have either been in reform school, prison or have been arrested at various times." "The females," she writes, "are all of a very low moral grade[,] nearly all of them being prostitutes at one time or another." "The children," she adds, "have been able to go only to a certain grade in school and are unable to make further progress." Reed concludes her letter by asking Davenport, "Will you please tell me how to go to work in making my thesis?"[45] Davenport encouraged Reed to send him her completed thesis, a family study she titled—using a pseudonym—"The Trix Family."[46] Reed resisted divulging the family's real name for reasons explained in a letter to Davenport accompanying the study: "Public opinion and the writer's personal acquaintance has to be relied upon to a great extent and much truth can be gained in this way as such people do not hesitate in telling their family and private affairs" (3). When Davenport nevertheless pressures her to reveal the family's real name, Reed demurs: "I would be glad to send the real names if they would be held in confidence at the station and would not get back to the state as it might cause me some trouble for I had to compile my data very carefully."[47] She receives prompt reassurance from Davenport: "In case you send the names, as I trust, we will mark the copy 'extra confidential. No names to be divulged to State Agents.' "[48] Clearly, Reed aims to establish a professional life far from her rural New Hampshire roots, while using her knowledge of the town's illegitimacy in order to lend legitimacy to her own professional status as researcher. But her real genius lies in her self-referential conclusion to "The Trix Family": "Someone must be held responsible, and it is the state's duty to assume responsibility. In the first place there should be a census taken yearly or oftener of the school children, and a test applied in order to determine each pupil's mentality. This work should be done by expert workers employed by the state" (17). More significant than Reed's self-promotion here (which could be subsumed under a conventional professionalization model) is her insistence on "the state's duty"—the institutionalization and nationalization of a conservative eugenics platform thus comes to the fore even within an individual volunteer worker's conclusion of her family study. Again, the aims of the family studies and the field workers are far broader than individual professionalization, reflecting and inscribing national anxieties regarding modern social formations and preoccupations as various (though also clearly connected) as morality, intelligence, ethnicity, urbanization, productivity, competitiveness, labor, and gender.

BERNICE REED WAS on the right track in her networking with Davenport. Although, as Nicole Rafter has observed, women were rarely the credited authors of published family studies, the male eugenicists at the ERO actively recruited them to become field workers. Superintendent Harry Laughlin conducted summer classes in field work at Cold Spring Harbor from 1910 to 1924—classes aimed specifically at college women. Of the 258 field workers trained, 219 were women.[49] At the peak of the ERO's family study activity, from about 1915 to 1917, at least 90 professional field workers were actively collecting and recording an enormous amount of data regarding families from at least 22 states; of these more than 90 workers, at least 80 were women.[50] A pamphlet included in the ERO's 1912 summer training course, "Directions for the Guidance of Field Workers," suggests some of the reasons the male eugenicists of the 1910s sought female field workers: "First of all, unfailing courtesy and regard for and sympathetic (humanistic) attitude toward the persons you are interviewing are essential. . . . To get the truth requires great tact."[51] The field workers were being selected, then, according to stereotypical feminine criteria; among the field worker evaluation instruments, there was even a "tenderness-sympathy test." In other words, the feebleminded women were not the only women being studied within the context of the family studies. In this instance, the field workers were clearly experiencing the period's gender restrictions, just as the period's more liberal women reformers did.

The role of the social scientific field worker, like the role of the settlement house worker or social worker, did represent a new professional alternative for middle-class, college-educated women (and one less conflicted between profession and politics), but clearly there was a catch. As Robyn Muncy puts it, if women "donned the behavioral garb appropriate to professional life, they invited criticism for being unfeminine," but "if they refused to wear the suit, they lost the aura of professional authority" (xiii). "Qualities Desired in a Eugenical Field Worker," a list prepared by Harry Laughlin in 1921, illustrates the quandary faced by the field workers. According to Laughlin, the ideal field worker would possess the positive stereotypical feminine traits— including "Industry," "Loyalty," "Social ability," "Obedience"—yet lack the negative ones—such as "Gossip" and an absence of "Analytic" ability.[52] Moreover, not only were the field workers expected to exploit their positive womanly attributes (industry, courtesy, tenderness, and so on), they were, as data collectors for the studies, also being replaced rather firmly within the context of the "family," however dysgenic that family might be. Finally, like the newly professionalizing nurses of the same period, the eugenics field workers were assigned strictly limited duties by their male superiors. Dr. Davenport, director of the ERO, advised them during a summer 1915 field worker meeting: "*Do not diagnose.* Let the one studying the history diagnose, but make the case history complete so that diagnosis will be possible."[53] The ERO doctors and sociologists ranked analytic skills well below interpersonal skills for effective field work (in fact, they ranked number ten on the list of thirteen desirable field worker traits).

The male eugenicists were probably correct that courtesy and tact would be essential prerequisites for such work. The field workers traveled to generally rural study sites throughout the country, where they conducted interviews of family members and their neighbors, acquaintances, pastors, and physicians—taking notes all the while. The workers then recorded their own observations of dysgenic family members' abilities and behaviors—all with the aim of documenting the genetic unworthiness of their subjects. Apparently, the field workers' tested-and-proven "tenderness and sympathy" usually did work to elicit a great deal of genetically incriminating information, if not from the family members themselves, then from those who knew them. One field worker described her methodology in this way: "[Only] those *all* agreed were feebleminded were listed [as such]. In this way at least four persons passed [judgment] upon each family reported, which served to verify [their feeblemindedness when] . . . these people could not be

Letter from a volunteer collaborator to Eugenics Record Office director Charles Davenport, March 1916. Courtesy of the American Philosophical Society.

first marriage have either been in reform school, prison or have been arrested at various times. The females are all of a very low moral grade nearly all of them being prostitutes at one time or another. The children have been able to go only to a certain grade in school and are unable to make further progress. The family has received state and town aid at various times but mostly when the family was largest. The man has been a stage driver for twenty years, his occupation being interrupted by drunks. I think it will be possible for me to get records of the family for one or two generations back.

Crime, drunkardness, prostitution shiftlessness and prostitution all exist within this family.

Will you please tell me how to go to work in making my thesis?

Thanking you, I am most sincerely,

Bernice Reed

New Hampshire College

Durham, N. H.

TENDERNESS - SYMPATHY TEST.

Suppose that there were placed before you a series of
individually *strong* ~~stronger~~ animals each of which you were to kill by
crushing. Record below your natural reaction as each animal is
presented to you.

ANIMALS, in order:
of presentation: :   Your reaction:

1. Amoeba   :   No difficulty

2. Beetle   :   Little difficulty

3. Earthworm   :   No difficulty

4. Small fish   :   Rather difficult

5. Harmless snake   :   Very difficult

6. Ground squirrel   :   Impossible

7. Medium sized   :
   chicken   :

8. Medium sized   :
   cat   :

9. Medium sized   :
   dog   :

10. Condemned human   :
    criminal   :

Date: _July 31, 1918_   Name: _Miriam Silver_

"Tenderness-Sympathy Test" administered to field workers in training
during the 1910s and 1920s. Courtesy of Harry H. Laughlin Collection,
Pickler Memorial Library, Truman State University, Kirksville MO 63501.

visited personally."[54] Clearly, then, despite Dr. Davenport's admonishment not to diagnose, the field workers frequently used whatever information they could get, from any source, to establish dysgenic diagnoses of the families they encountered.[55]

Sadie Devitt, ERO class of 1910, studied several rural Minnesota families and was one of the most successful and prolific data collectors as well as one of the most evocative and creative writers among the field workers. Her unpublished 1917 notes about a family in southeastern Minnesota, titled "Timber Rats" (the local nickname used for the family), demonstrate her remarkable narrative—as well as ideological— agility:

> My first introduction to these people happened thus—It was a hot, summer's day and we had driven from Preston to Whalan. At Whalan we found that the man I wished to see lived farther down the ravine. The road lead [sic] up for a ways and then we began going down and down. In reality we went down but about 200 feet but the horses had to seemingly sit down and slide over rocks most of the way so it seemed much farther. Then we drove along the rocky road at the foot of the ravine. . . .
>
> Soon we met a wagon, drawn by one bony horse. The driver was a boy of about 17 years, with all the earmarks of a mental defective. Thinking he might be acquainted with the inhabitants of the valley I asked him if he could tell me where Hawkin Hawkinson lived. The answer came in one of the slowest drawls I've ever heard, "He-e don't live here no more." "Has he moved?" I asked. "Yes, he's moved, he's dead," came the answer.
>
> "Oh Lord!" my driver shouted and burst into convulsions of laughter. The boy drove on, wondering what had happened to the driver that he laughed. I have a suspicion that I smiled. However, I warned my driver he must be more careful next time, for no one's feelings could be hurt. . . .
>
> That day, in that sparcely [sic] settled ravine, I saw at least five feeble-minded people so another trip, for more extensive study was planned. . . .
>
> The first family visited was that of Halvor Hagen, an uncle who had married his own neice [sic]."

Devitt, apparently struggling to maintain her "courtesy and regard for and sympathetic (humanistic) attitude toward" the family, tracks down

the niece who had married her own uncle and describes their encounter:

> She is a feebleminded woman, of the moron type; who can neither
> read nor write. She is very slovenly in her appearance and neglects
> her home. . . .
>
> Upon my return from visiting this family, I asked one of the cit-
> izens of Peterson how they came to allow such conditions to exist in
> their community. He said, "People don't bother about that bunch
> for they are nothing but a lot of 'timber rats.' "[56]

Devitt takes up the term, and she encounters a number of families in
the region that she labels "timber rats"—so named for their means of
survival in rural Minnesota in 1917: timber cutting, along with hunt-
ing and subsistence farming.

But the field workers' travels were not always so arduous as Devitt's.
Sadie Myers, a volunteer worker in rural Utah in 1916, described in
lively third-person narration, in another unpublished work, her data
collection style: "As soon as the field secretary finished her work in one
town, she usually took an automobile in order to save time, and in this
way was able to make as many as three towns in one day."[57] Though her
travels are easier than Devitt's, Myers finds similarly appalling dysgenic
families in her chosen region (three rural Utah counties): "Frequent
cases of goitre were noticed," she writes, and "in one small community
three separate families of Cretins were found." She also finds "incest
and illegitimacy running rampant," with many feebleminded children
the result. She visits local schools in order to confirm this widespread
feeblemindedness among the counties' children, and she describes one
particularly trying day: "While testing in one of the schools, the field
worker was much annoyed by the janitress who kept dropping the mop
and stumbling over the seats." But overall, Myers seems quite upbeat
about her job; it was not all about facing feeblemindedness in the
field: "Many of the women's clubs [in the area]," she reports, "invited
the field secretaries to speak to them and all showed great interest in
the work."

The potentially feminist, intraclass, intergender politics of both
Myers's and Devitt's studies (and of other unpublished studies) are certainly worth noting. First, both field workers have clearly wrested the
power of diagnosis from their male supervisors. They readily note the
"mental defectives" they encounter: the "feebleminded," the "moronic,"

the "Cretins." Indeed, the women come across in their field notes as experts hard at work in an exciting field. But, with a salary of $600 a year in 1916, plus the requirement of frequent progress reports to the ERO, the women did not possess wide-ranging professional or economic freedom (Harry Laughlin's salary that same year was $3,600).[58] At the same time, the field workers' ability to seize diagnostic power was limited by the ideological imperatives of their male supervisors and of eugenics itself.

The workers' diagnoses would be permitted to stand only if they served to bolster the aims of the movement as a whole. The workers actually appear at times to be aware of eugenic ideology's power to limit their revision of the studies' conduct as well as any challenge of the eugenical "truth" they had been selected to "get." For example, a Miss Kendig, a field worker assigned to study delinquent girls at Monson State Hospital in New Jersey, reported at a 1913 Field Workers Conference: "I was rather horrified that I was getting no results from the standpoint of heredity. There was no epilepsy, no feeble mindedness and no one became insane. I began to feel as if I had been careless. Even tho [sic] I tried to double my care I could not reproduce the same number of defectives that I had in adult cases. . . . There is a great danger of snap judgments. I want to avoid it. We must strive against premature publishing. The Binet tests should be given to all the members of the family and see if there are stigmata of degeneration."[59] No one at the conference takes up Kendig's call for caution or careful testing; indeed, she is followed in discussion by a Miss Robinson, who asks, "What is the best avenue of approach to a family [of a delinquent girl] to get results? Our best entrance," she decides, "is as a friend of the girl" (47).[60]

This remarkable moment in the field workers' conference proceedings leads us away from their intraclass, intergender feminism and toward their interclass, intragender politics—which, as it turns out, are far less progressive. In the case of Robinson's remarks, the field worker is decidedly *not* a "friend of the girl," whom the worker is likely seeking to have compulsorily institutionalized or sterilized. The conduct and content of the studies depend on a dialectic of eugenic/college-educated/professional female field worker versus dysgenic/feebleminded/working-class family member. Occasionally, however, and perhaps not surprisingly, the field workers encountered resistance, as was reported by Lucile Field Woodward at the 1913 conference: "My work is with epileptics in

New Jersey. . . . There is one town [there] made up almost entirely of mulattoes. They think the information I am trying to get is to be used against the Negro race. The children all go to one school. There are no children in the school who are not mulattoes. The teacher was also a member of this family. She has heard lectures on eugenics. She . . . said [to me], 'I am proud of my ancestors and I do not care to give information against them' " (42). Here, Woodward recognizes the teacher's overt resistance as "Negro" solidarity, although the teacher, if "mulatto," has both white and black ancestors. The field workers frequently had trouble not only interpreting but also simply perceiving less overt acts of resistance. Even the possibility of more subtle, class-based forms of resistance seems not to have registered with the workers. Like Ida M. Mellen's "charwoman," Sadie Myers's "janitress" can only be a stumbling, feebleminded sort—an inefficient, and thus dysgenic, working-class woman. Study subjects may either ease or hinder the investigation, but they can never function as agents for their own genetic vindication. Perhaps most chilling are the multiple instances in which inmates of state institutions have been called on to type up field workers' notes. In 1914, volunteer collaborator Dorothy Gardner submitted a case history on a patient "who was in the New Jersey State Hospital from Nov. 19, 1913 to Jan. 9, 1914," noting in longhand on the cover sheet that the report was "typewritten by a patient of the N.J.S.H."[61] Here, the institutionalized are literally inscribing, with the tools of modern record keeping, if not their own confinement, then the confinement of other study subjects much like them.

Feebleminded women were being placed in custodial care for eugenic reasons as early as 1878—not coincidentally, just as the New Woman was emerging. Although they established a new professional role for women, the family studies (along with mainline eugenics in general) also constituted part of a cultural backlash against the period's feminist activism and against the idea of sexually, or politically or professionally, liberated women. Such a typically eugenic measure (one advocated by all of the studies and all of the field workers) as the institutionalization of feebleminded women stands, then, as a modern adaptation of long-used strategies for curbing women's socially subversive behavior.[62] As the following excerpts from two studies (among the few published family studies written or coauthored by women field workers) disclose, "feeblemindedness" attains identity with socially undesirable (often sexual) behavior by women, almost always in the absence of any "Binet tests" to establish their "stigmata":

> III 15 [genealogical code] is probably feebleminded. She appears of average intelligence, for she is sharp-tongued and voluble.[63]
>
> A daughter [in the family] . . . has an uncontrollable temper and is subject to hysterical spells. Can read and write and has a fairly large vocabulary. Is dull of comprehension. Contrary and complaining, is probably on the borderline of feebleminded.[64]

Repeatedly, the field workers note the women's "immorality," their "slovenliness," their failure to take good care of their homes and children. Here, the family studies do seem to be partaking of, and promoting, maternalism, with its values of female nurturance, higher morality, and dependency. Certainly the studies and the field workers tautologically interpret women's failure to embrace appropriate, bourgeois feminine and maternal behaviors as a sign of feeblemindedness, and feeblemindedness itself as a sign of a proclivity toward such unacceptable behaviors. Unlike the progressive maternalists, however, the field workers are less concerned with the effect of feebleminded mothers and fathers on the welfare of the nation's children than they are with the effect of such parents, along with their children, on the nation's genetic makeup. The family studies do not aim to improve poor and feebleminded children's lives so much as they aim to prevent them. Such final solutions do not fit comfortably under the rubric of "maternalism."

Ironically, the eugenics field worker herself is, to a degree, contained by the gendered national eugenics program she is helping to enact. The workers, too, have been "tested" for their adherence to acceptable standards of femininity—it is just that they have already passed a "tenderness-sympathy" (and eugenics) test that their subjects are presumed, always already, to have failed. In one of the most famous family studies, *Mongrel Virginians: The Win Tribe* (1926), one of its male co-authors, Arthur Estabrook (who had been one of the few male field workers, but who later became a successful study director and author), sums up the role and status of the field worker when he cites, in a single prefatory sentence, "the highly efficient college women who assisted in the field work" and "must remain unnamed."[65] The anonymous eugenics field worker thus represents a counterpart to the anonymous dysgenic mother; both sets of women—the field workers and the feebleminded mothers—are functionally responsible, indeed necessary, for the production of the family studies—even as they remain "unnamed" or pseudonymous. For example, "the nameless feeble-minded girl" in Henry Goddard's famous family study *The Kallikak Family* (1912), who mothered the "kakos," or the genetically bad/ugly line of the Kallikak family, has her eugenic counterpart in Goddard's field worker, Elizabeth Kite, who collected the data for the study.[66] The women of the Kallikak, Timber Rat, and other feebleminded families produce dysgenic progeny; the field workers in turn replicate those offspring in the form of the study data. Thus dysgenic mothers and female eugenics field workers together are accountable for the production and for the narrative reproduction of a contaminated lineage. To put this another way, the field workers laboriously produce exhaustive catalogs of family members in a metaphorical replay of the reproductive labors of the fertile women of the family. *Eugenical News* regularly published the number of pages of family study data that had been submitted each month by the field workers, setting up a kind of productivity competition among them:

> Miss Helen Martin has reported 59 pages of single spaced notes, equivalent to somewhat over 100 pages of the usual double spaced form, collected mostly in Brooklyn, N.Y.
>
> Miss Edith Douglass has sent in 23 pages of data, about half of which is single spaced, collected chiefly in Hartford, Conn., and vicinity.[67]

The workers' productivity is always thoroughly entangled with the reproductivity of their dysgenic subjects. The field workers represent, as educated professionals, New Women (in stark contrast to the dysgenic women they observe); but their own work serves, in part, to re-contain them, as well as their subjects, on the grounds of parenthood.

That re-containment represents potential common ground between the field workers and their more liberal counterparts. Indeed, gender restrictions limited the professional options for reactionary New Women just as much as for progressive New Women, yet contemporary scholars of the New Woman and the reform era have not included the field workers in their studies. Granted, the field workers' conscious, willing, and active restriction of others by gender and class distinguishes them from the period's socially progressive reformers, and it perhaps renders them discomfiting exemplars of New Womanhood. Yet despite the fact that the field workers (unlike the settlement house workers) found that their social and political thinking meshed well with the nature of their work, they often found it just as difficult to reconcile their professional ambitions with their personal lives; the field workers, too, had to confront and cope with the period's prevailing gender roles. On the one hand, the field workers were quite conscious of—and defended—their professional status, as in the following excerpt from the 1913 summer field worker conference proceedings:

> Miss Brown;—Every field worker has a feeling of rebellion at being called a field worker. . . .
> Miss Ruth Moxcey;—. . . The name of "field worker" is a silly term especially as it is confused so much with the name of "social worker." It sounds amateur, trivial. I wish you too would bring it up at the Conference and see if they will change it. It is bad enough in the United States to be mistaken for an agriculturalist. (42–43)

On the other hand, the field workers, like many of their more progressive counterparts in the reform movement, were also reinforcing and enforcing some decidedly old-fashioned forms of womanhood and motherhood—certainly for their study subjects, and often even for themselves. For example, several of the field workers ended up marrying physicians and administrators at the institutions where they worked. The *Eugenical News* kept track of these and other blessed eugenic events— thereby setting up a reproductivity competition, both in addition to and in contradiction of, the productivity competition (regarding pages of data submitted), as in the April 1917 issue:

> Mrs. Alan Finlayson, née Anna Wendt [a field worker], '12 [the year that she took the summer course at the ERO], is the mother of a son, Malcolm Wendt, born January 24, 1917. On March 13 Mrs. Finlayson reported that the boy was growing splendidly and so far as temperamental traits were concerned she could diagnose only "hunger and a fondness for attention" as extraordinarily striking.
> The engagement of Miss Edith Atwood, '14, to Dr. Ralph E. Davis, one of the physicians at the Southeastern Hospital for the Insane, Cragmont, Madison, Indiana, is announced.[68]

These announcements must be understood in the context of long-standing concerns that college education and professional work for women led them to marry in smaller numbers and to have fewer chil-

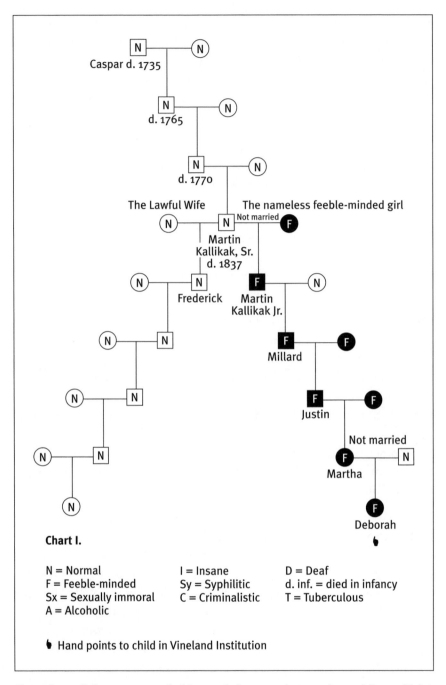

Chart I.

N = Normal
F = Feeble-minded
Sx = Sexually immoral
A = Alcoholic

I = Insane
Sy = Syphilitic
C = Criminalistic

D = Deaf
d. inf. = died in infancy
T = Tuberculous

❦ Hand points to child in Vineland Institution

Genealogical charts tracing feeblemindedness and normalcy in Martin Kallikak's two lineages, one descended from a "nameless feeble-minded girl," the other from "the lawful wife." The charts appeared in the most famous family study, *The Kallikak Family* (1912) by Henry Herbert Goddard.

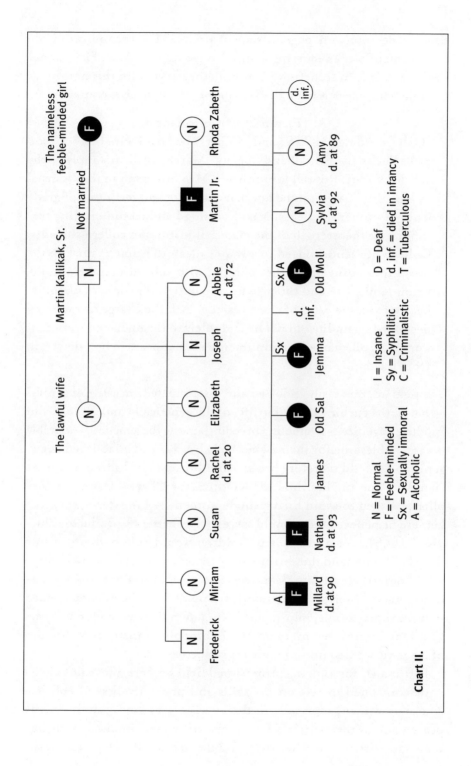

Chart II.

dren—a decidedly un-eugenic state of affairs. "The Fecundity of College Women" was a recurring feature in the *Eugenical News*. Field workers contended, in sometimes contradictory ways, with this notion, as the following excerpt from the October 1916 *Eugenical News* attests:

Fecundity of Collegians

"College Women as Wives and Mothers" by Miss Laura E. Lockwood of Wellesley in "School and Society" March, 1916, is a reply to the article by Prof. Roswell Johnson and Miss Stutzman in the "Journal of Heredity" based on the low marriage rate and fecundity of graduates of women's colleges. Miss Lockwood adduces interesting testimony on the strength of the maternal instinct in college students. College life tends indeed to advance ideals of women's work in the world to a point where they conflict with subordination to humdrum family life and the prosaic physiological processes of childbearing and the cares of child rearing. Still the charge of inducing decreased fecundity can not be laid solely to the higher education of women. Collegian education in either sex appears to be a deterrent from the family ideal.[69]

The field workers easily endorsed and disseminated "negative eugenics" —that is, the curbing of the fertility of the genetically undesirable. But "positive eugenics"—promoting breeding among the genetically desirable —was troublesome for them. They had already been established as eugenic and should therefore breed—and breed a lot. Indeed, as historian Amy Sue Bix has shown, ERO director Charles Davenport explicitly wished to avoid hiring single women "as long-term workers," because he believed they "would serve society better by producing children" (636). Yet having many children would rule out continuing their field work (and thus maintaining their New Woman status), which would nevertheless quite clearly serve to protect and improve the nation's genetic quality. For Davenport, Bix points out, the solution seemed to lie in short-term employment of women in their reproductive years (636), an interesting inversion of the compulsory institutionalization of dysgenic women during their reproductive years.

Fortunately for aspiring professional field workers, the male eugenicists continued to rely on the skills and perceptiveness of college-educated women, especially in the late 1910s as family study activity peaked and as their criteria for mental normalcy simultaneously became more stringent. After 1929 and throughout the Depression, the

ERO and other U.S. eugenics organizations suffered from lack of funds; as a result, the number of ongoing family studies dwindled, but volunteer women field workers (if not so many professionals) remained in demand. Harry Laughlin, in response to an inquiry from Kathryn Stein of the zoology department at Mount Holyoke, wrote to her in 1931: "There are so many interesting problems which advanced students, under direction, may tackle in the field of eugenics that I hardly know where to begin in making suggestions. There is always the opportunity for a student with interest in differences in people to seek out some trait in some accessible family, which trait is known by rumor 'to run in the family.' . . . Of course all these studies to be of value require extensive first-hand field work which involves careful description, diagnosis and measurement of human qualities."[70] Laughlin's letter suggests that field workers are valuable in that they can, with care, detect dysgenic human qualities, such as feeblemindedness, even in their subtlest expressions; they also represent relatively cheap (and sometimes free) labor for the ever more precise business of measuring genetic quality. Stephen Jay Gould aptly described the increasingly stringent taxonomy of mental deficiency that U.S. and English eugenicists advanced from the 1910s to the 1930s:

> Idiots and imbeciles could be categorized and separated to the satisfaction of most professionals, for their affliction was sufficiently severe to warrant a diagnosis of true pathology. They are not like us.
>
> But consider the nebulous and more threatening realm of 'high-grade defectives'—the people who could be trained to function in society, the ones who established a bridge between pathology and normality and thereby threatened the taxonomic edifice.[71]

Henry Herbert Goddard offered Deborah Kallikak, protagonist of *The Kallikak Family*, as an example of just such a taxonomic (and genetic) threat. He knows that Deborah looks normal.[72] And he suggests that this is exactly the problem: "A large proportion of those who are considered feeble-minded in this study are persons who would not be recognized as such by the untrained observer. They are not the imbeciles or idiots who plainly show in their countenances the extent of their mental defect" (102–4). Just so, Deborah "has no noticeable defect" (7). For the modern white eugenicist, the menace of the "feebleminded" goes hand in hand with the menace of the mulatto. It is the unnoticeably mentally inferior, the feebleminded rather than the obviously re-

Frontispiece of *The Kallikak Family* (1912), a photograph of Deborah Kallikak, who was institutionalized at the Vineland Training School in New Jersey.

tarded, who constitute a national menace because they can *pass* for normal, just as the racially mixed threaten to pass for white.[73] The family studies promise to eradicate the menace of the feebleminded, thereby restabilizing the "taxonomic edifice" of color and intelligence, along with the nation's competitiveness. The field workers function as the trained observers who, even in the absence of the male eugenicist (trainer) himself, can always and everywhere detect, sometimes with just a glance, the intellectually liminal.[74] And after detection comes treatment: institutionalization and sterilization. The June 1917 issue of *Eugenical News* sums up one such field worker's extensive labor and its eugenical outcome: "Ethel H. Thayer, '13, reports that at Letchworth Village from January 1, 1916, to April 1, 1917, she has spent 176 days in the field, has traveled about 10,000 miles, has interviewed 472 individuals and charted 1,984 and prepared 348 pages of descriptive material. . . . 7 were retained at the institution by the vote of the Board of Managers."[75] Here lies a (partial) solution for the eugenics field workers who must negotiate the conflicting demands of their own professional ambitions, the eugenic imperative that they breed, and the period's gender restrictions. While they must be considered New Women, whose lives and labor challenge Victorian gender restrictions, the field workers are nevertheless able to "pass" as acceptable, conventionally feminine women because their work functions to restrict the unacceptable gendered and reproductive behaviors of others.[76]

The field workers, like all professional and activist women of the era, were at risk of being labeled by their critics as unfeminine or unnatural.[77] The field workers' particular professional activity—the identification and diagnosis of "feebleminded" women who otherwise would be "passing" for normal—permits them to "pass" for normal women themselves and concomitantly to help protect the nation, its gene pool, its womanhood, and its economy. In the context of the family studies, the primary perceived threat to healthy U.S. capitalism and its requisite gender roles is the mentally, rather than the racially, liminal; in other words, white feeblemindedness is the problem. And in fact, with the significant exception of Estabrook's 1926 *Mongrel Virginians*, the family studies focus almost exclusively on the detection and elimination of those who are feebleminded rather than those who are of mixed race. There emerges in the family studies, then, an alternative version of the period's "passing" narratives, with gender/class/intellect occupying the place customarily reserved for race. Authenticated as feminine by the "tenderness-sympathy" test and certified as intelligent by their college degrees, the field workers can thus legitimately test others for mental adequacy and for their adherence to middle-class gender roles.

WE MUST ACKNOWLEDGE that the field workers were expected to study and test dysgenic men as well as women; as a result, there are interclass, intergender politics embedded in the family studies as well—politics that have been largely overlooked.[78] Perhaps because of scholars' reliance on a maternalism-feminism model to theorize women's activism in the reform era, we have been slow to theorize the ways that women exerted (sometimes damaging) power over men in the name of social reform in the 1910s and 1920s.[79] The family studies show that the men in dysgenic families were also targets of eugenic gender policing and punishment often enacted, or at the very least enabled, by women field workers. Bernice Reed noted several "sissy" and "very feminine" men in the "defective" Trix family she knew from rural New Hampshire, men who were prone to "crime, drunkardness, and pauperism."[80] Typically in the family studies, a dysgenic woman was one who, as one

Photographs from *The Kallikak Family* of family members who were not institutionalized. The original 1912 captions read, on the left, "Great-
grandson of 'Daddy' Kallikak. This boy is an imbecile of the Mongolian
type"; and, on the right, "Malinda, Daughter of 'Jemima.'" As Stephen
Jay Gould first noted, the photographs have apparently been retouched,
giving the subjects a menacing appearance.

woman field worker and study author put it, could not "order her life
in accordance with the standards of morality in vogue in twentieth
century society,"[81] whereas the quintessential dysgenic man violated
modern gender-economic-workplace standards, rather than gender-
moral-domestic ones. In other words, while the tasks of the eugenicists
were allotted according to a gendered division of labor (female field
worker/data collector versus male author/diagnostician), dysgenic behaviors, too, were gendered. The earliest U.S. family study, Robert
Dugdale's *The Jukes* (1877) had from the start established this model of
gendered dysgenics, which would characterize all the later family studies. Dugdale had argued that "prostitution in the woman is the ana-
logue of crime and pauperism in the man."[82] Of course, these two aspects of eugenic prescriptiveness—the moral and the economic, the
female and the male—were also inextricably linked from the start.

The connection between a new form of economy and explicitly gendered forms of national subjectivity emerges quite clearly in the family studies. Both men and women in the increasingly post-rural/agri-
cultural, industrial U.S. economy of the late nineteenth and early

twentieth centuries must prove their fitness, their ability to add to na-tional moral, economic, and genetic value in distinctly modern—and distinctly gendered—ways. In the family studies, the field workers are seeking reform within the social and historical context of this new economy and its new workplace. But, in contrast to the settlement house progressives who campaigned for antisweatshop legislation, the field workers sought to cull workers, like rural Minnesota's "Timber Rats," who appear incapable of surviving in such institutions of second-wave industrial capitalism as the sweatshop and the assembly line. James Knapp notes that as of "the end of the nineteenth century . . . it was widely believed that the advance of industry would not be able to con-tinue at its past rate unless future improvements in the tools of work were accompanied by appropriate—and planned—changes in the work-ers themselves. Predictable uniformity was one of the changes most earnestly sought."[83] As of the 1910s, Fordism and Taylorism had con-joined to transform the nature of much American labor, as well as the ideal American laborer. Henry Ford's Highland Park auto factory opened in 1910; it operated according to a production system (later termed Fordism) that "depended on standardization, mechanization, speed, efficiency, and careful control of production and workers."[84] Freder-ick Taylor published *The Principles of Scientific Management* in 1911. Accord-ing to his principles, which came to be known as Taylorism, laborers were first to be selected to do work for which they were fit; they were then to be trained to perform ever more specialized tasks in an ever more tightly regulated and efficient system of manufacture.[85] As a number of labor and cultural historians have noted, this system also effectively removes power and knowledge from the worker/craftsman and reas-signs them to the managers, creating a self-perpetuating hierarchy of production and class.[86]

Granted, though Taylor's system is certainly hierarchical, his empha-sis on training appears decidedly anti-eugenic. However, his worker-selection process, as detailed below, sounds remarkably similar to the diagnostic process of the family studies. Here, Taylor describes his ex-periment in selecting one worker, from among a number of manual laborers, to haul pig iron: "A careful study was made of each of these men. We looked up their history as far back as was practicable and thor-ough inquiries were made as to the character, habits, and the ambition of each of them. Finally, we selected one from among the four as the most likely man to start with."[87] Taylor selects this person in part be-

cause he is "a man of the mentally sluggish type" (46), who "is suited
to handle pig iron" and therefore "cannot possibly understand [the
science behind producing and handling pig iron], nor even work in
accordance with the laws of this science, without the help of those who
are over him" (48). Like this particular expression of Taylorism, the
family studies aim to select suitable modern male workers who can
conform to the compartmentalized, fast-paced, and increasingly regulated workplace of the twentieth century. Unlike the family studies,
however, Taylor's hierarchical but at least partially progressive principles permit him to include immigrants and even the "mentally sluggish" in his ideal modern workplace. The family studies' social con-
servatism, by contrast, leads them to construct both male producers
and female reproducers according to an inherited nineteenth-century
patriarchal, capitalist model: the family as the unit of consumption.[88]
In this view, the father, as worker, need only provide ever-increasing
income, while the mother sustains home, morality, and ever-increasing spending.[89] To the study authors and field workers, dysgenic families appeared mentally, behaviorally, and biologically unable to conform
to such a "uniform, predictable" model of an ideal gendered economic
unit—that is, the modern eugenic family first envisioned in Dugdale's
1877 *The Jukes*.

The later family studies followed Dugdale's original pattern of perceiving a gendered dysgenics in opposition to a mature, increasingly
urban and industrial capitalist economy, but they also refined that pattern. As Rafter points out, in the "late family studies, disinterest in accumulation is a sure sign of feeblemindedness."[90] Their feebleminded
subjects must not be maintained at the expense of a rapidly progres-
sing nation; ever more people who cannot adhere to modern standards
of either morality or production will necessarily be left behind. Calvin
Coolidge, in his 1925 inaugural address, succinctly expressed these
national imperatives: "The very stability of our society rests upon production and conservation. For individuals or for governments to waste
and squander their resources is to deny these rights and disregard these
obligations. The result of economic dissipation to a nation is always
moral decay."[91] No other form of discourse more effectively accommodated a national platform of production, conservation, efficiency, and
morality than did the family studies. As scientific management and assembly line production emerge as the predominant techniques of labor
control, the family studies show a concomitant "tailoring" of the cri-

teria for fitness.[92] One such study, coauthored by a woman field worker and the male superintendent of the Minnesota School for the Feeble-Minded and Colony for Epileptics, *Dwellers in the Valley of Siddem* (1919), readily acknowledges this narrowing trend in the determination of mental fitness: "Our definition of feeblemindedness is a shifting one. A few years ago we did not recognize the high-grade moron as feeble-minded. And, as Dr. Terman [reviser of the Stanford-Binet test] says, '. . . It becomes merely a question of the amount of intelligence necessary to enable one to get along tolerably with his fellows and to keep somewhere in sight of them in the thousand and one kinds of competition in which success depends upon mental ability. . . . It is possible that the development of civilization, with its inevitable increase in the complexity of social and industrial life, will raise the standard of mental normality higher still.' "[93] Thus the family studies' standards of normalcy, particularly for men, rose from the studies' origin in 1877 to their peak in the late 1910s. Overall, the studies' criteria become ever more stringent and more explicitly economic, as the ability to compete in the twentieth-century marketplace almost fully supplants appropriate moral behavior as their measure of male worth.

Family study author A. E. Winship, in his 1900 revision of Dugdale's *The Jukes*, marks this transition by observing that "it is much easier to reform a criminal than a pauper."[94] In 1877, Dugdale had focused on the habitually criminal, whereas turn-of-the-century studies like Winship's generally worried most about feeblemindedness and its possible results—immorality and sexual degeneracy among women, shiftlessness and unemployment among men. But even keeping a job becomes inadequate evidence to establish male genetic worth after the turn of the century and especially during World War I. A study coauthored by field worker Florence Danielson (published in 1912) focused on a "rural community of hereditary defectives" and noted about one dysgenic subject: "He was a good workman but lacked judgment and any idea of the value of money."[95] In 1918, field worker Mina Sessions published *The Happy Hickories*, a study of "the feeble minded in a rural county in Ohio." She used a measure even more abstract and subjective than the IQ test to determine mental (and so genetic) adequacy. According to Sessions, those who were incapable "(a) of competing on equal terms with their normal fellows or (b) of managing themselves and their affairs with ordinary prudence" must be considered feebleminded.[96] So by 1918, in order not to be labeled dysgenic, male study subjects had to be not only law-abiding and of at least average intelligence; they also had to know the value of a dollar and be competitive and prudent.[97] World War I was clearly adding urgency to the project of establishing competitive national subjectivity; increasingly, international political and economic terms of engagement seemed to call for an ever purer and fitter nation.[98] And some families were clearly not fit to produce or reproduce in a new global market, a new "Taylorized" workplace, or a new industrial economy. The danger lay in their continuing to reproduce anyway, in a kind of unnatural modern selection process. The field workers were thus essential for locating, diagnosing, and documenting those dangerously fecund dysgenic families who were, generation after generation, impairing the nation's efficiency. As Justice Oliver Wendell Holmes remarked in 1927, "Three generations of imbeciles are enough."

THE EUGENICS field workers represent a group of reformers who cannot be fully understood via historians' maternalism and professionalization-versus-reform paradigms for explicating women's reform activism in the 1910s and 1920s. First, they were participating in what has been considered the "male dominion," including discourse surrounding modern techniques of labor management and production, along with the concomitant discourse of economic and international competitiveness. Second, unlike the progressive women reformers, the field workers faced no contradiction between their professionalism and their politics; to restrict and confine their "clients"—through institutionalization and sterilization—precisely matched their reform agenda. Third, the field workers actually managed to finesse the period's gender restrictions inasmuch as those restrictions might have conflicted with their own status as professionals; their eugenics work focused on improving American families even as it required the workers to possess and exercise their positive feminine attributes. As volunteers and professionals in a field that reinforced old-fashioned gender behaviors along with new-fashioned controls of population and labor, the field workers managed to remain "true" women even while they acted as New Women. The field workers must be viewed, then, as particularly successful examples of the New Woman who—though they always had to operate within the bounds of eugenic and capitalist ideologies and therefore remained constrained by a gendered family structure and a disciplinary economy—nevertheless exerted both discursive and literal power over women and men in a quite flexible and creative fashion. Indeed, in their unpublished writings, the field workers created a new genre. Combining personal narrative, travel narrative, interviews, genealogical data, and statistical analysis, the eugenics field workers wrote quintessentially modern national family stories.

So now then we begin again this history of us and always we must keep in us the knowledge of the men and women who as parents and grandparents came together and mixed up to make us and we must always have in us a lively sense of these mothers and these fathers, of how they lived and married and then they had us and we came to be inside us in us.
—Gertrude Stein, *The Making of Americans* (1925)

We are learning at a very rapid clip how we are all the same and all different.—Francis Collins, National Genome Research Institute (2003)

CONCLUSION

This project carries implications for our understanding of both the modern period and the contemporary moment. First, we must acknowledge that our current views of the Progressive Era, of American modernism, and of the New Negro movement may not be so much aided by hindsight as they are occluded by present-day moral and political debates and standards. We in the twenty-first century know that eugenic thinking led quite directly to the worst violation of the human pact ever known. Because of the Holocaust, if not because of the eugenic sterilizations that were taking place in the United States in the decades before it, the very word *eugenics* has, since the mid-1940s, connoted ugliness and immorality. Since then, to label any sort of social policy or theory "eugenic" has been effectively, and usually rightly, to malign it. But it was not until May 2002 that Virginia governor Mark Warner and not until December 2002 that North Carolina governor Mike Easley formally apologized for the compulsory sterilizations their states had performed between the 1920s and the 1970s.[1]

Such renewed attention to modern eugenic practices emerges out of a potentially neo-eugenic contemporary context. The recent development of new genetic and prenatal tests, especially preimplantation genetic diagnosis, has reignited debates surrounding the selection of human beings.[2] As we conduct such debates, we must acknowledge and understand that the United States, among other nations, has a lengthy history regarding not only the social and aesthetic but also the scientific and legislative construction of ideal state and racial subjects. The site of the Eugenics Record Office in Cold Spring Harbor, New York—where the eugenic family studies of the 1910s and 1920s were developed and written—now houses a number of labs and databases for research on the human genome project. Cold Spring Harbor Laboratory's Web site acknowledges the troubling aspects of its own institutional history, noting that "in a classic example of well-intentioned but tragically misinformed science, [Charles] Davenport established the Eugenics Record Office at Cold Spring Harbor. . . . Shut down in 1940, for over 20 years the ERO was the main U.S. setting for this dark chapter in the history of genetics. Today it is a vivid reminder of the power genetics can have over the general public, and of the important role for ethics in science."[3] But the laboratory's attempt at a careful distinction between past and present is too facile. As the Web site itself acknowledges, "The flow of people and events at Cold Spring Harbor is an allegory of the development of modern American science." Allegories by their nature include social lessons: in their time, Davenport and Laughlin and the ERO field workers did not perceive themselves as "tragically misinformed."

For English and American thinkers of the 1920s across a wide political spectrum and regardless of race, eugenics was not a dirty word. As one scholar has argued, aside from G. K. Chesterton, "almost no one of importance spoke out against it."[4] Yet a number of literary scholars have seen T. S. Eliot as a eugenics sympathizer but have not categorized W. E. B. Du Bois as such, in part because Eliot's racial and class politics trouble them whereas Du Bois's do not. In its time, the deep wrongness of eugenic thinking was not as apparent as it is now. Indeed, to the degree that Du Bois was progressive, especially regarding sexuality and birth control, he was also sympathetic to the notion of selective biological reproduction, of scientific intervention to improve the race—at least during the 1920s. As he put it in 1922: "Birth control is science and sense applied to the bringing of children into the world, and of all who need it we Negroes are the first. We in America are becoming sharply divided into the mass who have endless children and the class who through long postponement of marriage have few or none."[5]

Du Bois's belief that the country (for him, the Negro race in particular) was suffering from a kind of modern, unnatural selection process was widely shared in the 1910s and 1920s. Across lines of race and
politics, many Americans worried that the conditions and events of the
modern period — from demographic shifts to public health measures
to World War I — had undermined the process of natural selection.
Anglo-American and African American writers and activists, including Margaret Sanger, Lothrop Stoddard, A. E. Wiggam, Nella Larsen,
E. Franklin Frazier, and A. Philip Randolph, worried about overpropagation among the inferior (generally the lower class) within their race.
Even Gertrude Stein, long considered a relatively apolitical, avant-garde
modernist, entered the debate over the nature and quality of American
identity and nativity. In general, modern writers were prone to self-
selection, seeing their own form of subjectivity as "best." Stein was, after
all, a self-proclaimed genius: "I know," she said, "that I am the most
important writer writing today."[6] T. S. Eliot declared of the *Criterion*: "I
have gone on the principle of trying to secure the best people of each
generation and type."[7] In her notes about her play *Rachel*, Angelina
Weld Grimké wrote: "I drew my characters, then, deliberately from the
best type of colored people."[8]

Indeed, eugenics, along with that self-selection process, serves quite
well to reveal the commonalities — as well as the distinctions — between
American modernism and the Harlem Renaissance. Most obviously,
the prevalence of eugenic discourse in both movements demonstrates
that modern African American and white thinkers participated in, and
contributed to, many of the same intellectual and social trends. Their
common participation in eugenic discourse also shows that many writers, regardless of race, were confronting characteristically modern
tensions between collective and individual subjectivity. As select individuals, they were positioned as arbiters and representatives of the collective good. When modern artists and writers linked cultural production to selective biological reproduction, they were thereby linking
their aesthetic and cultural experiments to political and social ends.
Of course, those ends differed according to the individual thinker.
W. E. B. Du Bois's or George Schuyler's or Alice Dunbar-Nelson's political vision certainly did not match Margaret Sanger's or T. S. Eliot's
or Lothrop Stoddard's. Such competing, indeed incompatible, versions of eugenics emerged, at least in part, out of the profound and

intensively enforced racial segregation that characterized the United States in the first three decades of the twentieth century. As a result of that segregation, Du Bois's version of eugenics was just as intraracial as Stoddard's was.

A number of literary scholars and historians over the last decade have considered the connections between American modernism and the Harlem Renaissance. Ann Douglas in *Terrible Honesty: Mongrel Manhattan in the 1920s* (1995), George Hutchinson in *The Harlem Renaissance in Black and White* (1995), and Walter Benn Michaels in *Our America: Nativism, Modernism, and Pluralism* (1995) have all emphasized the intellectual and geographical terrain shared by modern black and white writers. Houston Baker, in his landmark *Modernism and the Harlem Renaissance* (1987), points to the "radical uncertainty" and technical innovativeness shared by Anglo-American and African American modern writers. But Baker ultimately emphasizes their separateness and the "*distinctive* set of 'family' sounds, standards and criteria" that characterize "Afro-American modernism."[9] More recently, Seth Moglen has argued that a legacy of "politically narrow and racially exclusionary" Anglo-American modernist criticism in conjunction with African Americanist scholars' having "accepted the notion that modernism's formal practices and social concerns were largely alien to black writers of the early 20th century" has led to the neglect of a writer like Langston Hughes, who in his view was clearly a modernist.[10] Moglen concludes that "an expanded modernist canon" will correct for such exclusions (1191). I would argue, by contrast, that we should not seek simply to "expand" modernism to include—and then perhaps to subsume—the Harlem Renaissance, yet neither should we hold the two movements utterly apart. *Unnatural Selections* thus occupies a middle ground between Baker's and Hutchinson's (or Douglas's) studies. An exclusive, racial-familial model, such as Baker's, understates the commonalities between American modernism and the Harlem Renaissance; Hutchinson's model of "long-forgotten and repressed [interracial] *kinship*" overstates them, as does Douglas's "wider pattern of trans-race needs and debts."[11] There was certainly a degree of cultural and political cooperation, as well as some common social experience and aesthetic experimentation among modern African American and white thinkers. But such shared cultural and social practices were severely constrained by the particular material conditions, the daily lived experiences, of "the color line."

In his 1940 autobiography, *Dusk of Dawn*, Du Bois says that in 1918, his fiftieth year (when he was editor of a highly influential journal with a circulation of over 100,000 and had published a number of landmark books, essays, and plays), he "had one of my curiously seldom intimate contacts with human beings across the color line" at a "dinner in Boston with Glendower Evans, Margaret Deland and William James."[12] "I would like to have known other and wider circles of Americans in this manner," explains Du Bois, "but it was not easily possible" (743–44). For his part, he "early assumed that most Americans did not wish my personal acquaintance or contact with me except in purely business relations, and that many of them would repay any approach on my part with deliberate insult. . . . Probably I was often wrong in this assumption, but I was right often enough to prove to myself that my rule was wise and a great help to my own peace and quiet" (744). Du Bois says of the next year in the United States (ironically, the same year that the second Pan-African Congress took place in Paris):

> The facts concerning the year 1919 are almost unbelievable as one looks back upon them today. During that year seventy-seven Negroes were lynched, of whom one was a woman and eleven were soldiers; of these, fourteen were publicly burned, eleven of them being burned alive.
>
> That year there were race riots large and small in twenty-six American cities. . . . There was an open and wide revival of the Ku Klux Klan. (747–48)

Ultimately, Du Bois distanced himself from eugenic thinking; I would argue that it was the very relentlessness of Jim Crow and of racial terrorism in the United States that helped him to gain that distance. Also in *Dusk of Dawn*, Du Bois describes his debate with a white man who insists, first, that the white race is superior to the black race and, second, that some whites are better than other whites. "Is it possible," says the white man to Du Bois, "that you have never heard of the Jukes, or of the plain results of hereditary degeneration and the possibilities of careful breeding?" (659). Du Bois replies: "It is not possible; they have been served up to me ad infinitum. But they are nothing. I know greater wonders: Lincoln from Nancy Hanks, Dumas from a black beast of burden, and Kant from a saddler, and Jesus Christ from a manger" (660). Like Angelina Weld Grimké, Georgia Douglas Johnson, and Mary Burrill, Du Bois knew all too well that the modern United States was not a meritocracy and that the talented did not necessarily receive opportunities that matched their abilities. As Du Bois puts it: "To be sure, good seed proves itself in the flower and the fruit, but the failure of seed to sprout is no proof that it is not good. It may be proof simply of the absence of manure — or its excessive presence" (660). Just as the antilynching dramatists argued, the only "unnatural selection" taking place in the modern United States had not resulted from new technologies or public health measures or charity; it originated in a radically uneven distribution of advantages and penalties. The United States has yet to provide an equivalent environment, the same amount of manure, to use Du Bois's words, for all its citizens.

It may be that Du Bois's later skepticism about eugenics contains a lesson for us now. We should consider the possibility that just as we have misread the past — have misread both Eliot and Du Bois — we may be misreading the present. What do progressives now believe (and believe in as thoroughly and unquestioningly as modern Americans believed in eugenics) that in seventy years will look not only wrong, but decidedly unnatural, and perhaps even evil? And which citizens are we excluding from our pictures of ideal postmodern citizenry? In order to uncover the contemporary equivalent of eugenics, we could do worse than return to that still-tangled intersection of science, race, class, and nation, reminding ourselves that current struggles going on over the production and reproduction of ideal national subjects have antecedents in the modern era.

There has been very little scholarship to date on the eugenics field workers I discussed in the preceding chapter. Ironically enough, contemporary disregard of these troubling "New Women" may testify to a kind of unintentionally selective scholarly memory that prevents the workers from being acknowledged as authentic New Women. In current literary, political, and social histories of the family studies and of the eugenics movement, the field workers appear to have failed an updated version of the "tenderness-sympathy" test; certainly, unlike the liberal reformers of their day, the eugenics field workers rarely sympathize with the poor and working-class families they work among and study, while the family stories they create, however original and powerful, are certainly ugly. In general, the field workers appear to be quite willing to use their power to limit the (literal and social) mobility and fertility of the dysgenic women and men they encounter. V. P. Robinson, for example, seems to have no sympathy for the inmate of the

Bedford Hills New York State Reformatory for Women who "asks frequently if she can go out tomorrow and offers me a crate of berries if I will take her away."[13] The fact that the inmate "tests 7 years by the Binet" provides the only justification required for her life-long institutionalization.[14] Likewise, field worker Mary Storer Kostir has no trouble sentencing a man afflicted with "mental immaturity" not only to sterilization but also to segregation and "farm work all his life long."[15]

The family studies did not signal the century's last instance of middle-class mobility predicated on the immobility of others, particularly concerning matters of reproduction and labor. We may observe similar (although certainly not identical) interclass and intragender politics today centering on Americans' work and fertility. Once again, the advent of yet another new form of national economy, this time one based on "information" or "knowledge," seems to call for social reform and for new kinds of workers. Indeed, a number of present-day projects at Cold Spring Harbor Laboratory—bioinformatics, computational genomics, and genome informatics—tightly bind the nature and structure of this new economy to human genetic structures. Even as information and genetics have thus become intertwined in scientific discourse, a number of neo-eugenic social policies have been considered and sometimes put in place during the last two decades, especially at the state level. As Thomas Shapiro explains, "Changes in the state's role in promoting contraception, abortion, and sterilization correspond to the shifting interests and strategies of the dominant groups in society, as well as to changing social conditions."[16] In the 1980s and 1990s, state legislators debated, and in some cases approved, "welfare caps" that would block an increase in AFDC benefits for a woman who has another child while on welfare. Coercive policies aimed at decreasing poor women's fertility—cash rewards for the use of Norplant by welfare recipients, for example—were also introduced in a number of state legislatures during the 1980s and 1990s.[17]

Clearly, then, Americans still seek to determine which citizens are worthy of reproducing—and then to enforce that determination. Currently, poor teens are advised to abstain from sex, whereas Ivy League teens are bribed into becoming egg donors. At the same time, medical insurance companies are being increasingly pressured to cover the costs of in vitro fertilization.[18] Thus, even as the poor and very young are being urged to reproduce less, there is an attendant project being enacted to preserve the fertility of middle- and upper-class women, especially that of aging professionals. As Barbara Ehrenreich's recent work has shown, in general, the American professional middle-class—including and sometimes especially women—still neither perceives nor acknowledges the ways that others—again, particularly women—enable their class privilege and their relatively comfortable work and family lives.[19] There is a historical precedent in the New Women eugenics field workers of the 1910s and their relationship to their clients, such as the "charwoman" whom Ida Mellen derided as "cracked" on religion, the "janitress" whom Sadie Myers found so annoying, the "delinquent girls" whom V. P. Robinson pretended to befriend, and the putatively criminal, feebleminded, and destitute men and boys who, like the "immoral" and "feebleminded" women of the time, were subjected to negative eugenic practices in the United States of the "Progressive" Era.

Annalee Newitz and Matt Wray warn us about the enduring legacy of the eugenic family studies, pointing out that the studies' "stereotypes of rural poor whites as incestuous and sexually promiscuous, violent, alcoholic, lazy, and stupid remain with us to this day."[20] But unlike modern Americans with their focus on the eugenic quality of intraracial national subjects, we are now engaged in struggles over selective human reproduction interracially and internationally as well as domestically and intraracially. Population control measures are being enacted in developing countries and in "inner city" U.S. neighborhoods at the same time that infertility treatment has become an exclusive and extraordinarily costly perquisite of the American middle and upper classes. Granted, contemporary writers and bioethicists are certainly far more alert to the dangers of eugenic thinking than were modern thinkers. Nevertheless, hopes persist in scientific literature, in science fiction, and in cutting-edge cultural and social theory that we can create a better sort of human being—in part through biological and technological means. But there is no "natural" selection possible via social intervention and public policy, or even through biotechnology and genetic testing, because the criteria for selection themselves are always contingent, always produced by social contexts and historical circumstances, and even by particular developments in science and technology. Just as the eugenic family studies' criteria for normalcy changed over time, with the ideal American looking ever more like the field workers and their supervisors, notions of human perfection are temporary and are often imagined via a process of self-selection. As we seek to improve the human race, we must be sure that those improved beings, whether cyborgs or clones, look not just at (and like) ourselves but also outward toward others and back toward the past, even as they look to a new future.

NOTES

Introduction

1. There is a growing body of first-rate scholarship on the history of the eugenics movement in the United States. See Chase, *Legacy of Malthus*; Degler, *In Search of Human Nature*; Lisa Lindquist Dorr, "Arm in Arm"; Duffy, *Sanitarians*; Duster, *Backdoor to Eugenics*; Gould, *Mismeasure of Man*; Gugliotta, " 'Dr. Sharp with His Little Knife' "; Haller, *Eugenics*; Kevles, *In the Name of Eugenics*; Kline, *Building a Better Race*; Kühl, *Nazi Connection*; Larson, *Sex, Race, and Science*; Paul, "Genes and Contagious Disease"; Pickens, *Eugenics and the Progressives*; Rafter, "Claims-Making and Socio-Cultural Context"; Rafter, *White Trash*; Reilly, *Surgical Solution*; Roberts, *Killing the Black Body*; Selden, *Inheriting Shame*; J. David Smith, *Minds Made Feeble*; Stepan, "*Hour of Eugenics*"; Stepan, *Idea of Race in Science*; Thomson, *The Problem of Mental Deficiency*; Trent, *Inventing the Feeble Mind*; Weeks, *Sex, Politics, and Society*; Zenderland, *Measuring Minds*.

2. See Childs, *Modernism and Eugenics*; Doyle, *Bordering on the Body*; Kadlec, "Marianne Moore, Immigration, and Eugenics"; León, " 'Meeting Mr. Eugenides' "; Richardson, "Eugenization of Love"; and Seitler, "Unnatural Selection."

3. Bauman, *Modernity and Ambivalence*, 36.

4. This is not to say that eugenics can, in either theory or practice, represent politically, socially, or morally neutral ground. Eugenics emerges from a model of human normativity designed to exclude, even to eliminate, those designated biologically inferior or genetically flawed on the basis of inevitably contingent, historically specific criteria.

5. Malthus, *Essay on the Principle of Population*, 2; further citations will be parenthetical in the text.

6. Historian Carl Degler points out that Darwin "later accepted the phrase [survival of the fittest] as a kind of shorthand for natural selection." Degler, *In Search of Human Nature*, 11.

7. Spencer, *Social Statics*, 262.

8. Ibid., 147–48. In *Illness as Metaphor*, Susan Sontag objects to such troping of social problems as literal, physical ailments. She pursues "liberation" from these "lurid metaphors," because they stigmatize both the truly physically ill and the group pigeonholed by the metaphor (*"Illness as Metaphor,"* 4). She argues, for example, that TB first had to assume a sufficiently malevolent aura before Hitler could accuse "Jews of 'producing a racial tuberculosis among nations'" in an early rhetorical step (in 1919) toward genocide (82–83). Although Sontag is certainly right to challenge the figurative equation of human beings with disease, she does not fully address the antecedent trope of the "body politic." To envision the nation as a body is to fantasize that it can and should work as a synchronous system. The socially inferior or deviant—the object of negative eugenics—becomes then the "monkey wrench" (to adopt Slavoj Žižek's phrase) that proves the system already exists as a working unit with expected and fixable glitches—for Hitler, that would mean Jews, among others. As Žižek explains, "By transposing onto the Jew the role of the foreign body which introduces into the social organism disintegration and antagonism, the fantasy image of society *qua* consistent, harmonious whole is rendered possible" (*Enjoy Your Symptom!*, 90). The very phrase "body politic" automatically suggests that some body parts will be subject to Spencerian excision or excretion; thus, the trope can never be innocent. As Hannah Arendt has pointed out, "The truth is that race-thinking entered the scene of active politics at the very moment when the European peoples had prepared, and to a certain extent had realized, the new body politic of the nation" ("Race-Thinking before Racism," 41).

9. Darwin, *Origin of Species*, 68; further citations will be parenthetical in the text.

10. In *The Origin of Species*, Darwin veered away from any overt consideration of humans, yet he concluded the book with the remark that his "theory of descent with modification through natural selection" (342) might eventually mean that "light will be thrown on the origin of man and his history" (458). But even in *Origin*, Darwin had ventured some speculation about human evolution, and he almost always did so in racial terms, speaking of "the differences in races of man, which are so strongly marked" (227) and describing "negroes [*sic*] of the interior of Africa" as "the lowest savages" (92–93). Darwin here violated his own potentially egalitarian injunction, stated early on in *Origin*, against using "the words higher and lower" when comparing forms of life (33).

11. Darwin, *Descent of Man*, 108; further citations will be parenthetical in the text.

12. In *Descent*, Darwin does not even commit himself to a monogenetic

theory of the origins of humankind. The mid-nineteenth century witnessed a controversy in Britain and the United States over polygenesis, the theory that human races constituted different species with distinct origins, versus monogenesis, the theory that the human races shared a common ancestral origin. Polygenesis bolstered the views of the proslavery South in the United States, even if it implied deviation from the biblical version of the Adamic origin of all humankind. Some slaveholders speculated that to identify African Americans as a distinct, lesser species would justify the continued practice of slavery. Abolitionists generally insisted on the potentially more egalitarian, monogenetic origin of all human beings.

13. Galton, *Hereditary Genius*, v; further citations will be parenthetical in the text.

14. Gould, *Mismeasure of Man*, 75–77.

15. Indeed, as Stephen Jay Gould observed, not until the advent of the IQ test in the early 1900s did the measurement of inherent, hierarchical race and class differences receive another such boost. When French psychologist Alfred Binet published his original intelligence quotient test in 1905, he intended it to provide one technique for the identification of what we would now term learning-disabled children (*Mismeasure of Man*, 149). Lawrence Terman, a professor at Stanford, published his revised version of the test, the Stanford-Binet, in 1916, with much broader applications in mind (ibid., 175–76). Terman, along with a colleague, Harvard professor Robert Yerkes, initiated the testing of 1.75 million U.S. Army recruits in 1917–18. They found that recent immigrants (especially those from central, southern, and eastern Europe) and African Americans achieved, on average, lower scores. These results were later used as propaganda in the campaign for immigration restriction. See Gould for a definitive analysis of the flaws and biases of the army IQ test, its administration, and the interpretation of test data.

16. Other eugenic thinkers followed this authorial convention of self-genealogy. Havelock Ellis continued the tradition in his 1904 *A Study of British Genius*. So did W. E. B. Du Bois, who, on the occasion of his fiftieth birthday in 1918, delineated his genetic and racial inheritance for the *Crisis*: "So, with some circumstance, having finally gotten myself born, with a flood of Negro blood, a strain of French, a bit of Dutch, and thank God! no 'Anglo-Saxon,' I come to the days of my childhood." In the same passage, Du Bois compares his grandfather to "a thoroughbred" ("The Shadow of Years," 168). Eugenics popularizer A. E. Wiggam offered a particularly transparent version of the authorial self as eugenic exemplar: "The present writer is descended quite directly from Nordic Vikings" (*Fruit of the Family Tree*, 82).

17. Galton, *Inquiries into Human Faculty*, 24; further citations will be parenthetical in the text.

18. I am grateful to a reader for the University of North Carolina Press for suggesting "unnatural selections" as a part of the title and as a uniting concept for this book.

19. Spencer, *Principles of Biology*, 532.

20. Spencer, *Social Statics*, 146. Spencer also helped establish a crucial, long-lived distinction between the "unfortunate worthy" and the "innately unworthy," the "deserving" and the "undeserving poor," the "vicious poor" and the "virtuous poor" (ibid., 354–55, 361, 363). The vicious poor do not merit even voluntary charity; they are "good-for-nothings" (298) who should, rightly, be culled. The virtuous poor, on the other hand, might deserve "a lift into some self-supporting position" (144). Spencer's distinction resonates throughout the century and into current social policy debates. Even Marx's distinction between the lumpen proletariat and the proletariat arguably has something in common with Spencer's binary classification of the poor. See also Chase, *Legacy of Malthus*, 316.

21. Spencer, *Social Statics*, 147.

22. Spencer, *Principles of Biology*, 510.

23. See Innes, *Devil's Own Mirror*, and Lott, *Love and Theft* for more on the nineteenth-century equating of Africans with the Irish.

24. Spencer, *Principles of Biology*, 521.

25. Ibid., 512.

26. Bederman, *Manliness and Civilization*, 28.

27. Spencer, *Social Statics*, 359. Galton, like Spencer, was aware of and appreciated Dugdale's contribution to the project of improving human breeding. In his 1883 book, *Inquiries into Human Faculty and Its Development*, Galton opines that "fairly distinct types of criminals" have been permitted to "breed true to their kind" in what is, for him, one of "the saddest disfigurements of modern civilisation" (15). Galton supports his cultural diagnosis of modernity—criminal overbreeding—by citing "the history of the infamous Jukes family in America" (63).

28. In 1809, the French naturalist Jean-Baptiste Lamarck (1744–1829) had published *Philosophie zoologique*, wherein he proposed that species evolve as a result of the hereditary transmission to offspring of traits acquired by the parents during their lifetimes. Until and even after Darwin published *The Origin of Species* in 1859, Lamarckian inheritance was widely accepted as the most reasonable explanation for the evolution of species and their adaptation to changing environmental conditions.

29. Obviously, Lamarckianism provides no assurance of egalitarian or progressive social policy, as both Dugdale's policies and Spencer's social philosophy show. In fact, a belief in Lamarckian inheritance was what made monogenesis palatable to some racists and slavery advocates: if acquired traits are hereditary, then even given a common origin of all races, those races will

promptly evolve in very different ways. Proslavery factions could then argue that Africans had evolved to be slaves and whites to be masters. Unfortunately, as I will discuss in chapter 1, the rediscovery of Mendel's work in 1900 did not necessarily advance egalitarian racial or class politics. See Degler, *In Search of Human Nature*, 24.

30. Dugdale, *Jukes*, 66; further citations will be parenthetical in the text.

31. There were, as well, hundreds of unpublished eugenic family studies in the United States, as I will discuss at length in chapter 5.

32. Stoddard, *Revolt against Civilization*, 97.

33. Finlayson, "Dack Family," 251.

34. Sessions, "Happy Hickories," 294.

35. Goddard, *Kallikak Family*, 101, 115.

36. Rafter, *White Trash*, 2.

37. Childs, *Modernism and Eugenics*, 1–5.

38. Larson, *Sex, Race, and Science*, 28; Duster, *Backdoor to Eugenics*, 30; Chase, *Legacy of Malthus*, 16; Reilly, *Surgical Solution*, xiii.

39. Eugenics emerged with such force in the early-twentieth-century United States that it must be seen as an "over-determined product," to use Robert Young's words, much like its eighteenth- and nineteenth-century antecedent, European scientific racism. According to Young, French and English scientific racism emerged out of "a loss of belief in Biblical explanation and its replacement by apparently authoritative scientific laws, a sense of European cultural and technological pre-eminence accompanied by working-class unrest at home, revolution and colonial rebellion abroad, and a Civil War in the U.S. focused on the issue of slavery" (*Colonial Desire*, 120).

40. Childs, *Modernism and Eugenics*, 1–5.

41. Bederman, *Manliness and Civilization*, 195.

42. For further discussion of the post–World War I rise of eugenics in the United States, see Nies, *Eugenic Fantasies*, 23–26.

43. Bederman, *Manliness and Civilization*, 201.

44. As Matthew Guterl points out, 1920s eugenic anxiety also stemmed from the widespread perception that the Great War had been distinctly dysgenic because not only was it a conflict wherein " 'Nordics were killing Nordics' " (quoting Henry Fairfield Osborne) but it also was " 'destructive of the best strains, spiritually, morally, and physically' " (quoting Madison Grant). See Guterl, *The Color of Race*, 35; further citations will be parenthetical in the text.

45. John F. Kennedy Library and Museum. "Calvin Coolidge's Inaugural Address." Further quotations of Coolidge's address are from this source.

46. Biggs, *Rational Factory*, 105.

47. See JoAnne Brown, *Definition of a Profession*, for a fine analysis of the concept and the term "efficiency" in relationship to new forms of labor control,

industrial organization, and intelligence testing in the context of World War I (110–13).

48. Rogers and Merrill, *Dwellers in the Vale of Siddem*, 346.

49. Holmes's opinion: "We have seen more than once that the public welfare may call upon the best citizens for their lives. It would be strange if it could not call upon those who already sap the strength of the State for these lesser sacrifices . . . in order to prevent our being swamped with incompetence. . . . The principle that sustains compulsory vaccination is broad enough to cover cutting the fallopian tubes. . . . Three generations of imbeciles are enough." Novick, *Honorable Justice*, 352.

50. Granted, eugenics is not the only context in which to understand Coolidge's remarks. He is also certainly referring to organized crime and to Prohibition Era liquor bootlegging and marketing. Even so, Prohibition itself speaks to the link between morality and nationality that eugenics also addresses. In fact, eugenicists generally viewed alcoholism as both an inherited-biological and an immoral-behavioral condition.

51. Quoted in Reilly, *Surgical Solution*, 60.

52. See Douglas, *Terrible Honesty*, 304. Also see Morawska, "Sociology and Historiography of Immigration," 187–88.

53. See Reilly, *Surgical Solution*, 18.

54. The act permitted immigration by nationality in numbers correlated to the proportions of nationalities already present in the U.S. population as reflected by the 1890 (*not* the 1920) census. As a result, the 1924 act cut by over 80 percent the numbers of immigrants coming from central, southern, and eastern European countries. See Chase, *Legacy of Malthus*, 300; and Kadlec, "Marianne Moore, Immigration, and Eugenics," 25. In other words, the act discriminated on the basis of national origin in order to ensure a much higher proportion of immigrants from northern Europe; it sought thereby to exclude the "duller and lower immigrant breeds" (Wiggam, *Fruit of the Family Tree*, 176–77), that is, immigrants from southern and eastern Europe, who had represented the bulk of immigration between 1890 and the passage of the act. By excluding most southern, central, and eastern European immigrants, the act also effectively excluded the majority of Jewish immigrants.

55. Michaels, *Our America*, 6; further citations will be parenthetical in the text.

56. See *Modernism/Modernity* 3, no. 3 (1996), for discussions of Walter Benn Michaels's *Our America*. Marjorie Perloff, in "Modernism without the Modernists" observes, rightly, that only a highly selective and partial view of modernism, in particular one that excludes Pound and Eliot, permits Michaels to apply a model of "nativism" to American modernism. Both Perloff and Charles Altieri, in "Whose America Is *Our America*," point out that Michaels omits not only a great deal of literature but also a lot of history and econom-

ics in his discussion of the dynamics of modern American citizenship. Altieri argues persuasively that one cannot reduce all of American modernism, with its undeniable ambiguities and tensions (especially around race) to "a single dominant set of beliefs" (107).

57. This is not to say that awareness always led to enforcement of these differences. There were, for example, socialist eugenicists like Havelock Ellis who promoted the erasure of class difference.

58. Historian Wendy Kline has recently made a compelling case for continued strong influence of eugenics in the United States throughout the 1930s (*Building a Better Race*, 93–101, 107) and beyond, even into the 1950s (156), and perhaps even up to the present (164). Kline argues persuasively that 1930s eugenicists sustained their agenda by shrewdly avoiding the potentially racist, purely biological connotations of 1920s eugenics; they combined notions of nature and nurture, advocating sterilization of the feeble-minded not so much because they might pass on mental deficiency but because they would not make good parents. As a result, the number of compulsory sterilizations during the 1930s was "nearly triple" the number in the 1920s (107). Certainly the ideology and practice of eugenics persisted well past the 1920s and the 1930s. Historian Gregory Dorr has shown that eugenics was being taught in the 1950s at the University of Virginia; see his "Assuring America's Place in the Sun." Likewise, historian Johanna Schoen has found that North Carolina performed sterilizations, approved through its Eugenics Board, until 1975. See Schoen, "Between Choice and Coercion." But Schoen also notes North Carolina's exceptional eugenics history, observing that the state "greatly expanded its sterilization program in the 1950s and 1960s when most states ceased eugenic sterilizations" (135). Overall, in most states and in terms of original legislation and jurisprudence (though not necessarily in the sheer number of eugenic sterilizations performed), the 1920s must still be seen as "mainline" (that is, purely hereditarian) eugenics's most successful American decade.

59. Leef Smith, "Lynchburg," B1.

60. Lewis, *W. E. B. Du Bois: The Fight for Equality*, 87 (hereafter, title shortened to *Fight for Equality*).

61. Wiggam, *New Decalogue*, 35.

62. Model, "Work and Family," 138; Lewis, *Fight for Equality*, 164.

63. Du Bois, *Philadelphia Negro*, 45, 7.

64. Du Bois, "Opinion," 24 (August 1922): 152–53.

65. Dunbar-Nelson, "Woman's Most Serious Problem," 73.

66. Kevles, *In the Name of Eugenics*, 174.

67. Du Bois, "Opinion," 32 (October 1926): 283.

68. Shawn Michelle Smith, *American Archives*, 188; further citations will be parenthetical in the text.

69. Conversely, there were, as well, black eugenics sympathizers (such as Marcus Garvey) who advocated racial purity. I discuss Garvey at greater length in chapter 1.

70. See Gillman, "Pauline Hopkins and the Occult," for a discussion of the eugenic underpinnings of Pauline Hopkins's late-nineteenth-century version of racial uplift.

71. Hopkins, *Hagar's Daughter*, 270.

72. Talalay, *Composition in Black and White*, 50.

73. Diana Williams, "Building the New Race," 190; further citations will be parenthetical in the text. Matthew Guterl likewise observes that Toomer believed that "he represented a new 'type' of American—new and decidedly superior" (*The Color of Race*, 168).

74. Von Hallberg, "Literature and History," 116.

75. Kevles, *In the Name of Eugenics*, 88, 90, 106, 114, 169.

76. "Fitter Families for Future Firesides," 9.

77. Von Hallberg, "Literature and History," 116.

78. Eliot, *Letters*, 573.

79. León, "'Meeting Mr. Eugenides,'" and Childs, *Modernism and Eugenics*.

80. Michael Levenson observes that "vague terms still signify": the term "modernism" is "at once vague and unavoidable." See Levenson, *Genealogy of Modernism*, vii. Marianne DeKoven simply quotes Levenson, while observing that "most discussions of modernism acknowledge both the indefinability of the term and also the desirability of giving it a working definition, or at least periodization." See DeKoven, "Gertrude Stein and the Modernist Canon," 5. Raymond Williams at first tries to identify modernism's beginnings with "the extraordinary innovations in social realism" of Dickens, Gogol, and Flaubert in the mid-nineteenth century. But he, too, ends up relying on more conventional periodizations as a result of what he calls "a series of breaks in all arts in the late nineteenth century." See Raymond Williams, *Politics of Modernism*, 32–33.

81. Felski, *Gender of Modernity*, 12–13. Thus, although most critics of modernism acknowledge that "modernity" in its loosest sense could be taken to signify merely the postfeudal, they usually deploy more familiar (and generally more useful) periodizations—say, 1890–1930—to designate "modernism."

82. There were just a few articles written by whites about birth control and population issues among "Negroes" in the *Crisis* during the 1920s, and there were two "Negro numbers" of Margaret Sanger's *Birth Control Review* (one in 1919 and one in 1932). Ironically, the period's intensively enforced segregation largely protected African Americans from the compulsory eugenic practices enacted on poor whites; sterilization and institutionalization generally took place in whites-only institutions. This dynamic would change in the postsegregation era, with African Americans increasingly and eventually dis-

proportionately being sterilized. See Schoen, "Between Choice and Coercion," and Roberts, *Killing the Black Body*.

83. Levenson, *Genealogy of Modernism*, vii.

84. In the second volume of his towering Du Bois biography, David Levering Lewis associates the beginning of the New Negro Renaissance with the return of black World War I veterans and with Du Bois's July 1918 *Crisis* editorial: "'Returning Soldiers' spoke to all of them in their new, self-proclaimed, exhilarating incarnation: The New Negro" (Lewis, *Fight for Equality*, 2). For further debate on the dates and significance of the Harlem Renaissance, see Gates, "Harlem on Our Minds," 2; English, "Selecting the Harlem Renaissance," 811–12; Gates et al., *Norton Anthology of African American Literature*, 932; Lewis, *When Harlem Was in Vogue*, xviii; and Huggins, *Harlem Renaissance*, 53–58.

85. Du Bois, "Winter Pilgrimage," 15.

86. Of course, there were other shared contexts as well, World War I, especially. But many of the other common contexts—eugenics, Prohibition, and so on—can be seen as part of a general spirit of reform.

87. North, *Political Aesthetic*, 6.

88. Lewis uses the term to describe Du Bois up until the time of his resignation as editor of the *Crisis* in June 1934. See Lewis, *Fight for Equality*, 347–50.

89. Eliot, *Letters*, 573.

90. Dunbar-Nelson, "Woman's Most Serious Problem," 73.

91. Angelina Weld Grimké Papers, box 38–13, folder 223, Manuscript Division, Moorland-Spingarn Research Center, Howard University.

92. *Rachel*, 49.

93. Ibid., 73.

94. Stoddard, *Revolt against Civilization*, 17.

95. See Bederman, *Manliness and Civilization*, 45–76, on lynching protest, particularly by Ida B. Wells, that relied on a discourse of "civilization."

96. Dugdale, *Jukes*, 114.

97. As Dana Seitler cogently argues, modern scientific discourses such as eugenics "helped bring about narrative innovation," while "new narrative forms," in turn, served as "a central device for the production and publicization of scientific rhetoric" ("Unnatural Selection," 64).

98. Lott, *Love and Theft*, 9.

99. I borrow the term "rigorous historicization" from Gambrell, "Serious Fun," 244.

100. "Fitter Families for Future Firesides," 9.

101. Ibid.

102. Whittier-Ferguson, "Stein in Time," 116; further citations will be parenthetical in the text.

103. Francis Collins quoted in Weiss, "Genome Project Completed," A6.

104. Toni Morrison, *Playing in the Dark*, 14.

105. Kühl, *Nazi Connection*. Zygmunt Bauman also reminds us of the "non-Nazi and pre-Nazi, 'scientific' roots of genocide" (*Modernity and Ambivalence*, 41).

Chapter One

1. Wheatley, "To the University of Cambridge."

2. Wheatley, "On Being Brought from Africa to America." Critics have occasionally—and anachronistically, I would argue—charged Wheatley with failure to challenge the dominant racialist discourse of her day. Not surprisingly perhaps, Wheatley did not entirely dismantle the eighteenth century's prevailing racial hierarchies; but, in this poem at least, she rather subversively places (converted) Africans alongside "angelic" white men in the "Great Chain of Being."

3. Gaines, *Uplifting the Race*, xiv.

4. Ibid.

5. Carby, *Race Men*, 9–10.

6. Ibid., 11.

7. See, for example, Frances Harper's *Iola Leroy*. Authors like Harper and Pauline Hopkins took their authority seriously and viewed their works, in Hazel Carby's words, as "cultural interventions." See Carby, introduction to *Iola Leroy*, xvi. Harper concludes her novel with the explicit desire that *Iola Leroy* (like the title character herself) "inspire" the folk to "embrace every opportunity, develop every faculty, and use every power God has given them to rise in the scale of character and condition, and to add their quota of good citizenship to the best welfare of the nation" (282). Carby argues that here Harper is not promoting material so much as moral uplift. See also Carby, *Reconstructing Womanhood*, 92–94. On the other hand, Charles Chesnutt offers an interesting exception to this late-nineteenth-century, generally intraracial, definition of uplift. Chesnutt stated in his journal that his goal as a writer was "not so much the elevation of the colored people as the elevation of the whites." See Chesnutt, *Journals*, 139. I am indebted to Mason Stokes for calling this reference to my attention.

8. Doyle, *Bordering on the Body*, 10.

9. Ibid., 12.

10. Shawn Michelle Smith, *American Archives*, 183; further citations will be parenthetical in the text.

11. Michele Mitchell's dissertation, "Adjusting the Race," offers a rare exception to the scholarly tendency to exclude African American intellectuals and activists from eugenic thinking; see especially her chapter on "sexuality,

reproduction, and African-American vitality" (144–226); further citations of Mitchell's dissertation will be parenthetical in the text. The handful of other scholars who acknowledge any degree of African American participation in eugenic thinking include Marouf Arif Hasian Jr., who in *The Rhetoric of Eugenics in Anglo-American Thought* notes a class-inflected black version of eugenics, though without mention of Du Bois (69–70); and Matthew Guterl, who in *The Color of Race in America* argues that Du Bois "shared" with Lothrop Stoddard "an aristocrat's faith in the power of birth and heredity: in eugenics" (144). But even a quite recent book on U.S. eugenics, Nies's *Eugenic Fantasies*, considers eugenics solely in the context of "whiteness studies" (xi–xii).

12. This is not to say that Du Bois embraced reactionary racist eugenics as it was constructed and promoted by white supremacists such as Lothrop Stoddard and Madison Grant. As Laura Doyle points out, in the twenties and thirties, Du Bois tirelessly worked to refute white supremacist and reactionary eugenic thinking (*Bordering on the Body*, 12). In the pages of the *Crisis*, he more than once referred to Stoddard as a fool. Werner Sollors has recently observed (regarding Du Bois's reportage of his 1936 trip to Nazi Germany) that Du Bois "had an exceptional ability to understand and analyze the paradoxes of Nazi Germany—and the courage to speak out about them. At the same time, he did not idealize race relations in the United States, and was able to make fascinating comparisons between racial systems in the two nations that were informed by his own experience as a black American." See Sollors, "W. E. B. Du Bois in Germany," B4. For a thorough discussion of Du Bois's Germany trip, see Lewis, *W. E. B. Du Bois: Fight for Equality*, 397–403 (hereafter cited as *Fight for Equality*). Lewis notes that "once out of the country, Du Bois would vent his bottled-up consternation" at the Nazi persecution of Jews (400); however, also according to Lewis, Du Bois's understanding was not completely clear regarding Nazi treatment of Jews, which he considered "legal" in contrast to the "unconstitutional" American treatment of Negroes (420), while his "abiding affection for the Germans . . . conduced to a surreal indulgence of Hitler and Nazism" in the early 1940s (467).

13. Gaines, *Uplifting the Race*, xvi.

14. A revisionary trend within recent African Americanist literary and philosophical scholarship challenges past assumptions that African American writers were isolated from the scientific, philosophical, and cultural currents of their day. I, with W. Lawrence Hogue, am "assuming that people of color in the United States are not outside (Western) history and rationality." See Hogue, *Race, Modernity, Postmodernity*, x. See also Adell, *Double Consciousness/ Double Bind*; Gaines, *Uplifting the Race*; Hutchinson, *Harlem Renaissance in Black and White*; West, *The American Evasion of Philosophy*; and Zamir, *Dark Voices*.

15. Du Bois, *Souls of Black Folk*, 209.

16. Du Bois, *Dusk of Dawn*.

17. Du Bois, *Autobiography*, 154–55.

18. Du Bois, "Opinion," 24 (August 1922): 152–53.

19. Activist-writers Mary Burrill and Angelina Weld Grimké, for example, were birth control advocates oriented more toward women's rights than eugenics, although they were not completely without eugenic sympathies. See chapter 4 of this book. Also see the two special "Negro numbers" of *Birth Control Review*: September 1919 and June 1932.

20. Douglas, *Terrible Honesty*, 98. Margaret Sanger incisively analyzed New Women's resistance to male eugenicists' calls for prolific breeding among the "well-to-do": "If women in fortunate circumstances gave ear to the demand of masculine 'race-suicide' fantasies they could within a few years be down to the condition of their sisters who lack time to cultivate their talents and intellects. A vigorous, intelligent, fruitfully cultured motherhood is all but impossible if no restriction is placed by that motherhood upon the number of children." Sanger, *Woman and the New Race*, 68.

21. Du Bois, "Opinion," *Crisis* 24 (October 1922): 248.

22. Gaines, *Uplifting the Race*, 205.

23. Up to that time, and even for a bit after, belief in Lamarckian transmission persisted.

24. See Degler, *In Search of Human Nature*, 24–25.

25. See Douglas, *Terrible Honesty*, 304. Also see Morawska, "Sociology and Historiography of Immigration," 187–88.

26. See Model, "Work and Family," 138.

27. See Reilly, *Surgical Solution*, 18.

28. These tracts included (among many others) Stoddard's *The Rising Tide of Color* (1920), Grant's *The Passing of the Great Race* (1916), and Wiggam's *The New Decalogue of Science* (1923) and *The Fruit of the Family Tree* (1924).

29. See Kevles, *In the Name of Eugenics*, 61–62; Chesler, *Woman of Valor*, 215.

30. See International Eugenics Congress, *Report of the Second International Congress of Eugenics*, 26.

31. See Larson, *Sex, Race, and Science*, 28; see also Duster, *Backdoor to Eugenics*, 30; Chase, *Legacy of Malthus*, 16; and Reilly, *Surgical Solution*, xiii.

32. Kevles, *In the Name of Eugenics*, 170–75. Kevles's book remains a landmark study of the history of eugenics, but it does present a somewhat oversimplified assessment of the U.S. movement. Kevles astutely analyzes the two politically distinct branches of the eugenic movement; however, perhaps as a result of this solely political reading, he tends to elide race in favor of class (347 n. 21) and fails to consider any nonwhite adherents of socially progressive eugenic thinking.

33. Ellis, *Problem of Race-Regeneration*, 23, 25, 34.

34. Sanger, "Function of Sterilization," 299. For a discussion of Sanger's eugenic sympathies, see Chesler, *Woman of Valor*. As Chesler points out, Sang-

er's alliances with eugenicists were at times more strategic than ideological; nevertheless, Sanger consistently supported " 'negative eugenics,' or the weeding out of the unfit," even while she "disdained the idea of promoting fertility [among the fit], or 'positive eugenics' " (195).

35. Chesler, *Woman of Valor*, 193.

36. Ibid.

37. Degler, *In Search of Human Nature*, 42.

38. At least theoretically, this bridge between individual and collective subjectivity remains a corollary even of our contemporary understanding of human "breeding": the double helix of DNA (rather than a Mendelian chi square) now seems to represent, accurately, our individual (biogenetic) relationship to our families and to our ethnic groups—indeed, to the entire human family. For example, the human genome project aspires to map a kind of collective identity within which each individual is, paradoxically enough, uniquely represented.

39. North, *Political Aesthetic*, 156.

40. Ibid.

41. Eliot, "Notes towards the Definition of Culture," 95–96.

42. Du Bois, "The Talented Tenth" (1903), 17.

43. Kristeva, "Word, Dialogue and Novel," 37.

44. Appiah, "Uncompleted Argument," 34.

45. Quoted in Moon, *Emerging Thought of W. E. B. Du Bois*, 152. Granted, Appiah's argument explicitly takes Du Bois's unstable construction of race almost as a "pretext," as he puts it, for discrediting a continued, contemporary (particularly academic) reliance on notions of racial difference.

46. Gilroy, *Black Atlantic*, 122. Interestingly, some more recent theorizing on race, including that in Gilroy's *Black Atlantic* and in Appiah's *In My Father's House*, while still anti-essentialist, nevertheless deemphasizes the utter fictionality of race in favor of an affirmation of common black, especially black diasporic, experience. This communal-minded approach serves to advance a transnational political goal—what Gilroy calls the "global project of black advancement" (35). Suggestively (and a bit ironically, given Appiah's careful prior dismantling of Du Bois's concept of "race"), both Appiah and Gilroy adopt such classic Du Boisian paradigms as "double consciousness" (Gilroy) and "Pan-Africanism" (Appiah) without subjecting those notions to much more than a de rigueur anti-essentialist, postnationalist update.

47. Du Bois, *Dark Princess*, 28; further citations will be parenthetical in the text.

48. Tate, *Psychoanalysis and Black Novels*, 10; further citations will be parenthetical in the text.

49. Du Bois, "The Talented Tenth" (1948), 85–86.

50. Ibid., 88.

51. Ibid., 86. Here I depart from Joy James, who argues that, in his 1948 Wilberforce address, Du Bois "recanted his race leadership dogma" and "disbanded the old club." I do agree, however, with her argument that Du Bois's 1948 model of leadership is grounded far more surely in internationalist and socialist thinking; however, as we have seen, even Du Bois's internationalism was tinged in the 1920s with notions of improved biological reproduction. See James, *Transcending the Talented Tenth*, 23–24. Overall, James offers incisive political and historical analyses of the remarkably persistent notion of uplift via the leadership of an intraracial intellectual elite.

52. Lewis, *Fight for Equality*, 2.

53. Du Bois, "Editorial," 4 (October 1912): 287.

54. Du Bois, "Immediate Program," 312.

55. Du Bois, "Opinion," 32 (October 1926): 283.

56. Du Bois, *Philadelphia Negro*, 310–11. Just four years later, in *The Souls of Black Folk*, Du Bois again applied this notion of a "lowest class" of African Americans, this time in the context of his analysis of the post-Reconstruction rural South, noting the "'submerged tenth' of croppers, with a few paupers" (315).

57. Frazier, *Negro Family in Chicago*, 152; further citations will be parenthetical in the text. Even Frazier's apparently "objective" sectioning of Chicago into seven concentric sociogeographic "zones" (the "poorer migrants from the South" settle in the "first zone," 137) owes much to Du Bois's grading system of three decades earlier.

58. Frazier did not sustain his faith in the "leavening power" of middle- and upper-middle-class African Americans. In his 1965 *Black Bourgeoisie*, he in fact demonizes middle-class African Americans for having adopted "white values" (15) and for having "broken with the traditional background of the Negro and rejected [their] social heritage" (96). Frazier even explicitly condemns Du Bois (whom he had, in his earliest works, claimed as a forefather) for what he terms educational "compensation" for a "deep-seated inferiority complex" (148, 188). Here Frazier is, of course, both participating in and helping to construct the agenda of the Black Power Movement which aimed, in part, to reclaim and celebrate African American folk culture, often at the expense of "inauthentic" middle-class African Americans. Frazier had begun distancing himself from Du Bois as early as the mid-1930s, however. See Martin, *Race First*, 298, 310.

59. Frazier, "Eugenics and the Race Problem," 92.

60. Robert E. Park taught sociology at the University of Chicago from 1914 to 1933. His influential research was focused on human ecology and on race and culture.

61. James Weldon Johnson, *Black Manhattan*, 152; further citations will be parenthetical in the text.

62. "Men of the Month," 12 (October 1916): 278.

63. Ibid.

64. Du Bois, "Opinion," 24 (August 1922): 153.

65. See Shawn Michelle Smith, *American Archives*, 157–86, for a discussion of the significance of photographs of African Americans included in the Paris Exposition of 1900. Smith rightly argues that the photographs, assembled by W. E. B. Du Bois and Frances Benjamin Johnston, helped construct a "racially codified identity," one that represented "national belonging" for African Americans (158). But Smith also suggests that the photographs "challenged the essentialized discourses of race and national identity dominant during this period" (158) by asserting the Americanness of their black subjects. She is right that to include African Americans fully in the nation is also to challenge white nativist notions of American identity; however, her suggestion that the photographs challenge essential racial identity is less persuasive. The photos certainly challenge the white supremacy–interracial hierarchy —but they do not as a result challenge racial essentialism or race itself. As Du Bois's 1897 "The Conservation of Races" shows, as of the turn of the century, he seemed to very much still believe in the reality of "race." See also Appiah, "Uncompleted Argument."

66. "The Horizon," 167.

67. The *Crisis* did not confine itself to reporting "good news" about the racial family. Although the journal never published lists of black-committed crimes (as white NAACP chair Oswald Villard requested in 1913; see Lewis, *W. E. B. Du Bois: Biography of a Race*, 471), it did cover crimes against African Americans. Reports on lynching, for example, were frequent, graphic, and grisly, and they often included photographs of victims. In the context of my argument, however, such coverage was not only permissible but in fact necessary, as it served both to document an external threat to the Negro race–family (indeed a dysgenic threat) and to mobilize race activism. See chapter 4 for a consideration of modern African American women's antilynching plays in the context of eugenic and psychoanalytic discourses.

68. See Mitchell, "Adjusting the Race," for a discussion of " 'better babies' contests among African Americans after 1910," 204–14.

69. "One of Manhattan's 'Finest' " appeared in *Crisis* 8 (October 1914): 269; "A Great Grandfather's Great Grandson" appeared in *Crisis* 8 (October 1914): 296. Another characteristic picture, "A Perfect Baby," appeared in the "Men of the Month" feature in *Crisis* 10 (May 1915): 14.

70. Du Bois, "Our Baby Pictures," 298.

71. Archibald Grimké, "Editorial," 288.

72. Du Bois, "Editorial," 12 (October 1916): 268.

73. "Five Exceptional Negro Children" appeared in *Crisis* 34 (October 1927): 258.

74. Du Bois, "Opinion," 20 (May 1920): 8.

75. Du Bois, "Opinion," 20 (June 1920): 72.

76. Michele Mitchell makes a similar point: "Uplift activists virtually ranked race households: some were presented as showcases where the nation could ostensibly witness Afro-American improvement, other homes were deemed spare but salubrious, still other domiciles were singled out and subjected to thoroughgoing evaluations which, at times, resulted in calls for their very elimination" ("Adjusting the Race," 228).

77. Du Bois, "Opinion," 26 (October 1923), 249.

78. Du Bois, "Opinion," 28 (September 1924), 199.

79. "Pictures of Distinguished Negroes" appeared in *Crisis* 34 (December 1927): 358.

80. This celebration of the (often male) "top of the race" in the *Crisis* stands in stark contrast to the preoccupations of the white eugenicists of the day, who sought primarily to crop from their intraracial family picture immigrants and "poor white trash." White eugenics of the 1910s and 1920s focused on the dysgenic (rather than the eugenic) within its own race-family. Du Bois, while he does worry about the propagation of lower-class Negroes (especially in his earlier work), seeks primarily in the *Crisis* to promote conception among the Negro middle class. White eugenicists, on the other hand, were more likely to advocate limiting the number of children born to (white) families of the underclass. Thus eugenics among whites was also intraracial. These contrasting modes of diagnosing and envisioning one's racial family represent the modern racial-cultural divide. Whereas the modern American white middle class imagines itself embattled, threatened by a "rising tide of color," the black middle class needs just to make itself felt, to write and picture itself into being. Logically, Du Bois for the most part pursues positive propaganda and eugenics by countering negative representation of African Americans and promoting breeding "in [Negro] families of the better class" ("Opinion" 32 [October 1926]: 283). Both eugenic methods are aimed at refining and restricting notions of "normal" intraracial subjectivity, but in the process they picture their perfect races differently. For example, the elegant photographs in *Crisis* stand in stark contrast to the visual record of the white family studies. See chapter 5, which is on the family studies and eugenics field workers.

81. In the review, Larsen stands as a dutiful daughter of the Harlem Renaissance (and so of Du Bois); McKay is its prodigal son. See Du Bois, "Two Novels," 202.

82. Du Bois, "So the Girl Marries," 192–93, 207–9; further references will be cited parenthetically in the text.

83. See Lewis, *Fight for Equality*, 107–8, on Du Bois's interference in Yolande's first engagement to jazz musician Jimmie Lunceford (whom he found

unsuitable); see 159 and 222 on his oversight of Yolande's later relationship with and marriage to Cullen. Lewis concurs that the Du Bois's view of the Du Bois–Cullen wedding carried distinct eugenic overtones; see 223. Lewis also suggests that Du Bois's eugenics was confined to "his own flesh and blood" (223); I am arguing, by contrast, that his eugenic ideals were not only familial, but intraracial and international.

84. Eric Garber, in his essay reconstructing the history of "the lesbian and gay subculture" during the Harlem Renaissance, notes that "Cullen was homosexual and maintained a lifelong relationship with Harlem schoolteacher Harold Jackman," whom Garber describes as an "elegant homosexual" (318, 327, 322). Garber, "Spectacle in Color," 318–31.

85. Du Bois, "Opinion," 24 (October 1922): 247–48.

86. It is tempting to read, anachronistically, Du Bois's strange wording in this passage (written in 1922) through the lens of Yolande and Countée's failed 1928 marriage. And, indeed, Du Bois's "diagnosis" of the "petted" New Negro son does sound very much like one classic, homophobic "explanation" of the gay man: namely, that he was produced by a domineering mother. At the very least, Du Bois does seem here to be falling prey, rather uncharacteristically, to an anti-intellectualism that links academicism with a lack of virility and productivity. In other words, the passage reflects his—and others'—anxiety over differential birth rate within the race and thereby sets the stage for his discussion of "birth control as science" for "Negroes." He is worried that the New Negro will not be sufficiently (re)productive.

87. Lewis, *When Harlem Was in Vogue*, 203.

88. Stokes, "Strange Fruits," 63. Stokes's article offers a brilliant reading of the Harlem Renaissance as perhaps "the queerest avant-garde in history" (60).

89. Lewis, *Fight for Equality*, 226. Stokes, "Strange Fruits," 66.

90. Quoted in Lewis, *When Harlem Was in Vogue*, 203.

91. Quoted in Stokes, "Strange Fruits," 66.

92. Du Bois was not alone in the 1920s and 1930s in his attempt to create a member of a master Negro race within his own family, and Yolande Du Bois was not the only example of "failed" breeding during the Harlem Renaissance. In her book, *Composition in Black and White*, Kathryn Talalay exposes the extraordinary and explicitly eugenic project that *was* Philippa Schuyler (1931–67). The daughter of George Schuyler, black satirist and journalist, and white Texan heiress Josephine Cogdell, Philippa Schuyler was conceived, at least partly, to carry out a kind of breeding experiment in which she was to become the product of "hybrid genetics, proper education, and intensive education" (50). Alienated and isolated as an adult, Philippa Schuyler died (childless) tragically after having repeatedly reinvented herself in various professional guises in order to circumvent the strictures that her upbringing,

gender, and racial identity imposed. The Schuylers' experiment demonstrates clearly an alternative, relatively progressive brand of eugenic thinking that associated "vigor," not with racial purity, but with "hybridity" (see the discussion of this "hybrid vigor" version of eugenics in my introduction). Moreover, like Du Bois, the parents rejected purely hereditarian thinking, as their emphasis on nutrition and education indicates.

93. Claudia Tate offers a biographical analysis of the production of a messianic male child of color in *Dark Princess*, arguing that the final scene points to Du Bois's "wistful yearning for his infant son Burghardt" (*Psychoanalysis and Black Novels*, 63). Mason Stokes makes a similar argument ("Strange Fruits," 72). Again, perhaps less compelling than the personal dimension of the fantasy is the wider, political vision it represents: Du Bois was linking the advancement of peoples of color with a particular kind of literary production and with literal reproduction.

94. Du Bois, *Philadelphia Negro*, 1.

95. Susan Gillman has argued persuasively for a partly biological (and nascently eugenic) underpinning for Pauline Hopkins's late-nineteenth-century version of racial uplift. See Gillman, "Pauline Hopkins and the Occult," 57–82. Also see Gaines, *Uplifting the Race*, for a discussion of evolutionary theory in racial uplift discourse of the late nineteenth and early twentieth centuries (189, 205).

96. Edwards, "Racial Purity," 122.

97. Quoted in Martin, *Race First*, 22. The creed was originally printed as "What We Believe" in *Negro World*, January 5, 1924. See Mitchell, "Adjusting the Race," for a discussion of pre-Garvey, late-nineteenth-century black antimiscegenationist and eugenic thought (169–80).

98. Garvey, of course, rejected the white supremacy of Stoddard and other mainline white eugenicists, yet he also advocated racial separatism (including not only a rejection of miscegenation but also the promotion of New World blacks' return to Africa) to such a degree that white racial extremists often found his message quite congenial. In 1924, Madison Grant (author of the popular 1916 book *The Passing of the Great Race*), wrote to a fellow white supremacist about Garvey's planned Black Star Line: "I think if I were you I should get in touch with Garvey as it might be worthwhile to back his proposition" (quoted in Edwards, "Racial Purity," 125). For his part, Garvey viewed white separatists as, in a way, kindred spirits holding world views compatible with his own, while his contacts with the Klan, including a "summit conference" in 1922, became one of his critics' rallying cries (see Martin, *Race First*, 344). William Edwards likewise notes Garvey's "meeting with the Imperial Wizard of the KKK in July 1922" ("Racial Purity," 127).

99. Du Bois, *Dusk of Dawn*, 626.

100. Du Bois, "Miscegenation," 90–102; further citations will be parenthetical in the text.

101. Ibid., 93, 100, 95.

102. Du Bois, "Marcus Garvey," 977.

103. Quoted in Martin, *Race First*, 273.

104. See Lewis, *Fight for Equality*, 60–84, 149–53.

105. Randolph and Owen, "Who's Who," 26 (my emphasis).

106. Ibid., 27.

107. Michael North succinctly describes this dialectic in his discussion of aesthetic modernism, citing its "attempt to rejoin subject and object, individual and community, fact and value." North, *Political Aesthetic*, 15.

108. Du Bois, "Winter Pilgrimage," 15.

109. Gaines, *Uplifting the Race*, xv.

110. Du Bois, "Opinion," 23 (November 1921): 5.

111. Lewis, *When Harlem Was in Vogue*, 148.

112. Ibid., xxiii–xxiv, 148, 306–7; Douglas, *Terrible Honesty*, 23.

113. North, *Political Aesthetic*, 6.

114. Douglas, *Terrible Honesty*, 323–24; Gaines, *Uplifting the Race*, 5, 78–80.

115. Brooks, introduction to *Understanding Poetry*, 15; Eliot, "Music of Poetry," 113.

116. Ellmann, *Poetics of Impersonality*, 50.

117. North, *Political Aesthetic*, 20.

118. Horkheimer and Adorno, *Dialectic of Enlightenment*, 130.

119. Du Bois, "Criteria of Negro Art," 296.

120. Ibid., 291, 293, 295.

Chapter Two

1. Winston, "Life on the Color Line," XI.

2. Tate, *Psychoanalysis and Black Novels*, 49.

3. Du Bois, "Opinion," 24 (October 1922): 247–48.

4. Du Bois, *Dark Princess*, 311.

5. See especially Childs, *Modernism and Eugenics*, and León, "'Meeting Mr. Eugenides.'"

6. See Bender, "'His Mind Aglow'"; Childs, *Modernism and Eugenics*, 12–13, and Nies, *Eugenic Fantasies*. Nies does acknowledge that Fitzgerald and Hemingway parodied eugenic thinking at times; she concludes that Hemingway ultimately sided with the eugenic "Nordic body" (64) but that Fitzgerald, while he remained committed to the notion of "the body" as a source for "identity," tried to expand social "hierarchies" to include bodies and types other than the Nordic (107).

7. Toni Morrison, *Playing in the Dark*.

8. For discussion of the antifeminist elements of modernism, see Clark, *Sentimental Modernism*; Douglas, *Terrible Honesty*, 7−8, 92; Felski, *Gender of Modernity*, 27; Rado, *Modernism, Gender, and Culture*; and Scott, *Gender of Modernism*. On antiromanticism in modernism, see Nelson, *Repression and Recovery*, 21.

9. Lamos, *Deviant Modernism*, 7.

10. Eliot, *Letters*, 94.

11. Letter dated March 28, 1935, in Pound, *Letters*, 272.

12. Lyndall Gordon, *T. S. Eliot*, 312, 422.

13. Ibid., 367; further citations will be parenthetical in the text.

14. Lamos, *Deviant Modernism*, 16.

15. In his 1928 preface to *For Lancelot Andrewes*, Eliot proclaimed himself to be "classicist in literature, royalist in politics, and anglo-catholic in religion" (ix).

16. León, " 'Meeting Mr. Eugenides' "; further citations will be parenthetical in the text. Also see León's dissertation, "A Literary History of Eugenic Terror."

17. Eliot, *Collected Poems*, 35.

18. Stoddard, *Revolt against Civilization*, 91; further citations will be parenthetical in the text, referred to as *Revolt*.

19. Levenson, *Genealogy of Modernism*, 206; further citations will be parenthetical in the text.

20. Eliot, "Idea of a Christian Society," 14−15; further citations will be parenthetical in the text, referred to as "Idea."

21. John F. Kennedy Library and Museum, "Calvin Coolidge's Inaugural Address."

22. Michaels, *Our America*; further citations will be parenthetical in the text.

23. North, *Political Aesthetic*, 6.

24. Wiggam, *New Decalogue*, 19, 22.

25. Ibid.

26. Hasian, *Rhetoric of Eugenics*, 89−111.

27. Fitzgerald, *Great Gatsby*, 14; further citations will be parenthetical in the text.

28. Eliot, "Marie Lloyd," 407; further citations will be parenthetical in the text. Barry Faulk has argued that Eliot's view of the middle class, including even this quite stark quotation, is more complicated than it appears, suggesting that "Eliot's polemic cannot be taken at face value." See Faulk's "Modernism and the Popular," 604. But I see no reason not to take Eliot "at face value" here; for him, the lower, not the middle, classes produce culture that is viable for reuse by the upper class.

29. Fitzgerald, *FIE! FIE! Fi-Fi!*, 66−68.

30. Quoted in Kevles, *In the Name of Eugenics*, 174.

31. Stoddard argued that "real Bolsheviks, real social rebels," "should be carefully watched, strictly punished whenever they offend, and where anything like real revolution is attempted—hunted down and extirpated" (*Revolt against Civilization*, 232–33).

32. For discussions of Eliot's assessment of mass and popular culture, see Asher, *T. S. Eliot and Ideology*; Bauman, *Modernity and Ambivalence*; Chinitz, "T. S. Eliot and the Cultural Divide"; Faulk, "Modernism and the Popular"; Jay, "Postmodernism in *The Waste Land*"; Marsh, *Money and Modernity*; Paul Morrison, *Poetics of Fascism*; Nelson, *Repression and Recovery*; Rainey, *Institutions of Modernism*; Ricks, *T. S. Eliot and Prejudice*; Spurr, *Conflicts in Consciousness*.

33. Faulk, "Modernism and the Popular," 605.

34. Eliot, "Notes towards the Definition of Culture," 183–84; further citations will be parenthetical in the text, referred to as "Notes."

35. Eliot, *Waste Land*, line 146.

36. Du Bois, *Souls of Black Folk*, 217.

37. Eliot, *After Strange Gods*, 20–21.

38. Eliot, "Function of Criticism," 68; further citations will be parenthetical in the text as "Function."

39. Eliot, *After Strange Gods*, 15; further citations will be parenthetical in the text as *ASG*.

40. Craig Raine, in his book *In Defence of T. S. Eliot*, argues for a more generous reading of this passage because, though "the wording is unfortunate," it "allows for limited numbers of free-thinking Jews" (338). Raine continues: "As for restrictions on immigration, both major political parties now accept the necessity" (338). Raine's argument clearly hurts Eliot more than it helps him; it shows that contemporary visions of national stability founded on homogeneity bear more resemblance to some of the worst modern politics of population and nation than we might like to believe.

41. For discussion of Eliot's anti-Semitism, see Julius, *T. S. Eliot, Anti-Semitism, and Literary Form*; Ricks, introduction to *Inventions of the March Hare*; Ricks, *T. S. Eliot and Prejudice*; Dutta, "Ideology into Criticism"; León, "'Meeting Mr. Eugenides'"; North, *Dialect of Modernism*; Ricks, "Eliot's Uglier Touches"; Spurr, *Conflicts in Consciousness*; and Wilk, *Jewish Presence*. For a refutation, particularly of Anthony Julius's views, see Raine, *In Defence of T. S. Eliot*, 320–32. Raine argues that there is indeed anti-Semitism in Eliot's verse, but that it belongs to the characters, such as the speakers in Eliot's "dramatic monologues" "Burbank" and "Gerontion" (326–27). Regarding "Burbank," Raine concludes: "In other words, we have not an anti-Semitic poem, but a poem about anti-Semitism" (328).

42. Bauman, *Modernity and Ambivalence*, 35–36.

43. I thank a reader for the University of North Carolina Press for providing this insight.

44. Keeping people in their place either literally or figuratively could be seen as precisely what the New Negro movement opposed most clearly and fundamentally.

45. Wiggam, *New Decalogue*, 227–28.

46. Wiggam, *Fruit of the Family Tree*, 330.

47. Wiggam, *New Decalogue*, 171.

48. Doyle, "The Flat, the Round, and Gertrude Stein," 250.

49. On Eliot's relationship to the culture and language of the working class, popular culture, and mass culture, see Rainey, *Institutions of Modernism*; Chinitz, "T. S. Eliot and the Cultural Divide," 237; Tratner, *Modernism and Mass Politics*, 2; Asher, *T. S. Eliot and Ideology*, 2–3.

50. Julius, *T. S. Eliot, Anti-Semitism, and Literary Form*, 92.

51. Stoddard, *Clashing Tides*, 78.

52. Ibid., 76, 368.

53. North, "Dialect in/of Modernism," 57.

54. Ibid., 70.

55. Ibid., 71.

56. The blackface correspondence between Eliot and Aiken and between Eliot and Pound can be seen as a racial version of the well-known Sedgwickian triangle, wherein black bodies, both male and female (here, King Bolo and his "kween") supplant the white female body as the vehicle through which white men express their homosocial desires.

57. Eliot, "Notes towards the Definition of Culture," 95–96.

58. Lott, *Love and Theft*, 6.

59. Eliot, *Letters*, 431.

60. Read, "T. S. E.—A Memoir," 15.

61. North, "Dialect in/of Modernism," 65. Michael Tratner, too, argues that Eliot had a "lifelong fear that he was himself a product of mixed immigration, that he had 'mixed blood' in him and could not then be a cultural producer, an artist" (*Modernism and Mass Politics*, 100).

62. Eliot, *Letters*, 86.

63. North, "Dialect in/of Modernism," 56.

64. Eliot, *Letters*, 455.

65. North, "Dialect in/of Modernism," 57.

66. I am grateful to a reader for the University of North Carolina Press for pointing out this similarity.

67. Joyce, *Ulysses*, 508.

68. In *Our America*, Walter Benn Michaels takes the novel far too seriously, using it as evidence in support of his model of nativist literary modernism, when the novel is actually poking fun at both the writerly and racial mistakes that such a model invites (94–95). Betsy Nies makes an argument similar to

Michaels's, suggesting that Hemingway's novel, "while a satire, also is inseparable from its modernist target, Sherwood Anderson's *Dark Laughter*" (*Eugenic
Fantasies*, 480). Both Michaels and Nies largely ignore Hemingway's pointed
parody of modernist literary *form* in its reliance on racialism.

69. Hemingway, *Torrents of Spring*, 74–75.

70. Interestingly, both Hemingway (directly) and Eliot (indirectly) were
involved in the prolonged project of getting Stein's *The Making of Americans* into
print. In 1924, Hemingway convinced Ford Madox Ford to publish installments of the book in the *Transatlantic* and later, when the review seemed to be
foundering, began trying to get the *Criterion* to publish them. When the publication of installments in the *Transatlantic* got back on track, Hemingway wrote
to Stein: "At any rate there will be regular and continuous publication [in the
Transatlantic] and after all that is better than embalmed in the heavy, uncut
pages of Eliot's quarterly." Quoted in Katz, introduction to *Fernhurst, Q.E.D.,
and Other Early Writings*, 190.

71. Eliot, *Letters*, 544.

72. Ibid., 573.

73. Eliot, "Music of Poetry," 113.

74. Ibid.

75. Childs, *Modernism and Eugenics*, 99.

76. Eliot quoted in Harding, *The "Criterion,"* 209.

77. León, "'Meeting Mr. Eugenides,'" 174.

78. Pound quoted in Harding, *The "Criterion,"* 186.

Chapter Three

1. Stein, *Making of Americans*, 34; further citations will be parenthetical in the
text.

2. Stein, *Fernhurst, Q.E.D., and Other Early Writings*, 4; further citations of *Fernhurst* and *Q.E.D.* are to this edition and will be parenthetical in the text.

3. Quoted in Meyer, introduction to *The Making of Americans*, xiv.

4. Sanger, *Woman and the New Race*, 68.

5. Du Bois, "Damnation of Women," 953.

6. Katz, introduction to *Fernhurst, Q.E.D., and Other Early Writings*, xxxvii.

7. It is not clear exactly what Stein means here by the term "race." I take it to
mean explicitly the human race, but implicitly white, middle-class Americans.

8. For discussion of Stein's racial-sexual-literary politics, see Cohen, "Black
Brutes and Mulatto Saints"; Cooley, "White Writers and the Harlem Renais-
sance"; Cope, "'Moral Deviancy' and Contemporary Feminism"; DeKoven,
Rich and Strange; Doyle, "The Flat, the Round, and Gertrude Stein"; English,
"Gertrude Stein and the Politics of Literary-Medical Experimentation";

Hovey, "Sapphic Primitivism"; Toni Morrison, *Playing in the Dark*; Nielsen, *Reading Race*; Saldívar-Hull, "Wrestling Your Ally"; and Smedman, "'Cousin to Cooning.'"

9. Katz, introduction, xxxvii.

10. Stimpson, "The Mind, the Body, and Gertrude Stein"; and Meyer, *Irresistible Dictation*, 84.

11. Marianne DeKoven, who rightly acknowledges the inconsistencies and problematics of modernist politics in general and of Stein's politics in particular, nevertheless seems to find comfort in what she calls Stein's move "beyond or outside modernism." DeKoven argues that Stein "exceeded" the "limits of what we think of as modernist innovation" ("Half In and Half Out of Doors," 81). See also DeKoven, *Rich and Strange*, 68; and DeKoven, "Gertrude Stein and the Modernist Canon," 15. Similarly, Ellen Berry argues that, as a result of her radical aesthetic practices, Stein can be distinguished from Eliot and Pound and identified as a postmodernist feminist (*Curved Thought*, 8−9).

12. Whittier-Ferguson, "Stein in Time," 117−18. An important exception to the many recent oversimplified—and overly progressive—analyses of Stein, Whittier-Ferguson's essay challenges and complicates in effective and necessary ways the historicizing and politicizing turn in Stein scholarship of the past decade as well as in literary criticism in general.

13. Hovey, "Sapphic Primitivism," 548, 549, 563; further citations will be parenthetical in the text.

14. Smedman, "'Cousin to Cooning,'" 571−72.

15. Doyle, "The Flat, the Round, and Gertrude Stein," 250. Doyle also argues that the "insidious racism" of *Three Lives* is manufactured for a white audience and that, while it exposes Stein's own "attachment" to that racism and helps create her authority as author, it also works to "expose" her audience's "investment" in racism (262). I am less sanguine than Doyle that Stein's aim in "Melanctha" is "calling her audience out of its ideological closets" (262).

16. Here I am adopting Juan León's term "eugenic anxiety," which he coined to describe T. S. Eliot's participation in the modern period's eugenic discourse. See "'Meeting Mr. Eugenides.'"

17. Brinnin, *Third Rose*, 49.

18. Mellow, introduction to *Three Lives*, xi.

19. Stein, *Three Lives*, 3, 5; further citations will be parenthetical in the text.

20. William Carlos Williams, "Work of Gertrude Stein," 23.

21. Geller and Harris, eds., *Women of the Asylum*, 179.

22. As Jayne Walker has noted, Stein's original title was probably also intended as an acknowledgment of the literary influence of Flaubert and his *Trois Contes*. See *Making of a Modernist*, 19.

23. Stein, "Composition as Explanation," 457.

24. The modern medical chart emerged out of physicians' need for efficient, standardized assessment and diagnosis of ever-increasing numbers (and types) of patients. But, as of 1909, the publication date of *Three Lives*, the chart itself was still in an experimental stage; it represented a new genre highly susceptible to Stein's narrative innovations. *Three Lives* experiments with the chart's conventional categories of subjective information (supplied by the patient), objective information (observed by the clinician), assessment (diagnosis), and plan (prescription). By charting her characters via the medical gaze of a narrator-diagnostician, Stein at first appears to participate in a literary version of the epistemological hierarchy implied by the conventions of medical charting. However, her narrative technique also challenges such categorical assignment of authoritative knowledge by blurring the boundaries between "subjective" (patient) and "objective" (physician).

25. Foucault, *Birth of the Clinic*, 15.

26. Chessman, *Public Is Invited to Dance*, 28.

27. Critics have frequently observed that Jeff Campbell functions as a fictional stand-in for Stein herself, in a more veiled (by race and gender) version of the real-life love affair she had rendered earlier in *Q.E.D.* See Katz, introduction to *Fernhurst, Q.E.D., and Other Early Writings*, and Walker, *Making of a Modernist*. Lisa Ruddick, in *Reading Gertrude Stein*, persuasively argues that the "two lovers in the story, Melanctha and Jeff, are the products of Stein's imaginative self-splitting" (13). Ruddick goes on to suggest that Melanctha is "the locus of ambiguity in the story" (13). But Jeff Campbell represents an equally powerful site of narrative ambiguity. He clearly serves as another racialized locus of ambivalence around medical-literary authority.

28. DeKoven, *Rich and Strange*, 67.

29. Doane, *Silence and Narrative*, 54.

30. I am referring here to Wordsworth's well-known description of poetry as originating "from emotion recollected in tranquillity" (Preface to *Lyrical Ballads*).

31. As Toni Morrison has pointed out in *Playing in the Dark*, "For American writers generally, this Africanist other became the means of thinking about the body, mind, chaos, kindness, and love; provided the occasion for exercises in the absence of restraint [and] the presence of restraint" (47).

32. Stoddard, *Rising Tide*, 90; further citations will be parenthetical in the text.

33. All the mulatto characters in "Melanctha" are "sick": "Melanctha's pale yellow mother was very sick and in this year she died" (106). Jane Harden, "who was so white that hardly anyone would guess it" (100), was "very sick almost all day" (140).

34. The combination of anxiety over working-class fecundity and insis-

tence on white, middle-class genetic superiority represents the central eugenic paradox. Only through an ideologically tailored (fractured) Darwinism could the eugenicists simultaneously insist on their own greater fitness while fretting about what the Reverend James Marchant termed, in his introduction to C. W. Saleeby's *The Methods of Race Regeneration* (1911), "the uncontrolled multiplication of the degenerate, who threatened to swamp in a few generations the purer elements of our race" (4). According to "pure" Darwinian logic, the more reproductively successful species is, in fact, the "fitter" species. The upper class will shrink, therefore, only if selected against. Of course, the underlying flaw in the eugenicists' twisted Darwinism lies in their application of species theory to class and race—neither of which has any biological or genetic reality.

35. Laughlin, *Bulletin No. 10A*, 59.

36. Douglas, *Terrible Honesty*, 304.

37. Model, "Work and Family," 138, 141.

38. Stein entered the medical profession at a particularly significant historical moment—and at an equally significant institution. Johns Hopkins was, as public health historian John Duffy notes in *The Sanitarians*, at the forefront of the professionalization of medicine at the turn of the century and opened the first permanent U.S. school of public health in 1918. Duffy observes that Johns Hopkins "established the formula for public health schools" and was a leading force in the institutionalization of public health in the United States (253). The establishment of the Johns Hopkins School of Public Health and Hygiene stands as a symbolic culmination of a public health movement with roots in the mid-nineteenth century.

39. Rafter, *White Trash*, 15.

40. Crawford, *Modernism, Medicine*, 110.

41. Kevles, *In the Name of Eugenics*, 64; further citations will be parenthetical in the text.

42. Kobrin, "American Midwife Controversy," 197.

43. Bailey, "Control of Midwives," and Ziegler, "Elimination of the Midwife." Ziegler declared himself "unalterably and uncompromisingly opposed to any plan which seeks to give [the midwife] a permanent place in the practice of medicine" (32). One of his primary arguments for obstetricians' elimination of midwifery baldly discloses the contest's economic underpinnings: he cites the "$5,000,000 which it is estimated is collected [annually] by midwives in this country and which should be paid to physicians and nurses for doing the work properly" (34). By contrast, for examples of physician support for midwives during the period, see S. Josephine Baker, "Schools for Midwives," and Noyes, "Training of Midwives."

44. Baldy, "Midwife." Likewise, pioneering Boston obstetrician J. B. Huntington observed, in a 1912 issue of the *American Journal of Obstetrics and Gynecol-*

ogy, that "as soon as the immigrant is assimilated, then the midwife is no longer a factor in his home" (quoted in Kobrin, "American Midwife Controversy," 200). One obstetrician frankly assessed the situation in 1907, declaring that midwives "are un-American": see Mabbott, "Regulation of Midwives," 526.

45. Wertz and Wertz, *Lying-In*, 211, 215−17.

46. Kobrin, "American Midwife Controversy," 197.

47. Ibid., and Leavitt, " 'Science' Enters the Birthing Room," 97. Leavitt notes in *Brought to Bed* that by 1930 midwife-attended births had dropped to 15 percent of the total number (268).

48. In 1920 Lothrop Stoddard described the "negro" as the "quickest of the breeders" (*Rising Tide*, 90), while Harry Laughlin (probably the foremost U.S. eugenicist during the 1910s and 1920s) cautioned in 1914 that the "Federal Government" must undertake the task of "preventing the landing of inferior breeding stock" (*Bulletin No. 10A*, 62). At the same time (but not coincidentally), medical discourse was perfecting what Foucault termed the "thorough medicalization" of white, middle-class women's bodies and sexuality, a process "carried out in the name of the responsibility they owed to the health of their children, the solidity of the family institution, and the safeguarding of society" (*History of Sexuality*, 146−47). As C. W. Saleeby, a leading eugenicist of the day, put it, in "all times and places, women's primal and supreme function is or should be that of choosing the fathers of the future" (*Methods of Race Regeneration*, 36).

49. Kevles argues, correctly, for the existence of two strains of eugenics in the United States and Britain—one espoused by "social-radical eugenicists" such as George Bernard Shaw and Havelock Ellis, the other by eugenicists "of a conservative bent" such as Lothrop Stoddard and Karl Pearson (*In the Name of Eugenics*, 86−88).

50. Leavitt, " 'Science' Enters the Birthing Room," 91.

51. Antler and Fox, "Movement toward a Safe Maternity," 492. For period defenses by physicians of the safety of midwifery, see Levy, "Maternal and Infant Mortality in Midwifery Practice," and Zinke and Humiston, "Discussion on the Papers of Drs. Harrar and Levy." In " 'Science' Enters the Birthing Room," Leavitt explains the failure of early-twentieth-century obstetricians to improve on rates of maternal mortality as being a result of their readiness to intervene in the birth process. She argues that "when physician-directed obstetrics finally became master of the birthing room" (89), a "direct relationship existed between anesthesia and forceps" (91). Overuse and lack of skilled use of such interventions actually "increased the number of maternal deaths" (91).

52. Stein's allegorical rendition of the displacement of the female medical expert may also serve as an early critique of the emerging gender politics of

modernism. In other words, she is anxious to maintain her own status as the central figure of the modernist literary avant-garde, the expert of the experimental.

53. Stoddard, *Rising Tide*, 164–65.

54. Walker, *Making of a Modernist*, 27.

55. Stein, *Everybody's Autobiography*, 28.

56. Quoted in Gallup, "Making of *The Making of Americans*," 176.

57. Hemingway, *Torrents of Spring*, 86.

58. Meyer, *Irresistible Dictation*, 209 (emphasis in the original).

Chapter Four

1. Spillers, "Mama's Baby, Papa's Maybe," 272; further citations will be parenthetical in the text.

2. Jacobs, *Incidents*, 42; further citations will be parenthetical in the text.

3. An echo of Jacobs's analysis can be heard in Ida B. Wells-Barnett's later forthright and fearless analysis of the sexual dimensions of lynching (*On Lynchings*, 4–5).

4. Douglass, *Narrative*, 23.

5. Ibid., 61.

6. Carby, *Reconstructing Womanhood*.

7. Gourdine, "*Drama* of Lynching," 538.

8. This is not to say that such acts never occurred in reality. In addition to Margaret Garner's infanticide, there were several other documented cases of slave women who killed their own children. See Roberts, *Killing the Black Body*, 48–49. But substantive proof that slave women used infanticide and abortion as means of resistance may be impossible to obtain. It seems that slave women not infrequently tried to control their fertility by means of contraception and abortion, if not infanticide (which seems to have been relatively rare). See Giddings, *Where and When I Enter*, 46; Roberts, *Killing the Black Body*, 46–49; Bettina Aptheker, *Woman's Legacy*, 135. Here, I am concerned more with the political and literary usefulness of infanticide as a trope rather than as an actual act—that is, it offers a literary-figurative means to explore the modern politics of race and reproduction.

9. Goldsby, "High and Low Tech of It," 246.

10. Fuoss, "Lynching Performances," 6, 29.

11. Both Claudia Tate and Ann duCille have explored the different meanings that marriage and "coupling" could have for black women. Marriage and conventional civil and legal forms of bourgeois domestic life could in fact function as socially progressive and politically emancipatory for those historically denied access to such. See Tate, *Domestic Allegories*, and duCille, *Coupling Convention*.

12. Terrell, "Lynching from a Negro's Point of View," 862.

13. Hull, *Color, Sex, and Poetry*, 18.

14. Tate, *Domestic Allegories*, 217.

15. See Wells-Barnett, *On Lynching*; Trudier Harris, *Exorcising Blackness*; Stephens, "Racial Violence and Representation"; Hall, " 'The Mind That Burns' "; and Gunning, *Race, Rape, and Lynching*. Mason Stokes has recently added a convincing consideration of white men's sexuality in his analysis of lynching; see Stokes, *Color of Sex*, 133–34, 148–50. Robyn Wiegman, too, while considering "the double registers of sexuality and gender" nevertheless focuses primarily on "the black male rapist ethos" in her analysis of lynching, an analysis that foregrounds "interracial male contestations." See Wiegman, "Anatomy of Lynching," 467. By contrast, Bettina Aptheker has argued persuasively that the black women's antilynching movement "was also a movement—a Black women's movement—against rape" (54) and that Ida B. Wells-Barnett, among other antilynching activists, was defending black womanhood as much as she was protecting black manhood (*Woman's Legacy*, 62–63). Similarly, Jacquelyn Dowd Hall has offered an important analysis of the raping of black women as being inseparable from the lynching of black men in " 'The Mind That Burns in Each Body.' " As Hall argues, both depend on "racial subordination"; rape, like lynching, was used "as a political weapon" after the Civil War (331–32). My analysis considers not rape but voluntary heterosexual relations and fertility of African American women as necessary components in any analysis of the psychodynamics and history of lynching.

16. On lynching protest, see Aptheker, *Woman's Legacy*; Hall, *Revolt against Chivalry*; Gere, *Intimate Practices*; Giddings, *Where and When I Enter*; White, "Cost of Club Work"; White, *Too Heavy a Load*; Thompson, *Ida B. Wells-Barnett*. On lynching itself, see Trudier Harris, *Exorcising Blackness*; Gene L. Howard, *Death at Cross Plains*; Ayers, *Vengeance and Justice*; Brundage, *Under Sentence of Death*; Brundage, *Lynching in the New South*; Downey and Hyser, *No Crooked Death*; Walter Howard, *Lynchings*; McGovern, *Anatomy of a Lynching*; Rolph, *"To Shoot, Burn, and Hang"*; Tolnay and Beck, *Festival of Violence*; Wright, *Racial Violence in Kentucky*; Ginzburg, *100 Years of Lynchings*.

17. For recent scholarship on the antilynching plays, see Gourdine, *"Drama of Lynching."* Gourdine offers an insightful analysis of Angelina Weld Grimké's *Rachel* as a play that "establishes a relationship between the lived experiences of lynching and the textual manifestations of lynching" (535). Also see Schroeder, "Remembering the Disremembered." Schroeder emphasizes the mimetic and propagandistic elements of *Rachel*, *They That Sit in Darkness*, *Safe*, and several other plays. For a useful discussion of the literary-historical context and conventions of modern lynching dramas, see Stephens, "Racial Violence and Representation." Also see Stephens, introduction to *Strange Fruit*, and Krasner, "Walter Benjamin and the Lynching Play." For other critical

treatments of antilynching plays, see Tate, Storm, Herron, and Hull (all cited below).

18. Angelina Weld Grimké Papers, box 38-13, folder 223; Manuscript Division, Moorland-Spingarn Research Center, Howard University (hereafter Grimké Papers).

19. Du Bois, "Damnation of Women," 953.

20. Du Bois, "Opinion," 32 (October 1926): 283.

21. Spillers, "Mama's Baby, Papa's Maybe," 272.

22. Mitchell, "Adjusting the Race," 152; further citations will be parenthetical in the text.

23. The history of black women's participation in the birth control movement is elusive. In part because they were working against racist representations of black women as highly sexualized, African American club women, social workers, and nurses seem rarely to have documented birth control advocacy or practices. See Tone, *Devices and Desires*; Elsa Barkley Brown, "To Catch the Vision of Freedom"; Linda Gordon, "Black and White Visions of Welfare"; and Roberts, *Killing the Black Body*.

24. This is not to say that every African American woman activist of the modern era was utterly opposed to eugenic thinking. As White, Linda Gordon, and Weiss, among other historians, have demonstrated, quite a few believed that middle-class and sometimes light-skinned Negroes should have more children. See Linda Gordon, "Black and White Visions of Welfare," 220.

25. Tate, *Domestic Allegories*, 22.

26. Carby, *Reconstructing Womanhood*.

27. James Weldon Johnson, *Autobiography of an Ex-Colored Man*, 497; further citations will be parenthetical in the text.

28. Stephens, "Racial Violence and Representation," 2. For analyses of lynching as performance and ritual, also see Trudier Harris, *Exorcising Blackness*, x–xi; White, *Too Heavy a Load*, 25; and especially Fuoss, "Lynching Performances."

29. See Herron, introduction to *Selected Works of Grimké*, 6–7, 17–18.

30. As David Krasner suggests, "Allegory"—because of its excessive, historical, and collective dimensions—"is the artistic device appropriate for representing the response to the incomprehensibility of mass violence" (71), the "abundance of brutality" that is lynching (72). See Krasner, "Walter Benjamin and the Lynching Play."

31. Angelina Weld Grimké, *Rachel*, 33; further citations will be parenthetical in the text.

32. Note that the lynch mob's motivation in this instance is not an accusation of rape of a white woman but rather the political assertiveness and courage of Mr. Loving. Her analysis of lynching from the perspective of the victimized black family rather than from the perspective of the lynch mob

permits Grimké to supplant the normative representation of lynching as a defense of white womanhood, reassigning it its primary role as racial-political terrorism.

33. This representation of lynching as eliminating the best black men directly contradicts white supremacist justifications for lynching. Note, for example, several white southern newspapers' representations of Emmett Till in 1955, as described by Jacqueline Goldsby: "The documents insinuated that the criminal links between father and son were biological: Emmett Till was following in the footsteps of his lascivious and murderous father" ("High and Low Tech of It," 253).

34. This is not to say that only black men were lynched. As many historians have shown, there were black female as well as white female and white male victims of lynching. Furthermore, even at the representational level, there are other African American–authored versions of lynching and its victims. In *Autobiography of an Ex-Colored Man*, for example, James Weldon Johnson's narrator describes the victim of the lynching he witnesses as "a man only in form and stature, every sign of degeneracy stamped upon his countenance" (497). E. Franklin Frazier also associated black lynching victims with inferiority, offering a regional and intraracial eugenic analysis: "In the South where little notice is taken of the colored feebleminded, unless to lynch them when they commit crimes, they are permitted to breed at a rapid rate" ("Eugenics and the Race Problem," 92). But the idea that it is the strongest, most resistant black men who are most at risk of being lynched has dominated and persisted in writings by African American women and men (e.g., *The Autobiography of Malcolm X*, *Black Boy*, *Beloved*).

35. Fuoss, "Lynching Performances," 30 n. 9.

36. Tate, *Psychoanalysis and Black Novels*, 18.

37. Fuoss, "Lynching Performances," 23.

38. As David Krasner puts this, in Rachel's renunciation of childbearing, "there is no catharsis, no closure as such, but only an epiphany of endless, temporal mourning" ("Walter Benjamin and the Lynching Play," 73).

39. A number of critics have pointed to Grimké's envisioning a white audience for *Rachel*. See for example, Hull, *Color, Sex, and Poetry*, 120; and Tate, *Domestic Allegories*, 210. And many have taken Grimké at her word in her 1920 defense against charges that the play was advocating genocide for blacks: "Since I have been given to understand that 'Rachel' preaches race suicide, I should like to state at the start, that that was not my intention. To the contrary, the appeal is not primarily to the colored people, but to the whites" (Angelina Weld Grimké, "Synopsis and Purpose"). But the play was in fact predominantly performed by and for African Americans. As Hull remarks, "Even though [Grimké] aimed her appeal at white women, not many of them could have seen the play" (120). Despite Grimké's assertion of an intended

message for whites, then, given the play's performance history, considerations of black audience seem more pertinent and valuable. Furthermore, to accept Grimké's explanation is to leave unchallenged the original accusations about the play's advocacy of genocide. As Margaret Sanger concisely puts it, in decidedly feminist (if also elitist) terms: "If women in fortunate circumstances gave ear to the demand of masculine "race-suicide" fantasies they could within a few years be down to the condition of their sisters who lack time to cultivate their talents and intellects. A vigorous, intelligent, fruitfully cultured motherhood is all but impossible if no restriction is placed by that motherhood upon the number of children" (*Woman and the New Race*, 68). Not only do the genocide accusations emerge as antifeminist, but they also replicate the shortsighted, often masculinist, representational literary politics brought to the surface and analyzed by Deborah E. McDowell in her classic essay, "Reading Family Matters." As McDowell argues with regard to *The Color Purple*, Grimké's *Rachel* cannot and should not be read or viewed as either a cultural mirror or as a blunt social prescription.

40. Ford, "Katharsis," 113.

41. Barbara Freedman rightly notes "the long-standing debt of psychoanalysis to classical drama" ("Frame-up," 56).

42. Caruth, "Traumatic Awakenings," 89; further citations will be parenthetical in the text.

43. Storm, "Reactions of a 'Highly-Strung Girl,'" 462. Judith Stephens and Kathy Perkins have made the same observation; see Perkins and Stephens, *Strange Fruit*, and Stephens, "Racial Violence and Representation."

44. Livingston, "For Unborn Children," 122.

45. Georgia Douglas Johnson, *Safe*, 113.

46. Diamond, "Shudder of Catharsis," 158.

47. Cheng, *Melancholy of Race*, x.

48. Barbara Freedman, "Frame-up," 60; further citations will be parenthetical in the text.

49. A number of scholars have pointed out that Grimké repeatedly revised and retitled *Rachel*. Prior titles included *The Pervert*, *The Daughter*, and *Blessed Are the Barren*. See Hull, *Color, Sex, and Poetry*, 118–19; Herron, introduction to *Selected Works by Grimké*, 17; Tate, *Domestic Allegories*, 215. Each of the prior titles supports the dramatic and political reading of inversion, reproduction, and race that I am developing here. Also see Grimké Papers, boxes 38-13 and 38-14.

50. Grimké Papers, box 38-13, folder 222.

51. Larsen, *Quicksand*, 108; further citations will be parenthetical in the text.

52. Du Bois, "Opinion," 32 (October 1926): 283.

53. Frazier, "Eugenics and the Race Problem," 92.

54. Historian Linda Gordon notes that of sixty-nine black women who were "national leaders in welfare reform" ("Black and White Visions of Welfare," 217) between 1890 and 1945, 43 percent had no children (219). As Gordon puts it, the women's "fertility pattern was probably related to their independence" (219). She notes further: "In the black population in general, 7 percent of all married women born between 1840 and 1859 were childless, and 28 percent of those born between 1900 and 1919 were childless" (237 n. 28).

55. Mitchell, "Adjusting the Race," 190−91.

56. Burrill, "They That Sit in Darkness," 5−8; further citations will be parenthetical in the text.

57. Miss Shaw represents a very real type of figure in the rural South of the 1920s. Bettina Aptheker shows that "Black nurses worked to improve . . . public health conditions in the South. Unlike many of their colleagues, however, the Black public health nurses and midwives worked outside of institutional settings, with little income and few supplies and medicines. They provided care within the daily grind of poverty" (*Woman's Legacy*, 106).

58. Mrs. Jasper's desire for some form of fertility control supports Johanna Schoen's argument (in "Between Choice and Coercion") that, while many sterilizations were certainly coerced, significant numbers of poor women (in the 1960s, especially poor African American women) actively sought sterilization (137). Ironically, in the 1920s, African American women were both largely protected from compulsory sterilization and precluded from voluntary sterilization because of legalized institutional segregation; they simply were not permitted in most hospitals and asylums where sterilizations were being performed.

59. Roberts, *Killing the Black Body*, 215−16.

60. This picture of the poor as wholly ignorant of and without access to birth control has been challenged by a number of contemporary historians. Although relatively few women, regardless of class, had direct access to the clinics and devices provided by Margaret Sanger, working-class women, both black and white, seemed to have been aware of and used a wide variety of contraceptive devices and methods. Fertility rates of the period lend substantial support to this revised view of modern women's contraceptive practices. See Linda Gordon, "Professionalization of Birth-Control"; Roberts, *Killing the Black Body*; and Tone, *Devices and Desires*. Also see Schoen, "Between Choice and Coercion," for discussion of women who sought sterilization in North Carolina between 1929 and 1975.

61. Roberts, *Killing the Black Body*, 86.

62. Linda Gordon, "Black and White Visions of Welfare," 220.

63. Jacqueline Goldsby has pointed out, in her compelling 1999 analysis of the Emmett Till lynching, that Till's mother was violently forced to aban-

don any notion of northern identity as a protective contingency: "Mamie Bradley's dream state—her transplanted identity as a 'Northern Negro' safe from segregated harm—was shattered by the sight of her son's battered body in a box" ("High and Low Tech of It," 245).

64. Burrill, *Aftermath*, 82–93; further citations will be parenthetical in the text.

65. Holloway, "Body Politic," 489.

66. I began this chapter by making distinctions between nineteenth-century slave narrators' representations of infanticide and modern African American women writers' representations of lynching, infanticide, and barrenness. I do not wish to suggest now that the images of racial violence and infanticide in the works of these contemporary writers are identical to those images as they appeared in the works of modern African American women writers. As Deborah McDowell has argued, critics and historians of African American literature and culture must be cognizant of the distinct contemporary "material realities" along with "ever-worsening socioenvironmental factors that place black women's health at great risk" ("Afterword: Recovery Missions," 312). Images of assaulted black motherhood and fertility—and of violated and burnt black male bodies—in contemporary African American fiction and drama must be understood within their particular social, political, and scientific contexts, contexts that include Depo-Provera, Norplant, welfare caps, racial profiling, incarceration rates of black males, differential HIV infection and mortality rates, racially biased death penalty sentencing, and so on. See also Roberts, *Killing the Black Body*, and Louis, "Body Language."

Chapter Five

1. The term "new woman" seems to have been coined in 1894. See Richardson, "Eugenization of Love," 227; Felski, *Gender of Modernity*, 146. The image of a new kind of woman, struggling against Victorian sexual and social constraints, emerged as part of the turn-of-the-century zeitgeist. And indeed, first-wave feminism was well under way at the time, with its multiple women's (or at least primarily women's) movements, including suffragism, the campaign for birth control and reproductive rights led by Margaret Sanger (1883–1966) in the United States, influential white and African American women's clubs, and temperance activism. By the 1910s, with the "woman question" grown familiar, suffragist activity at its peak, and Sanger's birth control program well under way, many upper- and middle-class women had actively and, to a degree successfully, challenged Victorian gender restrictions; some had indeed seemed to become "new" sorts of women.

2. See Linda Gordon, "Professionalization of Birth-Control," 148–50;

Rafter, "Claims-Making," 24–25; and Richardson, "Eugenization of Love," 228.

3. Richardson, "Eugenization of Love," 228.

4. Bederman, *Manliness and Civilization*, 122.

5. Seitler, "Unnatural Selection," 63.

6. Sklar, "Historical Foundation of Women's Power," 72.

7. The actual degree of progressiveness, by today's standards, within the agenda of self-identified progressive women reformers (1890–1930) remains a contested issue among contemporary women's studies scholars. For some scholars, the reform movement's recurrent maternalist rhetoric—along with the class divide between the middle-class activists and the frequent objects of their reform activism (poor and working-class women)—render the reformers' efforts, to a degree, socially and politically suspect, if not downright reactionary. Other scholars view the reformers' maternalist rhetoric as a shrewd means to cloak radical reform with superficially acceptable ideologies of motherhood; they therefore interpret the reformers' interest in protective labor legislation as authentic progressiveness. Overall, questions remain regarding the progressive reformers' degree of personal agency as well as the political valence of their motivations in relationship to the period's institutional and social limitations for women.

Several historians have suggested that the era's progressive women may sometimes have ended up satisfying personal ambition at the expense of others, particularly other women. Robyn Muncy points to the "special tragedy" in the creation, in large part by professional women, of a welfare state that effectively served to confine other women. But Muncy does not seek, in her words, "to castigate" such women reformers. See Muncy, *Creating a Female Dominion*, xiv–xv. See also Fitzpatrick, *Endless Crusade*; Estelle Freedman, *Their Sisters' Keepers*; and Michel, "Limits of Maternalism."

On the other hand, many scholars, including Muncy, Fitzpatrick, and Michel, also emphasize the extraordinary commitment to public service and the hard work of the progressive women reformers, as well as their very real, if limited, successes in improving the lives of immigrants and the urban poor and working class. See Boris, "Power of Motherhood"; Kathleen A. Brown, " 'Savagely Fathered and Un-mothered World' "; Dilberto, *A Useful Woman*; Estelle Freedman, *Maternal Justice*; Ladd-Taylor, " 'My Work Came Out of Agony and Grief' "; and Ladd-Taylor, *Mother-Work*.

8. One graduate of Vassar, class of 1882, said in her contribution to *History of the Class of 1882, Vassar College*: "[Lucy Stone's] reasoning was, 'Why shouldn't I, an intelligent woman, vote when every ignorant ditch-digger may do so?' It was a stage of mind I had been in myself, but by the time I graduated from Vassar it had begun to seem to me a puerile view to take of the question, as I

had arrived at a very firm belief that to grant women the vote would be a grave mistake" ("Wyman, Anne Southworth," 154). Wyman also tells of leaving law school after two years, in part because "one of my classmates and myself had become rather interested in each other personally" (158). She decides to abandon her legal studies and settles down to a life of domesticity. The *History of the Class of 1882* was reviewed in the March–April 1933 issue of *Eugenical News*; the reviewer, Mrs. Lucien Howe, a Eugenics Record Office field worker, notes: "Eugenically it is clear that the class of '82 were made out of good hereditary stuff. It is also clear that as a class they have not perpetuated their own numbers or talents" ("Vassar '82," 38).

9. See Rafter, "Claims-Making," for a case-study of one such woman, Josephine Shaw Lowell, the "first female commissioner of New York's State Board of Charities in 1876," who successfully campaigned, on eugenic grounds, for a custodial asylum for feebleminded women in New York State (20). Also see Ellen Fitzpatrick's discussion of Katharine Bement Davis, superintendent of the Bedford Hills, New York, Reformatory for Women from 1901 to 1913, in *Endless Crusade*, 92–129. According to Fitzpatrick, Davis's corrections program for women had both eugenic and anti-eugenic aspects; Davis rejected "nativist and racist explanations of criminal behavior" (97–98) even as she argued for the segregation and colonization of women " 'who are dangerous to the community who are moral imbeciles, just as we have colonized the mental imbeciles' " (99). Like the family studies authors and field workers, Davis focused on lower-class white women as hereditary delinquents (99–100). Finally, see Kline, *Building a Better Race*, for a discussion of women's reform organizations' embrace of eugenic solutions to the problem of feebleminded (and so likely also promiscuous) women (27–29).

10. A 1997 article by Amy Sue Bix represents an important exception to the general scholarly neglect of the field workers, whom she treats as crucial for a full understanding of the U.S. eugenics movement. See Bix, "Experiences and Voices." However, I believe Bix is overgenerous in her analysis of both the workers' degree of resistance to eugenic thinking and the quality of their research methods.

Other than Bix, only a few scholars have even mentioned—and virtually none have treated in any detail—the women eugenics field workers of the reform era. See Zenderland, *Measuring Minds*, for a consideration of Elizabeth Kite, the field worker best known for her central role in the production of *The Kallikak Family* (1912); see especially 159–63, 173–77, 322–23. Also see Rafter, *White Trash*, 3, 20–23.

11. The first sterilization law, permitting sterilization of the mentally handicapped, was enacted in Indiana in 1907 (Kevles, *In the Name of Eugenics*, 100; Kühl, *Nazi Connection*, 17; and Reilly, *Surgical Solution*, 33). Between 1907 and 1930, twenty-four states enacted compulsory sterilization statutes. At least

60,000 people in the United States were compulsorily sterilized for eugenic reasons under those laws between 1907 and 1964 (Larson, *Sex, Race, and Science*, 28; Duster, *Backdoor to Eugenics*, 30; Chase, *Legacy of Malthus*, 16; and Reilly, *Surgical Solution*, xiii).

12. I thank Derek Nystrom for making this point and for contributing the idea of taxonomy in relation to varieties of New Womanhood.

13. Historian Molly Ladd-Taylor has already provided invaluable work toward such a taxonomy. As she argues, not all women reformers of the Progressive Era can be considered maternalists, and she rightly makes distinctions among three groups of women reformers: "sentimental maternalists, or club mothers," who embraced both maternalism and traditionalism; "progressive maternalists," who worked for broad social and labor reform only partly on the grounds of maternalist thinking and rhetoric; and "feminists," who largely rejected maternalist rhetoric in favor of "creating equal opportunities for women outside the home." See Ladd-Taylor, *Mother-Work*, 7–9. However, Ladd-Taylor neglects activists like the field workers, whose politics and reform agenda work are clearly not simply traditional but reactionary.

14. See especially Muncy, *Creating a Female Dominion*. Despite their progressive beliefs, Muncy argues, these professional women reformers "could succeed in satisfying their needs for respect, autonomy, and effectiveness only at the expense of other women" (xv). Further citations of Muncy are noted parenthetically in the text. Also see Fitzpatrick, *Endless Crusade*; Estelle Freedman, *Their Sisters' Keepers*; Kunzel, *Fallen Women, Problem Girls*; Odem, *Delinquent Daughters*; and Trent, *Inventing the Feeble Mind*.

15. In *Mother-Work*, Ladd-Taylor succinctly and effectively defines "maternalism" as: "a specific ideology whose adherents hold (1) that there is a uniquely feminine value system based on care and nurturance; (2) that mothers perform a service to the state by raising citizen-workers; (3) that mothers are united across class, race, and nation by their common capacity for motherhood and therefore share a responsibility for all the world's children; and (4) that ideally men should earn a family wage to support their 'dependent' wives at home" (3). For more on "maternalism" in women's reform, 1890–1930, see (though this is by no means an exhaustive list): Goodwin, *Gender and the Politics of Welfare Reform*; Linda Gordon, "Putting Children First"; Sklar, "Historical Foundation of Women's Power"; Skocpol, *Protecting Soldiers and Mothers*; and Weiner, "Maternalism as Paradigm." For challenges to the historical paradigm of maternalism, see Boris, "What about the Working of the Working Mother?"; and Cott, "What's in a Name?" For an excellent overview of the maternalist debate among historians, see Wilkinson, "The Selfless and the Helpless."

16. Mary Odem, in *Delinquent Daughters*, examines carefully and insightfully the role of women reformers in the regulation of "delinquent" girls' sexu-

ality: "They [reformers] did aim to shield teenage girls from sexual exploitation, unfit homes, and dangerous forms of work and recreation, but the protective work they advocated had a coercive side. It entailed using the state for
the purposes of surveillance, legal prosecution, detention, and institutionalization of young women and girls who engaged in suspect behavior" (109).
Although she discusses women judges, social workers, and parole officers,
Odem does not consider the less sympathetic figure of the eugenics field
worker, who seeks to "shield" the environment of the nation from the girls
rather than the girls from their environment.

17. As I will argue later in this chapter, the field workers still had to contend, as did the progressive women reformers, with the conflict between their
own status as workers and the period's dominant construction of women's
gender roles: that women should still function primarily in a domestic role,
while intelligent, middle-class women in particular should become mothers
of multiple children (itself a eugenic concept).

18. In *Creating a Female Dominion*, Muncy takes care to point out, however,
that professionalization and reform were not always and everywhere "in necessary opposition to each other during the Progressive era" (160). As she points
out, for some women, professional activities and relationships served to support and sustain their reform commitments and often enabled them to achieve
real reform successes (160–62).

19. Indeed, the many volunteer field workers further challenge the model
of professionalization.

20. As eugenics historian Daniel Kevles has shown, there were two distinct
"strains" of eugenic thinking in the modern United States: one was espoused
by progressive social reformers and the other, what he terms "mainline" eugenics, by social conservatives. The progressive eugenicists, Like Havelock
Ellis and Margaret Sanger, were far less likely to promote racialist versions of
eugenics and insisted on increased social equality as an accompaniment to
the better breeding of humans. The conservative eugenics of figures like Lothrop Stoddard and Harry Laughlin was racist, elitist, and strongly hereditarian in its orientation, with little or no concern for improving the environment of the poor and feebleminded. See Kevles, *In the Name of Eugenics*,
170–75. In general, both white and black eugenics can be seen as intraracial
movements, at least in the 1910s and 1920s.

21. One eugenics field worker documented the quality of her college grad-
uating class: "So we were preponderantly a Scotch-English group, harking
back to pioneer days. To your historian this seems significant" (Elizabeth
Howe, *History of the Class of 1882*, 4).

22. Rafter, *White Trash*, 3; Trent, *Inventing the Feeble Mind*, 178.

23. The depression of 1893 seemed to render the notions of class competition and social Darwinism even more plausible. The depression that began

in 1929, on the other hand, worked in a limited fashion to mitigate, though certainly not to stall, eugenics in the United States. During the years of the Great Depression, the American Eugenics Society soft-pedaled its "negative" eugenics platform—sterilization and institutionalization—in favor of "positive" eugenic measures—public health protection policies, health education, and so on. See Reilly, *Surgical Solution*, 78. As Donald Pickens points out, the Depression forced many eugenics advocates to realize that unemployment did not necessarily signify "individual weakness or lack of ability to compete successfully in the marketplace." See Pickens, *Eugenics and the Progressives*, 205. Environment simply had to enter into the explanation of such widespread financial failure. First, the Depression was clearly an external force; second, many middle- and even upper-class people were adversely affected. In general, eugenicists readily turned to environment/nurture to explain middle- and upper-class inadequacies and failures; heredity/nature explained them sufficiently in the working class.

The Great Depression cannot be viewed as wholly disruptive to eugenics, however. Skyrocketing unemployment also indicated a need for a smaller working class. Especially as technologies and techniques of production became more sophisticated, a mature capitalist economy required fewer working bodies. The minutes of a June 4, 1932, joint session of the American Eugenics Society and the Eugenics Research Association suggest that U.S. eugenicists hoped that the Depression would eventually redound to their benefit: "The activity of the Society in this time of depression was discussed. Dr. Little set forward the suggestion that the public was getting more and more of a grievance against the defective. He felt that this question, which was clearer now than at any other time, would force the public to come to eugenicists for a remedy" ("American Eugenics Society Minutes").

In fact, according to Edward Larson, the late 1920s and early 1930s witnessed a dramatic increase in the annual average number of compulsory eugenic sterilizations in the United States. See Larson, *Sex, Race, and Science*, 28. On the other hand, U.S. eugenics institutions did suffer setbacks during the Depression, as the above minutes also suggest. Both the American Eugenics Society and the ERO scaled back their staff, salaries, and activism.

24. For scholarly use of a "professionalization" paradigm to describe the U.S. eugenics movement, see especially Rafter, "Claims-Making" and *White Trash*. For a combined feminist and professionalization approach, see Bix, "Experiences and Voices," 633–37. For further elaboration of eugenics and professionalization, see Kevles, *In the Name of Eugenics*, 64, 77; and Haller, *Eugenics*, 76–77.

25. Rafter, *White Trash*, 21. As I argued above, such a model of "advancement" along with "segregation" of professional women has been applied to the era's more progressive reformers as well.

26. Ibid., 13.

27. Shawn Michelle Smith, *American Archives*, 124.

28. Haller, *Eugenics*, 138–39. The relative ease and lower risk of vasectomy (versus tubal ligation) may well be one reason for the frequency of male eugenic sterilization in the late 1800s and early 1900s. On the other hand, most of the early state sterilization statutes were written in distinctly gendered (male) rhetoric, often explicitly permitting sterilization of "confirmed criminals" and "rapists," as well as "idiots" and "imbeciles." Ibid., 50.

29. See Gugliotta, "'Dr. Sharp with His Little Knife.'"

30. See JoAnne Brown, *Definition of a Profession*, 97–105, for a fine analysis of "efficiency" as a central term and value in human, industrial, and mechanical engineering in the Progressive Era.

31. As prominent eugenics propagandist C. W. Saleeby put it, "Positive eugenics must largely take the form, at present, of removing such disabilities [impeding child rearing] as now weigh upon the desirable members of the community." He offers as an example of these disabilities the "tax which the propertied middle classes have to pay on marriage" (here he was quoting an article from the *Morning Post*). See Saleeby, *Parenthood and Race Culture*, 19. Recent debates in the U.S. Congress on the "marriage penalty" tax clearly echo this 1915 instance of eugenic thinking.

32. Eugenics historians report that the earliest targets of eugenic and punitive sterilization in the United States were institutionalized boys and men. In 1889, a number of feebleminded boys were castrated at the Pennsylvania Training School for Feebleminded Children; between 1894 and 1895, at least eleven boys and men were castrated at the Kansas State Asylum for Idiotic and Imbecile Youth. Throughout the 1890s, hundreds of feebleminded and delinquent males and females residing in state institutions were desexualized or unsexed (to use the jargon of the period) by castration, vasectomy, oopherectomy, or tubal ligation. See Kevles, *In the Name of Eugenics*, 93; Trent, *Inventing the Feeble Mind*, 192–202; Haller, *Eugenics*, 48–50. See also Mathew Thomson, *Problem of Mental Deficiency*, 181, 194–97.

See Gugliotta, "'Dr. Sharp with His Little Knife,'" for a first-rate discussion of the punitive and therapeutic, as well as eugenic, contexts for late-nineteenth-century use of vasectomy and castration on incarcerated and institutionalized males. Gugliotta argues persuasively that such "therapeutic (and punitive) understandings of sterilization were present from the beginning" (375). Castration, especially, was perceived and used in Indiana in the 1890s as a treatment of excessive masturbation (particularly among the institutionalized feebleminded) and as a means to punish and prevent sexual crime (particularly among incarcerated black men). Vasectomy was also perceived and used as a means to punish and prevent homosexual activity among prison inmates (377–78, 394).

33. Rafter, *White Trash*, 341. Patrick Ryan makes an argument similar to mine in his analysis of recent histories of mental retardation and intelligence testing. He suggests that the "concept of self-interest" has led some scholars to miss the "broader historical significance" as well as the public policy effects of the "'myth of the menace of the feeble-minded'" ("Unnatural Selection," 669).

34. A 1920s recruitment form letter sent to social workers by the American Eugenics Society said: "Without doubt you know that the application of Eugenics is a charity to lessen charity" ("Letter to Social Workers").

35. Weeks, *Sex, Politics, and Society*, 132.

36. For a description of the class collaboration involved in the founding of the ERO, see Kevles, *In the Name of Eugenics*, 54–55; and Haller, *Eugenics*, 65–66.

37. The fitter family contests took place at state and county fairs throughout the 1910s and 1920s. Administered by eugenics field workers and public health nurses, the contests involved the examination and evaluation of volunteer families for their health and overall genetic value. Winners received medals and ribbons. The fitter family evaluation form included the following categories for medical/eugenic findings and prescriptions: "Social and other history, psychometric [e.g., IQ scores], psychiatric, structural, medical, laboratory, teeth, special senses, health habits, summary and advice, Individual score, and Family score." Examples of "summary and advice" from fitter family contests conducted in Kansas in 1925 included:

"Outdoor exercise *very important* at your age."—8 years old
"Watch condition of pelvic organs"—age 39
"Clitoris adhered"—age 4
"Needs circumcision"—age 18 months
"Very fine child. Watch tonsils and adenoids and see about circumcision."
"Come back and take medal next year"
"You ought to take a medal next time!"

The evaluations show a clear preoccupation with the state of the families' genitalia ("Fitter Families Examinations").

38. Davenport, letter to Eugenics Record Office Board of Scientific Directors, December 13, 1913.

39. In a 1916 circular distributed to state institutions, the ERO explicitly outlined this policy, under the heading "Duration of Agreement": "The joint employment continues for one year from October 1st, after which the support of the Eugenics Record Office is withdrawn in order that it may send workers elsewhere to establish new centers of interest in eugenical study. The cooperative institution is then at liberty to discontinue the work or to continue it independently; in the latter case either taking over the jointly em-

ployed worker or employing another person. Most of the institutions have continued the joint worker, either for the family history studies exclusively or in connection with after-care work" (Eugenics Record Office, *Basis for the Joint Employment of Field Workers*, 2–3).

40. Ibid., 2.

41. The volunteer family studies were designed more for the eugenic than the dysgenic. The ERO encouraged potentially eugenic families to note their own genetic value, but to do so honestly. The voluntary family study kits from the 1920s included "Individual Analysis Cards" that noted, "If the study is to be of value, all statements—concerning both 'good' and 'bad' traits—must be frank and fair" ("Individual Analysis Cards"). The eugenic family studies, though fewer in number, represent a fascinating counterpart to the dysgenic family studies. The voluntary eugenic family studies often include photographs of individual subjects/family members posed standing while holding a mirror at an angle in front of him- or herself, in order to represent both a frontal and profile view (presumably to disclose the presence or absence of a weak or Hapsburgian chin). Dysgenic families, however, were not on the family study honor system. In such cases, field workers, along with their courtesy and tact, were assumed to be necessary for getting the unvarnished genetic truth.

42. Mellen, letter to Mr. H. H. Laughlin, August 11, 1912.

43. "Alumni Roster."

44. "Volunteer Collaborators."

45. Reed, letter to Dr. C. B. Davenport, March 31, 1916.

46. Reed, "The Trix Family"; further citations will be parenthetical in the text.

47. Reed, letter to Dr. C. B. Davenport, September 11, 1916.

48. Davenport, letter to Bernice Reed, September 13, 1916.

49. Laughlin even authored a "Memorandum on Eugenical Work as an Occupation for College Women." For more on the gender breakdown of field workers, see Bix, "Experiences and Voices," 627.

50. "Numbers of Eugenics Record Office Field Workers," 1–3.

51. Davenport, "Directions for the Guidance of Field Workers," 3.

52. Laughlin, "Qualities Desired in a Eugenical Field Worker."

53. Minutes of Cold Spring Harbor Meeting of the Field Workers, 12.

54. "Myers, Sadie," unpaginated.

55. As producers of a new and explicitly diagnostic form of discourse, the field workers expanded and revised their assigned role so as to create revised, more liberatory forms of professional subjectivity. Indeed, subjectivity (as opposed to objectivity) was central for their reportage, as their field notes attest. Most often taking narrative form, the notes disclose not only the workers' readiness to diagnose but also their active, even authorial role in the cre-

ation of what Rafter rightly terms the "distinctive form of discourse" that constitutes the family studies. That "discourse" partakes of a number of both social scientific and literary conventions; overall, the studies exist in a rather unstable space between fiction and nonfiction, with highly subjective and descriptive narration placed literally alongside genealogical charts. Here again, I differ from Bix, who acknowledges, but downplays, the "use of rumour in field-workers' reports" ("Experiences and Voices," 641). Bix implies that Charles Davenport's policies, advice, and pressure "led to" workers' occasional reliance on rumor (641). I found *many* examples of hearsay, rumor, gossip, and speculation in the field workers' notes; and, although the workers were undoubtedly pressured by Davenport to use any possible data, there seems to be little evidence that they themselves resisted incorporating neighbors' reports, physicians' judgments, and so on, in their study notes. Of course, one could argue that the diagnosis is in place before the data have even been gathered—the field workers are to identify and document the feebleminded; they must, therefore, be diagnosing from the outset. This is perhaps the fundamental flaw in the family studies' purported science.

56. Devitt, "Timber Rats," 2–4, 16.

57. "Myers, Sadie," unpaginated.

58. Charles Davenport, "E.R.O. Budget for 1916–1917." In 1916, however, $600 a year was a reasonably good salary, especially for a woman. Working-class women, by contrast, "rarely earned a 'living wage,' estimated to be $9.00 or $10.00 a week in 1910," according to Kathy Peiss ("'Charity Girls' and City Pleasures," 94).

59. Transcript of 1913 Field Workers Conference, 45–46; further citations will be parenthetical in the text.

60. Here again, I depart from Bix, who foregrounds the field workers who "voiced doubts about the validity and ethics of eugenic research, drawing on their field experiences and scientific ideals" ("Experiences and Voices," 626). Further citations of Bix will be parenthetical in the text. I found little evidence of widespread ethical or professional doubt among the field workers, although there were a few other scattered remarks (which Bix also notes) in the proceedings of the summer conferences that indicate some workers' misgivings about the way the studies were being conducted.

61. Gardner, "Case History," cover page.

62. The policing of women's sexual behaviors began in their youth in the reform era. As Mary Odem explains: "Juvenile court statistics from this period indicate that girls were, in fact, more likely to be institutionalized and less likely to receive probation than boys. . . . Between 1910 and 1920, twenty-three new reformatories [for delinquent and feebleminded U.S. girls] were founded," as compared to fewer than five between 1850 and 1910. Odem adds that "the vast majority (81 percent) of charges filed against girls

[in the 1910s and 1920s] were for moral offenses" (155). See Odem, *Delinquent Daughters*, 115–16, 155. Ellen Fitzpatrick confirms the presence of "this double standard": "While many more boys appeared before the juvenile court than girls, young female offenders received harsher punishments" (*Endless Crusade*, 185).

63. Danielson and Davenport, "Hill Folk," 135.

64. Sessions, "Happy Hickories," 320.

65. Estabrook and McDougle, *Mongrel Virginians*, 8.

66. Goddard, *Kallikak Family*, 33; further citations will be parenthetical in the text.

67. "Field Workers' Returns."

68. "Personals."

69. "Fecundity of Collegians."

70. Laughlin, letter to Miss Kathryn F. Stein.

71. Gould, *Mismeasure of Man*, 158.

72. The photographs of Deborah included in *The Kallikak Family* emphasize her domesticity and her apparently healthy and happy adjustment to her life-long institutionalization. The photographs of at-large Kallikaks, by contrast, emphasize their slovenliness. Moreover, as Stephen Jay Gould has pointed out, the photographs of the uninstitutionalized Kallikaks have been retouched, with heavy dark lines around eyes and mouths lending them an almost demonic appearance. See Gould, *Mismeasure of Man*, 170–72. There has been controversy regarding both the source and purpose of this retouching; Gould suggested that Goddard was responsible, whereas other scholars have argued that the publisher was probably to blame. See Fancher, "Goddard and the Kallikak Family Photographs," 588. Diane Paul has argued more recently that the retouched photographs would have undercut Goddard's own status as expert tester and detector of even the subtly, indeed invisibly feebleminded and therefore he was not likely to have done the retouching. See Paul, "Genes and Contagious Disease," 158. Granted, to render the feebleminded visually obvious does seem to contradict Goddard's goal of widespread testing of apparently normal people by experts in the field of human intelligence. But the photographs do support a second plank in his eugenic platform: that the uninstitutionalized feebleminded constitute a menace to society. Although we may never know who actually altered the photographs, we must acknowledge that Goddard had as much to gain ideologically as he had to lose by representing the institutionalized Deborah Kallikak as attractive and docile but the at-large Kallikaks as conspicuously feebleminded and threatening.

73. Lisa Lindquist Dorr makes a similar connection in her article "Arm in Arm." Dorr suggests that fear of "passing" by both " 'high grade morons' " and light-skinned African Americans worried "Northern and Southern eu-

genicists" (148). Dorr also argues persuasively that "fears about women's new freedoms and changing roles converged with eugenic concerns about racial order" and points out that it is no "coincidence that laws promoting immigration restrictions and sterilization of the 'feebleminded' were enacted contemporaneously" with Virginia's notorious 1924 Racial Integrity Act (149–50). But Dorr focuses almost exclusively on white male eugenicists and southern white male legislators as enactors of eugenic legislation in the 1920s and on their desire to curtail white women's newfound sexual and social freedoms. I wish to complicate this picture by focusing on ways that some white women benefited substantially and directly from the period's conservative eugenic activism.

74. This reliance on female intuition also rendered the family studies vulnerable to attack for lack of scientific rigor. One contemporary, Abraham Myerson, in 1925 offered a powerful and effective challenge to the field workers' methodology, attacking in particular *The Kallikak Family* and Goddard, who, in Myerson's words, "acting on this superior female intuition, founds an important theory of feeblemindedness, and draws sweeping generalizations, with a fine moral undertone, from [the field workers'] work" (quoted in Zenderland, *Measuring Minds*, 322).

75. "Work of a Field Worker." Letchworth Village, opened in 1910, was a New York state asylum for the feebleminded. See Trent, *Inventing the Feeble Mind*, 102, 227–30, for a history of Letchworth.

76. Kathleen Brown has recently made a similar point about the labor activist Ella Reeve Bloor, known as "Mother Bloor." See Brown, " 'Savagely Fathered and Un-mothered World.' " Brown argues that the "rubric 'Mother' provided a shield against accusations of 'free-love' " (562). I am suggesting that conservative women, too, often needed such a "shield" in order to function effectively as activist reformers.

77. See Tickner, *Spectacle of Women*, for a first-rate analysis of the fears and accusations of "masculinisation" of women associated with reform activism and suffragism. See 188–95, especially, for a consideration of the biological and eugenic aspects of the matter.

78. Wendy Kline, in *Building a Better Race*, rightly links the " 'menace of the feebleminded' " with the " 'girl problem' " (38). However, what might be termed a "man problem" was also very much on the minds of eugenicists in the 1910s and 1920s. Kline argues: "While social-purity reformers of the late nineteenth century sought to protect what they believed to be innocent women from moral ruin by male predators, twentieth-century social workers and eugenicists targeted working-class female sexuality as the source of moral ruin and racial degeneracy" (46). I wish to complicate this model of eugenic thinking by adding working-class and poor men's sexuality and fertility as an

equally clear target of eugenicist reformers. As Kline herself notes, between 1918 and 1934, "women represented only a slight majority of sterilized patients" at California's Sonoma State Home for the Feeble-Minded (53).

79. For example, although at times as many as a third of the residents at Hull House were male, Kathryn Kish Sklar argues that, "as a community of women, Hull House provided its members with a lifelong substitute for family life. In that sense it resembled a religious order, supplying women with a radical degree of independence from the claims of family life and inviting them to commit their energies elsewhere" ("Hull House in the 1890s," 56).

80. Reed, "Trix Family," 3, 14−15.

81. Kostir, "Family of Sam Sixty," 194. Kostir named the family "Sixty" because of the father Sam's IQ, which was "exactly sixty percent of the average adult"; see Rafter, White Trash, 185, 187.

82. Dugdale, Jukes, 26; further citations will be parenthetical in the text.

83. Knapp, Literary Modernism, 4.

84. Biggs, Rational Factory, 105.

85. See JoAnne Brown's discussion of "efficiency" as a national value in the 1910s, in Definition of a Profession, 110−13.

86. Ehrenreich and Ehrenreich, "Professional-Managerial Class"; Banta, Taylored Lives, 27. Banta's brilliant analysis of the many modern narratives that engaged the "one true theory" (39) of scientific management overlooks the family studies, which must be considered quintessential stories of human inefficiency and backwardness (waste) eliminated by means of social, scientific, and narratological intervention.

87. Taylor, Principles of Scientific Management, 43; further citations will be parenthetical in the text.

88. Historians Nancy Cott and Molly Ladd-Taylor point out that the period's "maternalists" were also "wedded to an ideology rooted in the nineteenth-century doctrine of separate spheres" (Ladd-Taylor, Mother-Work, 3; and Cott, "What's in a Name?" 821). They conclude that maternalist women reformers therefore cannot be considered feminists.

89. This emphasis on male work and female domesticity distinguishes the family studies' gender politics from those of the feminist, socially progressive reformers like Jane Addams and Frances Kellor, who readily acknowledged women's place in the work force. But it also establishes common ground between the eugenicists and the "sentimental maternalists" in Ladd-Taylor's analysis (Mother-Work, 7).

90. Rafter, White Trash, 17.

91. John F. Kennedy Library and Museum, "Calvin Coolidge's Inaugural Address."

92. Frederick Taylor's scientific management can be considered both eugenic and anti-eugenic. On the one hand, Taylor emphasized not only the

possibility but also the necessity of training workers for the modern industrial workplace. Moreover, Taylor was not a nativist or a white supremacist; he felt that the success of so many immigrants in the United States effectively proved his training hypothesis. On the other hand, the vocabulary of "making" workers also merges with notions of human engineering and a kind of Wellsian (and Spencerian) picture of labor as essentially and even biologically distinct from management. Banta points out that it was not "applied science and the social sciences" that had to "accommodate the presence of" women, children, blacks, and immigrants" in the nation and in the workplace, but rather the women, children, blacks, and immigrants themselves who "were expected to do the adjusting" (*Taylored Lives*, 28).

93. Rogers and Merrill, *Dwellers in the Vale of Siddem*, 346.

94. Winship, *Jukes-Edwards*, 13.

95. Danielson and Davenport, "Hill Folk," 132.

96. Sessions, "Happy Hickories," 256.

97. This modern construction of social and genetic standards ever more tailored to the cultural and economic moment finds a postmodern parallel in the current commonplace that those lacking computer literacy will necessarily be left behind in this, the "information" age. We are now, as then, concerned with identifying the economically and socially fit.

98. See Odem, *Delinquent Daughters*, 124–25, for a discussion of repressive measures put in place during World War I for the detention of "delinquent girls" perceived as disease-carrying threats to the purity and well-being of American soldiers stationed in the United States.

Conclusion

1. Branigin, "Warner Apologizes"; Associated Press, "Research Shows"; Schoen, "Between Choice and Coercion."

2. See, for example, D. S. King, "Preimplantation Diagnosis and the 'New' Eugenics."

3. Cold Spring Harbor Laboratory, "CSHL History."

4. Perry, foreword to *Eugenics and Other Evils*, 5.

5. Du Bois, "Opinion," 24 (October 1922): 248.

6. Stein, *Everybody's Autobiography*, 92.

7. Eliot, *Letters*, 573.

8. Angelina Weld Grimké, "Notes."

9. Houston Baker, *Modernism and the Harlem Renaissance*, xv.

10. Moglen, "Modernism in the Black Diaspora," 1189–90.

11. Hutchinson, *Harlem Renaissance in Black and White*, 31; Douglas, *Terrible Honesty*, 79. Hutchinson and Douglas rely heavily on the demography and geography of Manhattan to make their case for the interracial aspects of mod-

ernist cultural work. That reliance is itself telling, because once we expand our view of the New Negro movement (as opposed to the "Harlem Renaissance"), we must acknowledge that many other sites that produced the movement were more dispersed and less integrated than Manhattan.

12. Du Bois, *Dusk of Dawn*, 744.

13. "V. P. Robinson."

14. Ibid.

15. Kostir, "Family of Sam Sixty," 187.

16. Shapiro, *Population Control Politics*, 18.

17. See Thomas, "Race, Gender, and Welfare Reform"; and Roberts, *Killing the Black Body*.

18. See King and Meyer, "Politics of Reproductive Benefits." King and Meyer point out that "employees of the state of Illinois have broad insurance coverage of infertility treatments but no coverage of contraceptives; yet Illinois women insured by Medicaid receive benefits in just the opposite configuration" (8–9). They add that Illinois's requirement of "employer coverage of infertility treatments" resulted quite directly from the activism of "a very small group of professional, well-educated women and men" (18). Many states, they conclude, have similar policies in place: "The effect is a de facto [national] fertility policy that discourages births among poor women and encourages births among working- and middle-class women" (26).

19. Ehrenreich, "Maid to Order." Also see Ehrenreich, *Nickel and Dimed*. In her going "under cover" as a waitress and as a maid in the last several years, Ehrenreich can be compared with reform-era feminist and labor-reform activist Frances Kellor, whose 1902–3 investigative work Ellen Fitzpatrick describes in *Endless Crusade*: "Along with eight of her assistants, [Kellor] disguised herself as both employer and employee, personally visiting several agencies and even assuming a job as a domestic in a private home" (132).

20. Wray and Newitz, *White Trash*, 2.

BIBLIOGRAPHY

Manuscript Collections

Kirksville, Missouri
  Pickler Memorial Library, Truman State University
    Harry H. Laughlin Collection
Philadelphia, Pennsylvania
  American Philosophical Society Library
    American Eugenics Society Papers
    Charles Davenport Papers
    Eugenics Record Office Papers
Washington, D.C.
  Manuscript Division, Moorland-Spingarn Research Center,
      Howard University
    Angelina Weld Grimké Papers

Period Newspapers and Magazines

American Journal of Obstetrics
Birth Control Review
Crisis
Eugenical News
Journal of the American Medical Association
Messenger
Negro World

Published and Archival Sources

Ackroyd, Peter. *T. S. Eliot*. London: Hamish Hamilton, 1984.
Adell, Sandra. *Double Consciousness/Double Bind: Theoretical Issues in Twentieth-Century Black Literature*. Urbana: University of Illinois Press, 1994.

Altieri, Charles. "Whose America Is *Our America*: On Walter Benn Michaels's Characterizations of Modernity." *Modernism/Modernity* 3, no. 3 (1996): 101–13.

"Alumni Roster." *Eugenical News* 4 (March 1919): 23. Harry H. Laughlin Collection, Pickler Memorial Library, Truman State University, Kirksville, Mo.

"American Eugenics Society Minutes, 1925–1935." Folders 1 and 2, Eugenics Record Office Papers, American Philosophical Society Library, Philadelphia, Pa.

Antler, Joyce, and Daniel M. Fox. "The Movement Toward a Safe Maternity: Physician Accountability in New York City, 1915–1940." In *Sickness and Health in America*, edited by Judith Leavitt and Ronald Numbers, 375–92. Madison: University of Wisconsin Press, 1978.

Appiah, Kwame Anthony. *In My Father's House: Africa in the Philosophy of Culture.* New York: Oxford University Press, 1992.

———. "The Uncompleted Argument: Du Bois and the Illusion of Race." In *"Race," Writing, and Difference*, edited by Henry Louis Gates Jr. and Kwame Anthony Appiah, 21–37. Chicago: University of Chicago Press, 1985.

Aptheker, Bettina. *Woman's Legacy: Essays on Race, Sex, and Class in American History.* Amherst: University of Massachusetts Press, 1982.

Arendt, Hannah. *The Origins of Totalitarianism.* New York: Harcourt, Brace, 1951.

———. "Race-Thinking before Racism." *Review of Politics* 6 (January 1944): 36–73.

Asher, Kenneth. *T. S. Eliot and Ideology.* Cambridge: Cambridge University Press, 1995.

Associated Press. "Research Shows Sterilizations Killed at Least 3 N.C. Women." *Charlotte Observer*, February 17, 2003.

Ayers, Edward L. *Vengeance and Justice: Crime and Punishment in the Nineteenth-Century American South.* New York: Oxford University Press, 1984.

Bailey, Harold. "Control of Midwives." *American Journal of Obstetrics* 6 (September 1923): 293–98.

Baker, Houston. *Modernism and the Harlem Renaissance.* Chicago: University of Chicago Press, 1987.

Baker, S. Josephine. "Schools for Midwives." *American Journal of Obstetrics* 65 (1912): 256–70.

Baldy, J. M. "The Midwife." *Journal of the American Medical Association* 61 (January 1916): 56.

Banta, Martha. *Taylored Lives: Narrative Productions in the Age of Taylor, Veblen, and Ford.* Chicago: University of Chicago Press, 1993.

Bauman, Zygmunt. *Modernity and Ambivalence.* Ithaca, N.Y.: Cornell University Press, 1991.

Bederman, Gail. *Manliness and Civilization: A Cultural History of Gender and Race in the United States, 1880–1917*. Chicago: University of Chicago Press, 1995.

Bender, Bert. " 'His Mind Aglow': The Biological Undercurrent in Fitzgerald's *Gatsby* and Other Works." *Journal of American Studies* 32 (December 1998): 399–420.

Bennett, Michael, and Vanessa D. Dickerson, eds. *Recovering the Black Female Body: Self-Representations by African American Women*. New Brunswick, N.J.: Rutgers University Press, 2001.

Berry, Ellen E. *Curved Thought and Textual Wandering: Gertrude Stein's Postmodernism*. Ann Arbor: University of Michigan Press, 1992.

———. "Modernism/Mass Culture/Postmodernism: The Case of Gertrude Stein." In *Rereading the New: A Backward Glance at Modernism*, edited by Kevin Dettmar, 167–89. Ann Arbor: University of Michigan Press, 1992.

Biggs, Lindy. *The Rational Factory: Architecture, Technology, and Work in America's Age of Mass Production*. Baltimore: Johns Hopkins University Press, 1996.

Bix, Amy Sue. "Experiences and Voices of Eugenics Field-Workers: 'Women's Work' in Biology." *Social Studies of Science* 27 (1997): 625–68.

Boris, Eileen. "The Power of Motherhood: Black and White Activist Women Redefine the 'Political.' " In *Mothers of a New World: Maternalist Politics and the Origins of Welfare States*, edited by Seth Koven and Sonya Michel, 213–45. New York: Routledge, 1993.

———. "What about the Working of the Working Mother?" *Journal of Women's History* 5 (Fall 1993): 104–9.

Branigin, William. "Warner Apologizes to Victims of Eugenics." *Washington Post*, May 3, 2002, B1.

Brinnin, John Malcolm. *The Third Rose: Gertrude Stein and Her World*. Reading, Mass.: Addison-Wesley, 1987.

Brooks, Cleanth. Introduction to *Understanding Poetry: An Anthology for College Students*, edited by Cleanth Brooks and Robert Penn Warren. New York: H. Holt, 1938.

Brown, Elsa Barkley. "To Catch the Vision of Freedom: Reconstructing Southern Black Women's Political History, 1865–1880." In *Unequal Sisters: A Multicultural Reader in U.S. Women's History*, edited by Vicki L. Ruiz and Ellen Carol DuBois, 124–46. 3d ed. New York: Routledge, 2000.

Brown, JoAnne. *The Definition of a Profession: The Authority of Metaphor in the History of Intelligence Testing, 1890–1930*. Princeton: Princeton University Press, 1992.

Brown, Kathleen A. "The 'Savagely Fathered and Un-mothered World' of the Communist Party, U.S.A.: Feminism, Maternalism, and 'Mother Bloor.' " *Feminist Studies* 25 (Fall 1999): 537–69.

Brundage, W. Fitzhugh. *Lynching in the New South: Georgia and Virginia, 1880–1930*. Urbana: University of Illinois Press, 1993.

———, ed. *Under Sentence of Death: Lynching in the South.* Chapel Hill: University of North Carolina Press, 1997.

Burrill, Mary A. *Aftermath.* 1919. In *Strange Fruit: Plays on Lynching by American Women*, edited by Kathy A. Perkins and Judith L. Stephens, 82–91. Bloomington: Indiana University Press, 1998.

———. "They That Sit in Darkness." *Birth Control Review* 3 (September 1919): 5–8.

Carby, Hazel. Introduction to *Iola Leroy; or, Shadows Uplifted*, by Frances E. Harper. Boston: Beacon, 1987.

———. *Race Men.* Cambridge, Mass.: Harvard University Press, 1998.

———. *Reconstructing Womanhood: The Emergence of the Afro-American Woman Novelist.* New York: Oxford University Press, 1987.

Caruth, Cathy. "Traumatic Awakenings." In *Performativity and Performance*, edited by Andrew Parker and Eve Kosofsky Sedgwick, 89–108. New York: Routledge, 1995.

Chase, Allan. *The Legacy of Malthus: The Social Costs of the New Scientific Racism.* New York: Knopf, 1977.

Cheng, Anne Anlin. *The Melancholy of Race.* New York: Oxford University Press, 2000.

Chesler, Ellen. *Woman of Valor: Margaret Sanger and the Birth Control Movement in America.* New York: Simon and Schuster, 1992.

Chesnutt, Charles W. *The Journals of Charles W. Chesnutt.* Edited by Richard H. Brodhead. Durham, N.C.: Duke University Press, 1993.

Chessman, Harriet. *The Public Is Invited to Dance: Representation, the Body, and Dialogue in Gertrude Stein.* Stanford: Stanford University Press, 1989.

Chesterton, G. K. *Eugenics and Other Evils: An Argument against the Scientifically Organized State.* 1922. Edited by Michael W. Perry. Seattle: Inkling Books, 2000.

Childs, Donald J. *Modernism and Eugenics: Woolf, Eliot, Yeats, and the Culture of Degeneration.* Cambridge: Cambridge University Press, 2001.

Chinitz, David. "T. S. Eliot and the Cultural Divide." *PMLA* 110 (March 1995): 236–47.

Clark, Suzanne. *Sentimental Modernism: Women Writers and the Revolution of the Word.* Bloomington: Indiana University Press, 1991.

Cohen, Milton. "Black Brutes and Mulatto Saints: The Racial Hierarchy of Gertrude Stein's 'Melanctha.'" *Black American Literature Forum* 18 (1984): 119–21.

Cold Spring Harbor Laboratory. "Historical Highlights and Recent Achievements." <http://www.cshl.org/History/history.html>. September 26, 2003.

Cooley, John. "White Writers and the Harlem Renaissance." In *The Harlem*

Renaissance: Revaluations, edited by Amritjit Singh, William S. Shriver, and Stanley Brodwin, 13–22. New York: Garland, 1989.

Cope, Karin. "'Moral Deviancy' and Contemporary Feminism: The Judgment of Gertrude Stein." In *Feminism Beside Itself*, edited by Diane Elan and Robyn Wiegman, 155–78. New York: Routledge, 1995.

Cott, Nancy. "What's in a Name? The Limits of 'Social Feminism'; or, Expanding the Vocabulary of Women's History." *Journal of American History* 76 (December 1989): 809–29.

Crawford, T. Hugh. *Modernism, Medicine, and William Carlos Williams*. Norman: University of Oklahoma Press, 1993.

Crookshank, F. G. *The Mongol in Our Midst*. New York: E. P. Dutton, 1924.

Danielson, Florence H., and Charles B. Davenport. "The Hill Folk: Report on a Rural Community of Hereditary Defectives." In *White Trash: The Eugenic Family Studies, 1877–1919*, edited by Nicole Rafter, 81–163. Boston: Northeastern University Press, 1988.

Darwin, Charles. *The Descent of Man, and Selection in Relation to Sex*. London: J. Murray, 1871. Photoreproduction. Princeton: Princeton University Press, 1981.

———. *The Origin of Species by Means of Natural Selection; or, The Preservation of Favoured Races in the Struggle For Life*. 1859. Edited by J. W. Burrow. London: Penguin, 1985.

Davenport, Charles. "Directions for the Guidance of Field Workers." Cold Spring Harbor Series, B:D27, no. 2: 3, Charles Davenport Papers, American Philosophical Society Library, Philadelphia, Pa.

———. "E.R.O. Budget for 1916–1917." Cold Spring Harbor Series, B:D27, no. 2, Charles Davenport Papers, American Philosophical Society Library, Philadelphia, Pa.

———. Letter to Bernice Reed. Sept. 13, 1916. Series 8: Volunteer Collaborators, B:3, no. 15, Eugenics Record Office Papers, American Philosophical Society Library, Philadelphia, Pa.

———. Letter to Eugenics Record Office Board of Scientific Directors. December 13, 1913. Cold Spring Harbor Series, B:D27, no. 2, Charles Davenport Papers, American Philosophical Society Library, Philadelphia, Pa.

Degler, Carl N. *In Search of Human Nature: The Decline and Revival of Darwinism in American Social Thought*. New York: Oxford University Press, 1991.

DeKoven, Marianne. "Gertrude Stein and the Modernist Canon." In *Gertrude Stein and the Making of Literature*, edited by Shirley Neuman and Ira B. Nadel, 8–20. Boston: Northeastern University Press, 1988.

———. "Half In and Half Out of Doors." In *A Gertrude Stein Companion: Content with the Example*, edited by Bruce Kellner, 75–83. New York: Greenwood Press, 1988.

————. *Rich and Strange: Gender, History, Modernism*. Princeton: Princeton University Press, 1991.

Dettmar, Kevin, ed. *Rereading the New: A Backward Glance at Modernism*. Ann Arbor: University of Michigan Press, 1992.

Devitt, Sadie. "Timber Rats" (1917). Series 7: Field Worker Files, box 1, folder 2: 2–4, 16, Eugenics Record Office Papers, American Philosophical Society Library, Philadelphia, Pa.

Diamond, Elin. "The Shudder of Catharsis in Twentieth-Century Performance." In *Performativity and Performance*, edited by Andrew Parker and Eve Kosofsky Sedgwick, 152–72. New York: Routledge, 1995.

Dilberto, Gioia. *A Useful Woman: The Early Life of Jane Addams*. New York: Scribner, 1999.

Doane, Janice L. *Silence and Narrative: The Early Novels of Gertrude Stein*. Westport, Conn.: Greenwood Press, 1986.

Dorr, Gregory Michael. "Assuring America's Place in the Sun: Ivey Foreman Lewis and the Teaching of Eugenics at the University of Virginia, 1915–1953." *Journal of Southern History* 66 (May 2000): 257–96.

Dorr, Lisa Lindquist. "Arm in Arm: Gender, Eugenics, and Virginia's Racial Integrity Acts of the 1920s." *Journal of Women's History* 11 (Spring 1999): 143–66.

Douglas, Ann. *Terrible Honesty: Mongrel Manhattan in the 1920s*. New York: Farrar, Straus and Giroux, 1995.

Douglass, Frederick. *Narrative of the Life of Frederick Douglass, An American Slave, Written by Himself*. 1845. New York: Penguin, 1968.

Downey, Dennis, and Raymond Hyser. *No Crooked Death: Coatesville, Pennsylvania, and the Lynching of Zachariah Walker*. Urbana: University of Illinois Press, 1991.

Doyle, Laura. *Bordering on the Body: The Racial Matrix of Modern Fiction and Culture*. New York: Oxford University Press, 1994.

————. "The Flat, the Round, and Gertrude Stein: Race and the Shape of Modern(ist) History." *Modernism/Modernity* 7, no. 2 (2000): 249–71.

Du Bois, W. E. B. *The Autobiography of W. E. B. Du Bois*. New York: International Publishers, 1968.

————. "The Conservation of Races." In *W. E. B. Du Bois Speaks: Speeches and Addresses, 1889–1919*, edited by Philip S. Foner, 73–85. New York: Pathfinder Press, 1970.

————. "Criteria of Negro Art." *Crisis* 32 (October 1926): 290–97.

————. "The Damnation of Women." 1920. In *Writings*, edited by Nathan Huggins, 952–68. 1986. New York: Library of America, 1996.

————. *Dark Princess*. 1928. Introduction by Claudia Tate. Jackson: University Press of Mississippi, 1995.

———. *Dusk of Dawn: An Essay toward an Autobiography of a Race Concept.* New York: Harcourt, Brace, 1940.

———. "Editorial." *Crisis* 4 (October 1912): 287–90.

———. "Editorial." *Crisis* 12 (October 1916): 267–71.

———. "Editorial." *Crisis* 13 (January 1917): 111–17.

———. "The Immediate Program of the American Negro." *Crisis* 9 (April 1915): 310–12.

———. "A Lunatic or a Traitor." 1924. In *Writings*, edited by Nathan Huggins, 990–92. New York: Library of America, 1996.

———. "Manifesto of the Second Pan African Congress." *Crisis* 23 (November 1921): 5–6.

———. "Marcus Garvey." 1920–21. In *Writings*, edited by Nathan Huggins, 969–79. New York: Library of America, 1996.

———. "Miscegenation." In *Against Racism: Unpublished Essays, Papers, Addresses, 1887–1961*, edited by Herbert Aptheker, 90–102. Amherst: University of Massachusetts Press, 1985.

———. "Opinion of W. E. B. Du Bois." *Crisis* 20 (May 1920): 5–8.

———. "Opinion of W. E. B. Du Bois." *Crisis* 20 (June 1920): 72.

———. "Opinion of W. E. B. Du Bois." *Crisis* 23 (November 1921): 5.

———. "Opinion of W. E. B. Du Bois." *Crisis* 24 (August 1922): 152–53.

———. "Opinion of W. E. B. Du Bois." *Crisis* 24 (October 1922): 247–48.

———. "Opinion of W. E. B. Du Bois." *Crisis* 26 (October 1923): 247–50.

———. "Opinion of W. E. B. Du Bois." *Crisis* 28 (September 1924): 199–203.

———. "Opinion of W. E. B. Du Bois." *Crisis* 32 (October 1926): 283.

———. "Our Baby Pictures." *Crisis* 8 (October 1914): 298–300.

———. *The Philadelphia Negro: A Social Study.* Philadelphia/University of Pennsylvania: Ginn, 1899.

———. "The Shadow of Years." *Crisis* 15 (February 1918): 167–71.

———. "So the Girl Marries." *Crisis* 35 (June 1928): 192–93, 207–9.

———. *The Souls of Black Folk.* 1903. In *Three Negro Classics*, edited by John Hope Franklin, 207–389. New York: Avon Books, 1965.

———. "The Talented Tenth." 1903. In *Writings by W. E. B. Du Bois in Nonperiodical Literature Edited by Others*, compiled and edited by Herbert Aptheker, 17–29. New York: Kraus-Thomson, 1982.

———. "The Talented Tenth: Memorial Address." 1948. In *Writings by W. E. B. Du Bois*, edited by Herbert Aptheker, 4:78–88. New York: Kraus-Thomson, 1982.

———. "Two Novels." Review of *Quicksand* by Nella Larsen and *Home to Harlem* by Claude McKay. *Crisis* 35 (June 1928): 202, 211.

———. "A Winter Pilgrimage." *Crisis* 1 (June 1911): 15.

duCille, Ann. *The Coupling Convention: Sex, Text, and Tradition in Black Women's Fiction*. New York: Oxford University. Press, 1993.

Duffy, John. *The Sanitarians: A History of American Public Health*. Urbana: University of Illinois Press, 1990.

Dugdale, Robert L. *The Jukes: A Study in Crime, Pauperism, Disease, and Heredity*. 1877. 4th ed. New York: Putnam, 1910.

Dunbar-Nelson, Alice. "Woman's Most Serious Problem." *Messenger* (March 1927): 73, 86.

Duster, Troy. *Backdoor to Eugenics*. New York: Routledge, 1990.

Dutta, Ujjal. "Ideology into Criticism: The Case of T. S. Eliot." *Literary Criterion* 22, no. 3 (1986): 91–99.

Edwards, William A. "Racial Purity in Black and White: The Case of Marcus Garvey and Earnest Cox." *Journal of Ethnic Studies* 15 (Spring 1987): 117–42.

Ehrenreich, Barbara. "Maid to Order: The Politics of Other Women's Work." *Harper's*, April 2000, 59–70.

———. "Nickel-and-Dimed: On (Not) Getting By in America." *Harper's*, January 1999, 37–52.

———. *Nickel and Dimed: On (Not) Getting By in America*. New York: Metropolitan Books, 2001.

Ehrenreich, Barbara, and John Ehrenreich, "The Professional-Managerial Class." In *Between Labor and Capital*, edited by Pat Walker, 5–45. Boston: South End Press, 1979.

Eliot, T. S. *After Strange Gods*. New York: Harcourt, Brace, 1934.

———. *Collected Poems, 1909–1962*. 1963. New York: Harcourt Brace Jovanovich, 1991.

———. *For Lancelot Andrewes*. London: Faber and Faber, 1928.

———. "The Function of Criticism." 1923. In *Selected Prose of T. S. Eliot*, edited by Frank Kermode, 68–76. San Diego: Harcourt Brace Jovanovich, 1988.

———. "The Idea of a Christian Society." 1930. In *Christianity and Culture*, 1–77. New York: Harcourt Brace Jovanovich, 1988.

———. *Inventions of the March Hare, Poems 1909–1917*. Edited by Christopher Ricks. New York: Harcourt Brace, 1996.

———. *The Letters of T. S. Eliot*. Edited by Valerie Eliot. New York: Harcourt Brace Jovanovich, 1988.

———. "Marie Lloyd." 1923. In *Selected Essays*, 405–8. New York: Harcourt, Brace and World, 1964.

———. "The Music of Poetry." 1942. In *Selected Prose*, edited by Frank Kermode, 107–14. San Diego: Harcourt, Brace, 1988.

———. "Notes towards the Definition of Culture." 1949. In *Christianity and Culture*, 79–202. New York: Harcourt Brace Jovanovich, 1988.

———. *The Waste Land*. 1922. In *Collected Poems, 1909–1962*. New York: Harcourt Brace Jovanovich, 1991.

Ellis, Havelock. *The Problem of Race-Regeneration*. New York: Moffat, Yard, 1911.

———. *A Study of British Genius*. London: Hurst and Blackett, 1904.

Ellmann, Maud. *The Poetics of Impersonality: T. S. Eliot and Ezra Pound*. Sussex: Harvester Press, 1987.

English, Daylanne. "Gertrude Stein and the Politics of Literary-Medical Experimentation." *Literature and Medicine* 16 (Fall 1997): 188–209.

———. "Selecting the Harlem Renaissance." *Critical Inquiry* 25 (Summer 1999): 807–21.

Estabrook, Arthur H., and Ivan E. McDougle. *Mongrel Virginians: The Win Tribe*. Baltimore: Williams and Wilkins, 1926.

Eugenics Record Office. *Basis for the Joint Employment of Field Workers by the Eugenics Record Office and Institutions for the Socially Inadequate*. Eugenics Record Office Circular Number 1 (July 1, 1916): 2–3. Box D-2-5:3, Harry H. Laughlin Collection, Pickler Memorial Library, Truman State University, Kirksville, Mo.

Fancher, Raymond E. "Goddard and the Kallikak Family Photographs: 'Conscious Skullduggery' or 'Whig History'?" *American Psychologist* 42 (June 1987): 585–90.

Faris, Robert E. L. *Chicago Sociology, 1920–1932*. Chicago: University of Chicago Press, 1979.

Faulk, Barry J. "Modernism and the Popular: Eliot's Music Halls." *Modernism/Modernity* 8, no. 4 (2001): 603–21.

"Fecundity of Collegians." *Eugenical News* 1 (October 1916): 71. Harry H. Laughlin Collection, Pickler Memorial Library, Truman State University, Kirksville, Mo.

Felski, Rita. *The Gender of Modernity*. Cambridge, Mass.: Harvard University Press, 1995.

"Field Workers' Returns." *Eugenical News* 1 (January 1916): 3. Harry H. Laughlin Collection, Pickler Memorial Library, Truman State University, Kirksville, Mo.

Finlayson, Anna Wendt. "The Dack Family: A Study in Hereditary Lack of Emotional Control." In *White Trash: The Eugenic Family Studies, 1877–1919*, edited by Nicole Rafter, 210–51. Boston: Northeastern University Press, 1988.

"Fitter Families Examinations." Series 6: Fitter Families Examinations— Kansas #2, Eugenics Record Office Papers, American Philosophical Society Library, Philadelphia, Pa.

"Fitter Families for Future Firesides." Series 6: Kansas Free Fair, 1921–1924, Eugenics Record Office Papers, American Philosophical Society Library, Philadelphia, Pa.

Fitzgerald, F. Scott. *FIE! FIE! Fi-Fi!*. 1914. Book and lyrics by F. Scott Fitzgerald; music by D. D. Griffin et al. Edited by Matthew J. Bruccoli. Columbia: University of South Carolina Press, 1996.

———. *The Great Gatsby*. 1925. Edited by Matthew J. Bruccoli. Cambridge:
Cambridge University Press, 1991.

Fitzpatrick, Ellen. *Endless Crusade: Women Social Scientists and Progressive Reform*. New
York: Oxford University Press, 1990.

Ford, Andrew. "Katharsis: The Ancient Problem." In *Performativity and Performance*, edited by Andrew Parker and Eve Kosofsky Sedgwick, 109–32.
New York: Routledge, 1995.

Foucault, Michel. *The Birth of the Clinic*. Translated by A. M. Sheridan Smith.
New York: Pantheon, 1973.

———. *The History of Sexuality*. Vol. 1. Translated by Robert Hurley. New York:
Vintage Books, 1980.

Frazier, E. Franklin. *Black Bourgeoisie: The Rise of a New Middle Class*. New York:
Free Press, 1965.

———. "Eugenics and the Race Problem." *Crisis* 31 (December 1925):
91–92.

———. *The Free Negro Family: A Study of Family Origins before the Civil War*. Nashville,
Tenn.: Fisk University Press, 1932.

———. *The Negro Family in Chicago*. Chicago: University of Chicago Press, 1932.

Freedman, Barbara. "Frame-up: Feminism, Psychoanalysis, Theatre." In
Performing Feminisms: Feminist Critical Theory and the Theatre, edited by Sue-Ellen
Case, 54–76. Baltimore: Johns Hopkins University Press, 1990.

Freedman, Estelle. *Maternal Justice: Miriam Van Waters and the Female Reform
Tradition*. Chicago: University of Chicago Press, 1996.

———. *Their Sisters' Keepers: Women's Prison Reform in America, 1830–1930*. Ann
Arbor: University of Michigan Press, 1981.

Freud, Sigmund. *Civilization and Its Discontents*. 1930. Translated and edited by
James Strachey. New York: Norton, 1961.

Fuchs, Lawrence H. "The Reactions of Black Americans to Immigration."
In *Immigration Reconsidered: History, Sociology, Politics*, edited by Virginia Yans-
McLaughlin, 293–314. New York: Oxford University Press, 1990.

Fuoss, Kirk W. "Lynching Performances, Theatres of Violence." *Text and Performance Quarterly* 19 (January 1999): 1–37.

Gaines, Kevin. *Uplifting the Race: Black Leadership, Politics, and Culture in the Twentieth
Century*. Chapel Hill: University of North Carolina Press, 1996.

Gallup, Donald. "The Making of *The Making of Americans*." Appendix to *Fernhurst, Q.E.D., and Other Early Writings by Gertrude Stein*, 175–214. New York:
Liveright, 1971.

Galton, Francis. *Fingerprints*. 1892. Edited by Harold Cummins. New York:
DeCapo Press, 1965.

———. *Hereditary Genius: An Inquiry into Its Laws and Consequences*. 1869. New York: D. Appleton, 1870.

———. *Inquiries into Human Faculty and Its Development*. London: Macmillan, 1883.

Gambrell, Alice. "Serious Fun: Recent Work on Zora Neale Hurston." *Studies in the Novel* 29 (Summer 1997): 238–44.

Garber, Eric. "A Spectacle in Color: The Lesbian and Gay Subculture of Jazz Age Harlem." In *Hidden from History: Reclaiming the Gay and Lesbian Past*, edited by Martin Duberman, Martha Vicinus, and George Chauncey Jr., 318–31. New York: New American Library, 1989.

Gardner, Dorothy. "Case History." Series 8: Volunteer Collaborators, box 2, folder 8, Eugenics Record Office Papers, American Philosophical Society Library, Philadelphia, Pa.

Gates, Henry Louis, Jr. "Harlem on Our Minds." *Critical Inquiry* 24 (Autumn 1997): 1–12.

———. Introduction to *"Race," Writing, and Difference*, edited by Henry Louis Gates Jr. and Kwame Anthony Appiah. Chicago: University of Chicago Press, 1985.

Gates, Henry Louis, Jr., Nellie McKay, et al., eds. *The Norton Anthology of African American Literature*. New York: Norton, 1997.

Geller, Jeffrey L., and Maxine Harris, eds. *Women of the Asylum: Voices from Behind the Walls, 1840–1945*. New York: Anchor, 1994.

Gere, Anne Ruggles. *Intimate Practices: Literacy and Cultural Work in U.S. Women's Clubs, 1880–1920*. Urbana: University of Illinois Press, 1997.

Giddings, Paula. *Where and When I Enter: The Impact of Black Women on Race and Sex in America*. New York: William Morrow, 1984.

Gillman, Susan. "Pauline Hopkins and the Occult: African American Revisions of Nineteenth-Century Sciences." *American Literary History* 8 (Spring 1996): 57–82.

Gilroy, Paul. *The Black Atlantic: Modernity and Double Consciousness*. Cambridge, Mass.: Harvard University Press, 1993.

Ginzburg, Ralph, ed. *100 Years of Lynchings*. Baltimore: Black Classic Press, 1988.

Goddard, Henry Herbert. *The Kallikak Family: A Study in the Heredity of Feeble-Mindedness*. New York: Macmillan, 1912.

Goldsby, Jacquelyn. "The High and Low Tech of It: The Meaning of Lynching and the Death of Emmett Till." *Yale Journal of Criticism* 9 (1996): 245–82.

Goodwin, Joanne L. *Gender and the Politics of Welfare Reform: Mothers' Pensions in Chicago, 1911–1929*. Chicago: University of Chicago Press, 1997.

Gordon, Linda. "Black and White Visions of Welfare: Women's Welfare Activism, 1890–1945." In *Unequal Sisters: A Multicultural Reader in U.S. Women's History*, edited by Vicki L. Ruiz and Ellen Carol DuBois, 214–41. 3d ed. New York: Routledge, 2000.

———. "The Professionalization of Birth-Control." In *Women and Power in American History: A Reader*, edited by Kathryn Kish Sklar and Thomas Dublin, 2:146–59. Englewood Cliffs, N.J.: Prentice Hall, 1991.

———. "Putting Children First: Women, Maternalism, and Welfare in the Early Twentieth Century." In *U.S. History as Women's History: New Feminist Essays*, edited by Linda Kerber, Alice Kessler-Harris, and Kathryn Kish Sklar, 63–86. Chapel Hill: University of North Carolina Press, 1995.

Gordon, Lyndall. *T. S. Eliot: An Imperfect Life*. New York: Norton, 1998.

Gould, Stephen Jay. *The Mismeasure of Man*. New York: Norton, 1981.

Gourdine, Angeletta K. M. "The *Drama* of Lynching in Two Blackwomen's Drama, or Relating Grimké's *Rachel* to Hansberry's *A Raisin in the Sun*." *Modern Drama* 41 (Winter 1998): 533–45.

Grant, Madison. *The Passing of the Great Race; or, The Racial Bias of European History*. New York: Scribner, 1916.

Griffith, D. W., dir. *Birth of a Nation*. 1915. Los Angeles: Republic Pictures Home Video, 1991.

Grimké, Angelina Weld. "Notes on Revision of *Rachel*." Box 38-13, folder 222, Angelina Weld Grimké Papers, Manuscript Division, Moorland-Spingarn Research Center, Howard University, Washington, D.C.

———. *Rachel*. 1916. In *Strange Fruit: Plays on Lynching by American Women*, edited by Kathy A. Perkins and Judith L. Stephens, 27–91. Bloomington: Indiana University Press, 1998.

———. "*Rachel*, the Play of the Month: The Reason and Synopsis by the Author." *Competitor* 1 (January 1920): 51–52. In *Selected Works of Angelina Weld Grimké*, edited by Carolivia Herron, 413–16. New York: Oxford University Press, 1991.

———. "*Rachel* Synopsis and Purpose in Writing Play." Box 38-13, folder 223, Angelina Weld Grimké Papers, Manuscript Division, Moorland Spingarn Research Center, Howard University, Washington, D.C.

Grimké, Archibald. "Editorial." *Crisis* 19 (October 1915): 288, 290.

Gugliotta, Angela. " 'Dr. Sharp with His Little Knife': Therapeutic and Punitive Origins of Eugenic Vasectomy—Indiana, 1892–1921." *Journal of the History of Medicine* 53 (October 1998): 371–406.

Gunning, Sandra. *Race, Rape, and Lynching: The Red Record of American Literature, 1890–1912*. New York: Oxford University Press, 1996.

Guterl, Matthew Pratt. *The Color of Race in America, 1900–1940*. Cambridge, Mass.: Harvard University Press, 2001.

Hall, Jacqueline Dowd. " 'The Mind That Burns in Each Body.' " In *Powers of Desire: The Politics of Sexuality*, edited by Ann Snitow, Christine Stansell, and Sharon Thompson, 328–49. New York: Monthly Review Press, 1983.

———. *Revolt against Chivalry: Jessie Daniel Ames and the Women's Campaign against Lynching*. New York: Columbia University Press, 1979.

Haller, Mark. *Eugenics: Hereditarian Attitudes in American Thought*. New Brunswick, N.J.: Rutgers University Press, 1963.

Haraway, Donna. *Simians, Cyborgs, and Women: The Reinvention of Nature*. New York: Routledge, 1991.

Harding, Jason. *The "Criterion": Cultural Politics and Periodical Networks in Inter-war Britain*. Oxford: Oxford University Press, 2002.

Harper, Frances E. *Iola Leroy; or, Shadows Uplifted*. 1893. Boston: Beacon, 1987.

Harris, Elisha. Foreword to *The Jukes*, by Robert Dugdale. 4th edition; New York: Putnam, 1910.

Harris, Trudier. *Exorcising Blackness: Historical and Literary Lynching and Burning Rituals*. Bloomington: Indiana University Press, 1984.

Hasian, Marouf Arif, Jr. *The Rhetoric of Eugenics in Anglo-American Thought*. Athens: The University of Georgia Press, 1996.

Hemingway, Ernest. *The Torrents of Spring: A Romantic Novel in Honor of the Passing of a Great Race*. 1926. New York: Scribner, 1972.

Herron, Carolivia. Introduction to *Selected Works of Angelina Weld Grimké*, edited by Carolivia Herron. New York: Oxford University Press, 1991.

Hinman, Alan R. "1889 to 1989: A Century of Health and Disease." *Public Health Reports* 105 (July–August 1990): 374–80.

Hogue, W. Lawrence. *Race, Modernity, Postmodernity: A Look at the History and Literatures of People of Color since the 1960s*. Albany: State University of New York Press, 1996.

Holloway, Karla F. C. "The Body Politic." In *Subjects and Citizens: Nation, Race, and Gender from Oroonoko to Anita Hill*, edited by Michael Moon and Cathy N. Davidson, 481–95. Durham, N.C.: Duke University Press, 1995.

Hopkins, Pauline. *Hagar's Daughter: A Story of Southern Caste Prejudice*. 1901–2. In *The Magazine Novels of Pauline Hopkins*, introduced by Hazel V. Carby. New York: Oxford University Press, 1988.

Horkheimer, Max, and Theodor W. Adorno. *The Dialectic of Enlightenment*. 1944. Translated by John Cumming. New York: Continuum, 1969.

"The Horizon." *Crisis* 28 (August 1924): 167–68.

Hovey, Jaime. "Sapphic Primitivism in Gertrude Stein's *Q.E.D.*" *Modern Fiction Studies* 42, no. 3 (1996): 547–68.

Howard, Gene L. *Death at Cross Plains: An American Reconstruction Tragedy*. University: University of Alabama Press, 1984.

Howard, Walter. *Lynchings: Extralegal Violence in Florida during the 1930s*. Selinsgrove, Pa.: Susquehanna University Press, 1995.

Howe, Elizabeth, ed. *History of the Class of 1882, Vassar College*. Poughkeepsie, N.Y.: The College, 1933. Harry H. Laughlin Collection, Pickler Memorial Library, Truman State University, Kirksville, Mo.

Howe, Mrs. Lucien. " 'Vassar '82': A Stock-Taking of the Social and Eugenical Values of the Class of 39 Women Who Graduated from Vassar College in 1882." *Eugenical News* 18 (March–April 1933): 38–39. Harry H. Laughlin Collection, Pickler Memorial Library, Truman State University, Kirksville, Mo.

Huggins, Nathan. *Harlem Renaissance*. New York: Oxford University Press, 1971.

Hughes, Robert. *The Shock of the New*. New York: Knopf, 1982.

Hull, Gloria. *Color, Sex, and Poetry: Three Women Writers of the Harlem Renaissance*. Bloomington: Indiana University Press, 1987.

Hutchinson, George. *The Harlem Renaissance in Black and White*. Cambridge, Mass.: Harvard University Press, 1995.

Huyssen, Andreas. *After the Great Divide*. Bloomington: Indiana University Press, 1986.

"Individual Analysis Cards." Series 6: Individual Analysis Cards A–Ma #1, 1920–1936, Eugenics Record Office Papers, American Philosophical Society Library, Philadelphia, Pa.

Innes, Catherine Lynette. *The Devil's Own Mirror: The Irishman and the African in Modern Literature*. Washington, D.C.: Three Continents Press, 1990.

International Eugenics Congress. *The Report of the Second International Congress of Eugenics, American Museum of Natural History, New York, September 1 to 28, 1921*. Baltimore: Williams and Wilkins, 1923.

Jacobs, Harriet. *Incidents in the Life of a Slave Girl*. 1861. Edited by Jean Fagan Yellin. Cambridge, Mass.: Harvard University Press, 1987.

James, Joy. *Transcending the Talented Tenth*. New York: Routledge, 1997.

Jameson, Fredric. *The Political Unconscious: Narrative as a Socially Symbolic Act*. Ithaca, N.Y.: Cornell University Press, 1981.

Jay, Gregory S. "Postmodernism in *The Waste Land*: Women, Mass Culture, and Others." In *Rereading the New: A Backward Glance at Modernism*, edited by Kevin J. H. Dettmar, 221–46. Ann Arbor: University of Michigan Press, 1992.

John F. Kennedy Library and Museum. "Calvin Coolidge's Inaugural Address; Wednesday, March 4, 1925." <http://www.jfklibrary.org/coolidge_inaugural.html>. April 21, 2003.

Johnson, Georgia Douglas. *Safe*. 1929. In *Strange Fruit: Plays on Lynching by American Women*, edited by Kathy A. Perkins and Judith L. Stephens, 110–15. Bloomington: Indiana University Press, 1998.

Johnson, James Weldon. *The Autobiography of an Ex-Colored Man*. 1911. In *Three Negro Classics*, edited by John Hope Franklin, 391–511. New York: Avon, 1965.

———. *Black Manhattan*. New York: Knopf, 1930.

Joyce, James. *Ulysses*. New York: Modern Library, 1961.

Julius, Anthony. *T. S. Eliot, Anti-Semitism, and Literary Form*. Cambridge: Cambridge University Press, 1995.

Kadlec, David. "Marianne Moore, Immigration, and Eugenics." *Modernism/Modernity* 1, no. 2 (April 1994): 21–49.

Katz, León. Introduction to *Fernhurst, Q.E.D., and Other Early Writings by Gertrude Stein*. New York: Liveright, 1971.

Kenner, Hugh. *The Pound Era*. Berkeley: University of California Press, 1971.

Kevles, Daniel. *In the Name of Eugenics: Genetics and the Uses of Human Heredity*. New York: Knopf, 1985.

King, D. S. "Preimplantation Diagnosis and the 'New' Eugenics." *Journal of Medical Ethics* 25 (April 1999): 176–82.

King, Leslie, and Madonna Harrington Meyer. "The Politics of Reproductive Benefits: U.S. Insurance Coverage of Contraceptive and Infertility Treatments." *Gender and Society* 11 (February 1997): 8–27.

Kite, Elizabeth S. "The Pineys." In *White Trash: The Eugenic Family Studies, 1877–1919*, edited by Nicole Rafter, 164–84. Boston: Northeastern University Press, 1988.

Kline, Wendy. *Building a Better Race: Gender, Sexuality, and Eugenics from the Turn of the Century to the Baby Boom*. Berkeley: University of California Press, 2001.

Knapp, James. *Literary Modernism and the Transformation of Work*. Evanston, Ill.: Northwestern University Press, 1988.

Kobrin, Frances E. "The American Midwife Controversy: A Crisis of Professionalization." In *Sickness and Health in America*, edited by Judith Leavitt and Ronald Numbers, 217–25. Madison: University of Wisconsin Press, 1978.

Kostir, Mary Storer. "The Family of Sam Sixty." In *White Trash: The Eugenic Family Studies, 1877–1919*, edited by Nicole Rafter, 185–209. Boston: Northeastern University Press, 1988.

Koven, Seth, and Sonya Michel, eds. *Mothers of a New World: Maternalist Politics and the Origins of Welfare States*. New York: Routledge, 1993.

Krasner, David. "Walter Benjamin and the Lynching Play: Allegory and Mourning in Angelina Weld Grimké's *Rachel*." *Text and Presentation* 18 (1997): 64–80.

Kristeva, Julia. "Word, Dialogue and Novel." 1969. In *The Kristeva Reader*, edited by Toril Moi, 34–61. New York: Columbia University Press, 1986.

Kühl, Stefan. *The Nazi Connection: Eugenics, American Racism, and German National Socialism*. New York: Oxford University Press, 1994.

Kunzel, Regina G. *Fallen Women, Problem Girls: Unmarried Mothers and the Professionalization of Social Work, 1890–1945*. New Haven: Yale University Press, 1993.

Ladd-Taylor, Molly. *Mother-Work: Women, Child Welfare, and State, 1890–1930*. Urbana: University of Illinois Press, 1994.

———. "'My Work Came Out of Agony and Grief': Mothers and the Making of the Sheppard-Towner Act." In *Mothers of a New World: Maternalist Politics and the Origins of Welfare States*, edited by Seth Koven and Sonya Michel, 321–42. New York: Routledge, 1993.

Lamarck, J. B. *Zoological Philosophy: An Exposition with Regard to the Natural History of Animals*. 1809. Translated by Hugh Elliot. London: Macmillan, 1914.

Lamos, Colleen. *Deviant Modernism: Sexual and Textual Errancy in T. S. Eliot, James Joyce, and Marcel Proust*. Cambridge: Cambridge University Press, 1998.

Larsen, Nella. *Quicksand*. 1928. In *"Quicksand" and "Passing,"* edited by Deborah E. McDowell, 1–210. New Brunswick, N.J.: Rutgers University Press, 1986.

Larson, Edward J. *Sex, Race, and Science: Eugenics in the Deep South*. Baltimore: Johns Hopkins University Press, 1995.

Laughlin, Harry. *Bulletin No. 10A: Report of the Committee to Study and to Report on the Best Practical Means of Cutting off Defective Germ-Plasm in the American Population*. Cold Spring Harbor, N.Y.: Eugenics Record Office, 1914.

———. Letter to Miss Kathryn F. Stein. October 20, 1931. Box C-2-4:23, Harry H. Laughlin Collection, Pickler Memorial Library, Truman State University, Kirksville, Mo.

———. "Memorandum on Eugenical Work as an Occupation for College Women." Box D-5-3:12, Harry H. Laughlin Collection, Pickler Memorial Library, Truman State University, Kirksville, Mo.

———. "Qualities Desired in a Eugenical Field Worker." Box C-2-4:8, Harry H. Laughlin Collection, Pickler Memorial Library, Truman State University, Kirksville, Mo.

Leavitt, Judith. *Brought to Bed: Childbearing in America, 1750 to 1950*. New York: Oxford University Press, 1986.

———. "'Science' Enters the Birthing Room: Obstetrics in America since the Eighteenth Century." In *Sickness and Health in America*, edited by Judith Leavitt and Ronald Numbers, 81–97. 2d ed. Madison: University of Wisconsin Press, 1985.

León, Juan Enrique. "A Literary History of Eugenic Terror in England and America." Ph.D. diss., Harvard University, 1989.

———. "'Meeting Mr. Eugenides': T. S. Eliot and Eugenic Anxiety." *Yeats Eliot Review* 9 (Summer–Fall 1988): 169–77.

"Letter to Social Workers." Minutes of the American Eugenics Society, 1925–35, folder 1, American Eugenics Society Papers, American Philosophical Society Library, Philadelphia, Pa.

Levenson, Michael. "Does *The Waste Land* Have a Politics?" *Modernism/Modernity* 6, no. 3 (1999): 1–13.

———. *A Genealogy of Modernism: A Study of English Literary Doctrine, 1908–1922*. Cambridge: Cambridge University Press, 1984.

Levy, Julius. "The Maternal and Infant Mortality in Midwifery Practice in Newark, New Jersey." *American Journal of Obstetrics* 77 (January 1918): 41–53.

Lewis, David Levering. *W. E. B. Du Bois: Biography of a Race, 1868–1919*. New York: Henry Holt, 1993.

———. *W. E. B. Du Bois: The Fight for Equality and the American Century, 1919–1963*. New York: Henry Holt, 2000.

———. *When Harlem Was in Vogue*. New York: Oxford University Press, 1979.

Lifton, Robert Jay. *The Nazi Doctors: Medical Killing and the Psychology of Genocide*. New York: Basic, 1986.

Livingston, Myrtle A. Smith. "For Unborn Children." *Crisis* (July 1926): 122–25.

Locke, Alain, ed. *The New Negro*. 1925. New York: Atheneum, 1992.

Lott, Eric. *Love and Theft: Blackface Minstrelsy and the American Working Class*. New York: Oxford University Press, 1993.

Louis, Yvette. "Body Language: The Black Female Body and the Word in Suzan-Lori Parks's *The Death of the Last Black Man in the Whole Entire World*." In *Recovering the Black Female Body: Self-Representations by African American Women*, edited by Michael Bennett and Vanessa D. Dickerson, 141–64. New Brunswick, N.J.: Rutgers University Press, 2001.

Mabbott, J. Milton. "The Regulation of Midwives in New York." *American Journal of Obstetrics* 55 (April 1907): 516–27.

Malthus, Thomas. *An Essay on the Principle of Population*. 1798. 8th ed. London: Reeves and Turner, 1878.

Marchant, James. Introduction to *The Methods of Race Regeneration*, by C. W. Saleeby. New York: Moffat, Yard, 1911.

Marsh, Alec. *Money and Modernity: Pound, Williams, and the Spirit of Jefferson*. Tuscaloosa: University of Alabama Press, 1998.

Martin, Tony. *Race First: The Ideological and Organizational Struggles of Marcus Garvey and the Universal Negro Improvement Association*. 1976. Dover, Mass.: Majority Press, 1986.

Marx, Karl, and Friedrich Engels. *The Communist Manifesto*. Translated by Samuel Moore. 1888. London: Penguin, 1985.

McCulloch, Oscar C. "The Tribe of Ishmael: A Study in Social Degradation." In *White Trash: The Eugenic Family Studies, 1877–1919*, edited by Nicole Rafter, 48–65. Boston: Northeastern University Press, 1988.

McDowell, Deborah E. "Afterword: Recovery Missions: Imaging the Body." In *Recovering the Black Female Body: Self-Representations by African American Women*, edited by Michael Bennett and Vanessa D. Dickerson, 296–317. New Brunswick, N.J.: Rutgers University Press, 2001.

———. "Reading Family Matters." 1989. In *"The Changing Same": Black Women's Literature, Criticism, and Theory*, 118–37. New Brunswick, N.J.: Rutgers University Press, 1995.

McGovern, James R. *Anatomy of a Lynching: The Killing of Claude Neal*. Baton Rouge: Louisiana State University Press, 1982.

Mellen, Ida M. Letter to Mr. H. H. Laughlin, August 11, 1912. Series 8: Volunteer Collaborators, box 2, folder 12, Eugenics Record Office Papers, American Philosophical Society Library, Philadelphia, Pa.

Mellow, James R. Introduction to *Three Lives*, by Gertrude Stein. New York: Penguin, 1985.

"Men of the Month." *Crisis* 12 (October 1916): 278–79.

Meyer, Steven. Introduction to *The Making of Americans* by Gertrude Stein. Normal, Ill.: Dalkey Archive, 1995.

———. *Irresistible Dictation: Gertrude Stein and the Correlations of Writing and Science*. Stanford: Stanford University Press, 2001.

Michaels, Walter Benn. *Our America: Nativism, Modernism, and Pluralism*. Durham, N.C.: Duke University Press, 1995.

Michel, Sonya. "The Limits of Maternalism: Policies toward American Wage-Earning Mothers during the Progressive Era." In *Mothers of a New World: Maternalist Politics and the Origins of Welfare States*, edited by Seth Koven and Sonya Michel, 277–320. New York: Routledge, 1993.

Minutes of Cold Spring Harbor Meeting of the Field Workers. June 23, 1915. Series 7: Field Worker Files, box 1, folder 95, Eugenics Record Office Papers, American Philosophical Society Library, Philadelphia, Pa.

Mitchell, Michele. "Adjusting the Race: Gender, Sexuality, and the Question of African-American Destiny, 1877–1930." Ph.D. diss., Northwestern University, 1998.

Model, Suzanne W. "Work and Family: Blacks and Immigrants from South and East Europe." In *Immigration Reconsidered: History, Sociology, Politics*, edited by Virginia Yans-McLaughlin, 130–59. New York: Oxford University Press, 1990.

Moglen, Seth. "Modernism in the Black Diapora: Langston Hughes and the Broken Cubes of Picasso." *Callaloo* 25, no. 4 (2002): 1189–1205.

Moon, Henry Lee. *The Emerging Thought of W. E. B. Du Bois*. New York: Simon and Schuster, 1972.

Morawska, Eva. "The Sociology and Historiography of Immigration." In *Immigration Reconsidered: History, Sociology, Politics*, edited by Virginia Yans-McLaughlin, 187–238. New York: Oxford University Press, 1990.

Morrison, Paul. *The Poetics of Fascism: Ezra Pound, T. S. Eliot, Paul de Man*. New York: Oxford University Press, 1996.

Morrison, Toni. *Playing in the Dark: Whiteness and the Literary Imagination*. Cambridge, Mass.: Harvard University Press, 1992.

Muncy, Robyn. *Creating a Female Dominion in American Reform, 1890–1935*. Oxford: Oxford University Press, 1991.

"Myers, Sadie." Series 8: Volunteer Collaborators, box 3, 1916. Eugenics Record Office Library, American Philosophical Society Library, Philadelphia, Pa.

Nelson, Cary. *Repression and Recovery: Modern American Poetry and the Politics of Cultural Memory, 1910–1945*. Madison: University of Wisconsin Press, 1989.

Nielsen, Aldon. *Reading Race: White American Poets and the Racial Discourse in the Twentieth Century*. Athens: University of Georgia Press, 1988.

Nies, Betsy L. *Eugenic Fantasies: Racial Ideology and Popular Culture of the 1920s*. New York: Routledge, 2002.

North, Michael. "The Dialect in/of Modernism: Pound and Eliot's Racial Masquerade." *American Literary History* 4 (Spring 1992): 56–76.

———. *The Dialect of Modernism: Race, Language, and Twentieth-Century Literature*. New York: Oxford University Press, 1994.

———. *The Political Aesthetic of Yeats, Eliot, and Pound*. Cambridge: Cambridge University Press, 1991.

Novick, Sheldon M. *Honorable Justice: The Life of Oliver Wendell Holmes*. Boston: Little, Brown, 1989.

Noyes, Clara D. "Training of Midwives in Relation to the Prevention of Infant Mortality." *American Journal of Obstetrics* 66 (1912): 1051–59.

"Numbers of Eugenics Record Office Field Workers." Series 7: 1–3, Eugenics Record Office Papers, American Philosophical Society Library, Philadelphia, Pa.

Odem, Mary. *Delinquent Daughters: Protecting and Policing Female Sexuality in the United States, 1885–1920*. Chapel Hill: University of North Carolina Press, 1995.

Owen, Chandler. "Marriage and Divorce." *Messenger* 5 (April 1923): 664–65, 679.

Parker, Andrew, and Eve Kosofsky Sedgwick, eds. *Performativity and Performance*. New York: Routledge, 1995.

Paul, Diane B. "Genes and Contagious Disease: The Rise and Fall of a Metaphor." In *The Politics of Heredity: Essays on Eugenics, Biomedicine, and the Nature-Nurture Debate*, 157–71. Albany: State University of New York Press, 1998.

Perkins, Kathy A., and Judith L. Stephens, eds. *Strange Fruit: Plays on Lynching by American Women*. Bloomington: Indiana University Press, 1998.

"Personals." *Eugenical News* 2 (April 1917): 5. Harry H. Laughlin Collection, Pickler Memorial Library, Truman State University, Kirksville, Mo.

Peiss, Kathy. "'Charity Girls' and City Pleasures: Historical Notes on Working-Class Sexuality." In *Women and Power in American History: A Reader*, edited by Kathryn Kish Sklar and Thomas Dublin, 2:88–100. Englewood Cliffs, N.J.: Prentice Hall, 1991.

Perloff, Marjorie. "Modernism without the Modernists: A Response to Walter Benn Michaels." *Modernism/Modernity* 3, no. 3 (1996): 99–105.

———. "Modernist Studies." In *Redrawing the Boundaries: The Transformation of English and American Literary Studies*, edited by Stephen Greenblatt and Giles Gunn, 154–78. New York: Modern Language Association, 1992.

Perry, Michael W. Foreword to *Eugenics and Other Evils: An Argument Against the Scientifically Organized State* (1922), by G. K. Chesterton. Seattle: Inkling Books, 2000.

Phelan, Peggy. *Unmarked: The Politics of Performance*. London: Routledge, 1993.

Pickens, Donald K. *Eugenics and the Progressives*. Nashville: Vanderbilt University Press, 1968.

Pound, Ezra. *The Letters of Ezra Pound, 1907–1941*, edited by D. D. Paige. New York: Harcourt, Brace, 1950.

———. "The Serious Artist." 1913. In *Literary Essays*, 15–57. New York: New Directions, 1968.

Rado, Lisa. ed. *Modernism, Gender, and Culture: A Cultural Studies Approach*. New York: Garland, 1997.

Rafter, Nicole. "Claims-Making and Socio-Cultural Context in the First U.S. Eugenics Campaign." *Social Problems* 39 (February 1992): 17–34.

———, ed. *White Trash: The Eugenic Family Studies, 1877–1919*. Boston: Northeastern University Press, 1988.

Raine, Craig. *In Defence of T. S. Eliot*. London: Picador, 2000.

Rainey, Lawrence. *Institutions of Modernism: Literary Elites and Public Culture*. New Haven: Yale University Press, 1998.

Randolph, A. Philip, and Chandler Owen. "Editorials." *Messenger* 2 (July 1918): 8–15.

———. "Editorials." *Messenger* 2 (December 1919): 4–12.

———. "The Negro Radicals." *Messenger* 2 (December 1919): 20–21.

———. "Who's Who." *Messenger* 2 (May–June 1919): 26–27.

Read, Herbert. "T. S. E.—A Memoir." In *T. S. Eliot: The Man and His Work*, edited by Allen Tate, 11–37. New York: Delacorte, 1966.

Reed, Bernice. Letter to Dr. C. B. Davenport. March 31, 1916. Series 8: Volunteer Collaborators, box 3, folder 15, Eugenics Record Office Papers, American Philosophical Society Library, Philadelphia, Pa.

———. Letter to Dr. C. B. Davenport. September 11, 1916. Series 8: Volunteer Collaborators, box 3, folder 15, Eugenics Record Office Papers, American Philosophical Society Library, Philadelphia, Pa.

———. "The Trix Family." Series 8: Volunteer Collaborators, box 3, folder 15: 1–18, Eugenics Record Office Papers, American Philosophical Society Library, Philadelphia, Pa.

Reilly, Philip R. *The Surgical Solution: A History of Involuntary Sterilization in the United States*. Baltimore: Johns Hopkins University Press, 1991.

Rentoul, Robert Reid. *Race Culture; or, Race Suicide? A Plea for the Unborn*. 1906. Edited by Charles Rosenberg. New York: Garland, 1984.

Richardson, Angelique. "The Eugenization of Love: Sarah Grand and the Morality of Genealogy." *Victorian Studies* 42 (Winter 1999/2000): 227–55.

Ricks, Christopher. "Eliot's Uglier Touches." *Times Literary Supplement*, November 4–10, 1988, 1226, 1235.

———. *T. S. Eliot and Prejudice*. London: Faber and Faber, 1988.

Roberts, Dorothy. *Killing the Black Body: Race, Reproduction, and the Meaning of Liberty*. New York: Pantheon, 1997.

Rogers, A. C., and Maud A. Merrill. "Dwellers in the Vale of Siddem." In *White Trash: The Eugenic Family Studies, 1877–1919*, edited by Nicole Rafter, 341–78. Boston: Northeastern University Press, 1988.

Rolph, Daniel N. *"To Shoot, Burn, and Hang": Folk-History from a Kentucky Mountain Family and Community*. Knoxville: University of Tennessee Press, 1994.

Ruddick, Lisa. *Reading Gertrude Stein: Body, Text, Gnosis*. Ithaca, N.Y.: Cornell University Press, 1990.

Ruiz, Vicki L., and Ellen Carol DuBois, eds. *Unequal Sisters: A Multicultural Reader in U.S. Women's History*. 3d ed. New York: Routledge, 2000.

Ryan, Patrick. "Unnatural Selection." *Journal of Social History* 30 (Spring 1997): 669–85.

Saldívar-Hull, Sonia. "Wrestling Your Ally: Stein, Racism, and Feminist Critical Practice." In *Women's Writing in Exile*, edited by Mary Lynn Broe and Angela Ingram, 182–98. Chapel Hill: University of North Carolina Press, 1989.

Saleeby, C. W. *The Methods of Race Regeneration*. New York: Moffat, Yard, 1911.

———. *Parenthood and Race Culture: An Outline of Eugenics*. New York: Moffat, Yard, 1915.

Sanger, Margaret. "The Function of Sterilization." *Birth Control Review* 10 (October 1926): 299.

———. *Woman and the New Race*. New York: Brentano's, 1920.

Schoen, Johanna. "Between Choice and Coercion: Women and the Politics of Sterilization in North Carolina, 1929–1975." *Journal of Women's History* 13 (Spring 2001): 132–56.

Schroeder, Patricia R. "Remembering the Disremembered: Feminist Realists of the Harlem Renaissance." In *Realism and the American Dramatic Tradition*, edited by William W. Demastes, 91–106. Tuscaloosa: University of Alabama Press, 1996.

Scott, Bonnie Kime, ed. *The Gender of Modernism: A Critical Anthology*. Bloomington: Indiana University Press, 1990.

Seitler, Dana. "Unnatural Selection: Mothers, Eugenic Feminism, and Charlotte Perkins Gilman's Regeneration Narratives." *American Quarterly* 55, no. 1 (2003): 61–88.

Selden, Steven. *Inheriting Shame: The Story of Eugenics and Racism in America*. New York: Teachers College Press, 1999.

Sessions, Mina. "The Happy Hickories: The Feeble-Minded in a Rural County of Ohio." In *White Trash: The Eugenic Family Studies, 1877–1919*, edited by Nicole Rafter, 253–340. Boston: Northeastern University Press, 1988.

Shapiro, Thomas. *Population Control Politics: Women, Sterilization, and Reproductive Choice*. Philadelphia: Temple University Press, 1985.

Sklar, Kathryn Kish. "The Historical Foundation of Women's Power in the Creation of the American Welfare State." In *Mothers of a New World: Maternalist Politics and the Origins of Welfare States*, edited by Seth Koven and Sonya Michel, 43–93. New York: Routledge, 1993.

———. "Hull House in the 1890s: A Community of Women Reformers." In *Women and Power in American History: A Reader*, edited by Kathryn Kish Sklar and Thomas Dublin, 2:54–68. Englewood Cliffs, N.J.: Prentice Hall, 1991.

Skocpol, Theda. *Protecting Soldiers and Mothers: The Political Origins of Social Policy in the United States*. Cambridge, Mass.: Harvard University Press, 1992.

Smedman, Lorna. "'Cousin to Cooning': Relation, Difference, and Racialized Language in Stein's Nonrepresentational Texts." *Modern Fiction Studies* 42, no. 3 (1996): 569–88.

Smith, J. David. *Minds Made Feeble: The Myth and Legacy of the Kallikaks*. Rockville, Md.: Aspen Publications, 1985.

Smith, Leef. "Lynchburg." *Washington Post*, May 13, 2002, B1.

Smith, Shawn Michelle. *American Archives: Gender, Race, and Class in Visual Culture*. Princeton: Princeton University Press, 1999.

Sollors, Werner. "W. E. B. Du Bois in Germany: A Surprising, Prescient Visitor." *Chronicle of Higher Education*, November 12, 1999, B4.

Sontag, Susan. *"Illness as Metaphor" and "AIDS and Its Metaphors."* New York: Doubleday, 1990.

Spencer, Herbert. *The Works of Herbert Spencer*. Vol. 1, *The Principles of Biology*. 1864. Osnabrück: Proff, 1966.

———. *The Works of Herbert Spencer*. Vol. 2, *"Social Statics," Abridged and Revised, Together with "The Man Versus the State."* 1850. 4th ed. Osnabrück: Proff, 1966 [1904].

Spillers, Hortense. "Mama's Baby, Papa's Maybe: An American Grammar Book." 1987. In *African American Literary Theory: A Reader*, edited by Winston Napier, 257–79. New York: New York University Press, 2000.

Spurr, David. *Conflicts in Consciousness: T. S. Eliot's Poetry and Criticism*. Urbana: University of Illinois Press, 1984.

Stein, Gertrude. "Composition as Explanation." 1926. In *Selected Writings of Gertrude Stein*, edited by Carl Van Vechten, 453–61. New York: Random House, 1946.

———. *Everybody's Autobiography*. New York: Random House, 1937.

——. *Fernhurst, Q.E.D., and Other Early Writings*. Introduction by Leon Katz. New York: Liveright, 1971.

——. *The Making of Americans*. 1925. New York: Something Else Press, 1966.

——. *Three Lives*. 1909. New York: Penguin, 1985.

Steiner, Wendy. *Exact Resemblance to Exact Resemblance: The Literary Portraiture of Gertrude Stein*. New Haven: Yale University Press, 1978.

Stepan, Nancy. *"The Hour of Eugenics": Race, Gender and Nation in Latin America*. Ithaca, N.Y.: Cornell University Press, 1991.

——. *The Idea of Race in Science*. Hamden, Conn.: Archon Books, 1982.

Stephens, Judith L. Introduction to *Strange Fruit: Plays on Lynching by American Women*, edited by Kathy A. Perkins and Judith L. Stephens. Bloomington: Indiana University Press, 1998.

——. "Racial Violence and Representation: Performance Strategies in Lynching Dramas of the 1920s." *African American Review* 33 (Winter 1999): 655–72.

Stimpson, Catharine. "The Mind, the Body, and Gertrude Stein." In *Gertrude Stein*, edited by Harold Bloom, 131–44. New York: Chelsea House, 1986.

Stoddard, Lothrop. *Clashing Tides of Colour*. New York: Scribner, 1935.

——. *The Revolt against Civilization: The Menace of the Under Man*. New York: Scribner, 1924.

——. *The Rising Tide of Color against White World-Supremacy*. New York: Scribner, 1920.

Stokes, Mason. *The Color of Sex: Whiteness, Heterosexuality, and the Fictions of White Supremacy*. Durham, N.C.: Duke University Press, 2001.

——. "Strange Fruits." *Transition* 12, no. 2 (2002): 56–79.

Storm, William. "Reactions of a 'Highly-Strung Girl': Psychology and Dramatic Representation in Angelina W. Grimké's *Rachel*." *African American Review* 27, no. 3 (1993): 461–71.

Talalay, Kathryn. *Composition in Black and White: The Life of Philippa Schuyler*. New York: Oxford University Press, 1995.

Tate, Claudia. *Domestic Allegories of Political Desire: The Black Heroine's Text at the Turn of the Century*. New York: Oxford University Press, 1992.

——. *Psychoanalysis and Black Novels: Desire and the Protocols of Race*. New York: Oxford University Press, 1998.

Taylor, Frederick Winslow. *The Principles of Scientific Management*. 1911. New York: Norton, 1967.

Terrell, Mary Church. "Lynching from a Negro's Point of View." *North American Review* 178 (June 1904): 853–68.

Thomas, Susan L. "Race, Gender, and Welfare Reform: The Antinatalist Response." *Journal of Black Studies* 28 (March 1998): 419–46.

Thompson, Mildred I. *Ida B. Wells-Barnett: An Exploratory Study of an American Black Woman, 1893–1930*. Brooklyn, N.Y.: Carlson, 1990.

Thomson, Mathew. *The Problem of Mental Deficiency: Eugenics, Democracy, and Social Policy in Britain, 1870–1959*. Oxford: Clarendon Press, 1998.

Tickner, Lisa. *The Spectacle of Women: Imagery of the Suffrage Campaign, 1907–1914*. Chicago: University of Chicago Press, 1988.

Tolnay, Steward E., and E. M. Beck. *A Festival of Violence: An Analysis of Southern Lynchings, 1882–1930*. Urbana: University of Illinois Press, 1995.

Tone, Andrea. *Devices and Desires: A History of Contraceptives in America*. New York: Hill and Wang, 2001.

Trachtenberg, Alan. *Reading American Photographs: Images as History, Mathew Brady to Walker Evans*. New York: Hill and Wang, 1989.

Transcript of 1913 Field Workers Conference. Cold Spring Harbor Series, B:D27, no. 2: 45–46, Charles Davenport Papers, American Philosophical Society Library, Philadelphia, Pa.

Tratner, Michael. *Modernism and Mass Politics: Joyce, Woolf, Eliot, Yeats*. Stanford: Stanford University Press, 1995.

Trent, James W., Jr. *Inventing the Feeble Mind*. Berkeley: University of California Press, 1994.

"Volunteer Collaborators." Series 8: boxes 1–4, Eugenics Record Office Papers, American Philosophical Society Library, Philadelphia, Pa.

von Hallberg, Robert. "Literature and History: Neat Fits." *Modernism/Modernity* 3, no. 3 (September 1996): 115–26.

"V. P. Robinson." Series 7: Field Worker Files, box 1, folder 26, Eugenics Record Office Papers, American Philosophical Society Library, Philadelphia, Pa.

Walker, Jayne. *The Making of a Modernist: Gertrude Stein from "Three Lives" to "Tender Buttons."* Amherst: University of Massachusetts Press, 1984.

Warren, Robert Penn. "Pure and Impure Poetry." In *Understanding Poetry: An Anthology for College Students*, edited by Cleanth Brooks and Robert Penn Warren, 4–31. New York: H. Holt, 1942.

Weeks, Jeffrey. *Sex, Politics, and Society: The Regulation of Sexuality since 1800*. London: Longman, 1981.

Weiner, Lynn Y. "Maternalism as Paradigm: Defining the Issues." *Journal of Women's History* 5 (Fall 1993): 96–98.

Weiss, Rick. "Genome Project Completed." *Washington Post*, April 15, 2003, A6.

Wells-Barnett, Ida B. *On Lynchings: Southern Horrors, a Red Record, Mob Rule in New Orleans*. 1892. New York: Arno Press, 1969.

Wertz, Richard W., and Dorothy C. Wertz. *Lying-In: A History of Childbirth in America*. 1977. New Haven: Yale University Press, 1989.

West, Cornel. *The American Evasion of Philosophy: A Genealogy of Pragmatism*. Madison: University of Wisconsin Press, 1989.

Wheatley, Phillis. "On Being Brought from Africa to America." In *The Nor-*

ton Anthology of African American Literature, edited by Henry Louis Gates Jr., Nellie McKay, et al., 171. New York: Norton, 1997.

———. "To the University of Cambridge, in New England." In The Norton Anthology of African American Literature, edited by Henry Louis Gates Jr., Nellie McKay, et al., 170. New York: Norton, 1997.

White, Deborah Gray. "The Cost of Club Work, the Price of Black Feminism." In Visible Women: New Essays on American Activism, edited by Nancy A. Hewitt and Suzanne Lebsock, 247–69. Urbana: University of Chicago Press, 1993.

———. Too Heavy a Load: Black Women in Defense of Themselves, 1894–1994. New York: Norton, 1999.

Whittier-Ferguson, John. "Stein in Time: History, Manuscripts, and Memory." Modernism/Modernity 6, no. 1 (January 1999): 115–51.

Wiegman, Robyn. "The Anatomy of Lynching." Journal of the History of Sexuality 3 (January 1993): 445–67.

Wiggam, Albert Edward. The Fruit of the Family Tree. Indianapolis: Bobbs-Merrill, 1924.

———. The New Decalogue of Science. Indianapolis: Bobbs-Merrill, 1923.

Wilk, Melvin. Jewish Presence in T. S. Eliot and Franz Kafka. Atlanta: Scholars Press, 1986.

Wilkinson, Patrick. "The Selfless and the Helpless: Maternalist Origins of the U.S. Welfare State." Feminist Studies 25 (Fall 1999): 571–97.

Williams, Diana I., "Building the New Race: Jean Toomer's Eugenic Aesthetic." In Jean Toomer and the Harlem Renaissance, edited by Geneviève Fabre and Michel Feith, 188–201. New Brunswick, N.J.: Rutgers University Press, 2001.

Williams, Raymond. The Politics of Modernism: Against the New Conformists. Edited by Tony Pinkney. London: Verso, 1989.

Williams, William Carlos. "The Work of Gertrude Stein." 1930. In Gertrude Stein, edited by Harold Bloom, 19–24. New York: Chelsea House, 1986.

Winship, A. E. Jukes-Edwards: A Study in Education and Heredity. Harrisburg, Pa.: R. L. Meyers, 1900.

Winston, Michael R. "Life on the Color Line." Washington Post, November 5, 2000, X1.

"Work of a Field Worker." Eugenical News 2 (June 1917): 46. Harry H. Laughlin Collection, Pickler Memorial Library, Truman State University, Kirksville, Mo.

Wray, Matt, and Annalee Newitz, eds. White Trash: Race and Class in America. New York: Routledge, 1997.

Wright, George. Racial Violence in Kentucky, 1865–1940: Lynchings, Mob Rule, and "Legal Lynchings." Baton Rouge: Louisiana State University Press, 1990.

"Wyman, Anne Southworth." In History of the Class of 1882, Vassar College, edited

by Elizabeth Howe, 151–71. Poughkeepsie, N.Y.: The College, 1933.
Harry H. Laughlin Collection, Pickler Memorial Library, Truman State University, Kirksville, Mo.

Young, Joseph A. *Black Novelist as White Racist: The Myth of Black Inferiority in the Novels of Oscar Micheaux.* New York: Greenwood Press, 1989.

Young, Robert J. C. *Colonial Desire: Hybridity in Theory, Culture, and Race.* London: Routledge, 1995.

Zamir, Shamoon. *Dark Voices: W. E. B. Du Bois and American Thought, 1888–1903.* Chicago: University of Chicago Press, 1995.

Zenderland, Leila. *Measuring Minds: Henry Herbert Goddard and the Origins of American Intelligence Testing.* Cambridge: Cambridge University Press, 1998.

Ziegler, Charles. "The Elimination of the Midwife." *Journal of the American Medical Association* 60 (January 1913): 32–38.

Zinke, Gustav, and William Humiston. "Discussion on the Papers of Drs. Harrar and Levy." *American Journal of Obstetrics* 77 (January 1918): 114–16.

Žižek, Slavoj. *Enjoy Your Symptom!* New York: Routledge, 1992.

"Tradition and the Individual Talent," 81; *The Wasteland*, 69–70, 81, 85–86
See also *Criterion*
Eliot, Vivien, 68, 91
Ellis, Havelock, 14, 40–41, 63, 72, 189 (n. 16), 193 (n. 57), 213 (n. 49)
Estabrook, Arthur, 144, 161, 169
Eugenical News, 149, 162–63, 166, 168, 222 (n. 8)
Eugenics: acceptance of in United States, 2–3, 10–11, 14–15, 29–30, 33, 145, 169; contemporary expressions of, 32–34, 177, 183–85, 220 (n. 66), 233, (n. 97), 234 (n. 18); contradictions within, 8, 27, 106, 211–12 (n. 34); cross-political appeal of, 2–3, 17, 24, 29, 40–41, 62, 179, 224 (n. 20); cross-racial appeal of, 2–3, 14, 16–17, 22, 24–27, 29, 37–38, 40–41, 62, 179, 196–97 (n. 11), 216 (n. 24); history of, 1, 3–10, 38–39, 122, 145–47, 170–71, 191 (n. 39), 193 (n. 58); hybrid vigor version of, 17–18; intraracial forms of, 11, 16–17, 23, 28, 46, 169, 180, 202 (n. 80); legislation regarding, 10, 14–15, 24; men and boys as targets of, 143, 147, 169–70, 173–75, 181, 183, 226 (nn. 28, 32), 231–32 (n. 79); opposition to, 1, 7, 20, 22, 26–28, 73, 75–77, 122, 231 (n. 74); origins of term, 3, 6, 147; poor and working class as targets of, 147, 149–50, 158, 160, 171, 182–83, 190 (n. 20); women and girls as targets of, 143, 147, 159–61, 175,
183, 222 (n. 9), 229–30 (n. 62), 231–32 (n. 78). *See also* Family studies; Field workers
Eugenics Record Office, 13, 28, 144–52, 157, 159, 163, 166–67, 178, 225 (n. 23), 227–28 (n. 39), 228 (n. 41)
Expatriatism, 79–80, 88, 90

Family studies, 6, 9–10, 28, 144–75, 228 (n. 41), 232 (n. 86); *Dwellers in the Valley of Siddem*, 173; *The Happy Hickories*, 173; *The Jukes*, 9–10, 145, 170, 172–73, 181, 190 (n. 27); *The Kallikak Family*, 10, 144–45, 162, 167, 230 (n. 72), 231 (n. 74); *Mongrel Virginians*, 144–45, 161, 169; "Timber Rats," 157–58, 162, 171; "The Trix Family," 151–52, 169
Fauset, Jessie, 53
Feeblemindedness, 5, 7, 10, 13, 15, 27–28, 39, 74, 137, 142, 144, 147, 150–53, 158–62, 167–69, 172–74, 222 (n. 9), 226 (n. 28), 227 (n. 33)
Field workers, 20, 22, 28, 30, 142–75, 178, 182, 184, 228–29 (n. 55), 229 (n. 60); salaries of, 159, 229 (n. 58); summer training for, 148–50, 152, 163, 222 (nn. 9, 10), 223–24 (nn. 16, 17)
Fitter families contests and examinations, 19, 31, 39, 149, 227 (n. 37)
Fitzgerald, F. Scott, 2, 67, 75–77, 205 (n. 6); *FIE! FIE! Fi-Fi!*, 76–77; *The Great Gatsby*, 75
Ford, Henry, 11, 171
Fordism, 11–12, 171
Foucault, Michel, 101, 213 (n. 48)